WEB BASED TEACHING-LEARNING PROCESS

WEB BASED TEACHING-LEARNING PROCESS

Edited by

Dr. S.K. Panneer Selvam

Assistant Professor
Department of Education
Bharathidasan University
Tiruchirappalli
Tamil Nadu
(India)

DPH

DISCOVERY PUBLISHING HOUSE PVT. LTD.
NEW DELHI-110 002

Published by:
Tilak Wasan
DISCOVERY PUBLISHING HOUSE PVT. LTD.
4383/4B, Ansari Road, Darya Ganj
New Delhi-110 002 (India)
Phone : +91-11-23279245, 43596064-65
Fax : +91-11-23253475
E-mail : parul.wasan@gmail.com
discoverypublishinghouse@gmail.com
web : www.discoverypublishinggroup.com

***First Edition:* 2012**

ISBN: 978-93-5056-131-7

Web Based Teaching-Learning Process

Printed at:
Shree Balaji Art Press
Delhi

Preface

This is a compiled edition. The very purpose of this edition is to make the students and the teachers know what is going on around them in the academic world. Language learning is always a 'task', it requires patience and constant practice. Here comes the computer to render Tamil learning easy, entertaining and enriching. Concepts, contents and learning devices can attract young mind. Hearing, seeing and sharing involves in all the steps of learning Tamil. We can provide for students from primary class to university class and post university level. Beginners as well as scholars, researchers can benefit from computer teaching and learning of Tamil. Multimedia is a great boon to introduce and induces to learn all life long. We can construct the curriculum according to the hierarchy of learning. Though Tamil people live in small numbers in hundreds of foreign cities, towns and villages, they can imbibe and become familiar with all characteristic features of the life. There are many cultural features and fine things that can be taught orally. They could be presented in 'light and sound' technology. The internet and electronic media will play a major role in show caring Bharatha Natyam, Nadaswaram, the art and technique of sculpture. karagattam and other similar performing and non performing arts and fine arts.

It should be our prime endeavour and duty to establish and run a separate 'Teaching-learning Tamil' world wide web. This will enable the Tamil teachers working in far off places to update their language skills and teaching patterns. e-Learning is growing instantly like a censer cell and it should be exploited in appropriate manner to develop Tamil teaching-learning strategies to made learning through standardized teaching. I acknowledge their whole-hearted thanks again and again. This book provides an illuminations and in-depth analysis of modern technology's learning. All the articles are taken from the INFITT website—who gave the eminent persons in the field of IT to UTHAMAM of world Tamil union. The very purpose of this edition is to make the students and the teachers know what is going on around them in the academic world. Even the entrepreneurs in the realm of education find it more beneficial. Some of the articles are modified or simplified versions. As the author I am not able to trace out and contact the resource persons who were helpful in bringing out this book. I acknowledge their whole-hearted thanks again and again.

Author

Contents

List of Contributors

1. **Sabitha.Tammaneni, Madhan Karky**
Department of Computer Science and Engineering, College of Engineering Guindy, Anna University

2. **A.G. Tamilarasan, Madhan Karky**
Department of Computer Science and Engineering, College of Engineering Guindy, Anna University

3. **J. Jai Hari Raju, P. IndhuReka, Dr. Madhan Karky**
Department of Computer Science and Engineering, College of Engineering, Anna University, Guindy

4. **R. Indra Gandhi**
Mother Teresa Women's University, Tamil Nadu, India.

   Dr. K. Iyakutti
Madurai Kamaraj University, Tamil Nadu, India.

   Dr. C. Jothi Venkateswaran
Presidency College, Chennai,, Tamil Nadu, India.

5. **Dr. K. Kalyanasundaram**
Lausanne, Switzerland

6. **R. Jayabrabu**
Karunya University, Coimbatore – 641 114

   Prof. (Dr). V. Saravanan
Dr. N.G.P Institute of Technology, Coimbatore – 641 048

7. **D. Thenmozhi, Arun Balachandran Ganesan and C. Aravindan**
Department of Computer Science and Engineering SSN College of Engineering, Chennai, India

8. **B. Asadullah, Librarian**
Mazharul Uloom College, Ambur – 635 802.

9. **Mani M. Manivannan**
Senior Director of Engineering, Symantec Corporation, Chennai, India

10. **Dr. A. Vijaya Kathiravan, R. Vidhya**
Dept. of Master of Computer Applications, KSR College of Technology, Tiruchengode–637 215

11. **A.Parimaladevi, III MCA, A.Muthukumar, Professor,**
Kumaraguru College of Technology, Coimbatore

12. **Eric Miller**

13. **Saminatha Kumaran Veloo, Saravanan Mariappan**
Nexus IT Solutions, Malaysia,

14. **N D Loga Sundaram**
26/15 Kutchery Lane Mylapore, Chennai, India.

15. **Nethravathi B, Archana C P, Shashikiran K & A G Ramakrishnan,**
MILE Lab, Department of Electrical Engineering, IISc, Bangalore, India.

16. **R. DhivyaBharathi**
Bannari Amman Institute of Technology, Erode – 638 401

A. BalaMurugan
Anna University, Tiruchirappalli – 620 024

17. **S.Rajakumar, Dr.V.Subbiah Bharathi, J. Navarajan**
DMI College of Engineering, Chennai-602103

18. **Tushar Patnaik**
CDAC Noida

Shalu Gupta
CDAC CV Jawahar, IIIT Hyderabad

Santanu Choudhury
IIT Delhi A G Ramakrishnan, IISc, Bangalore–560012

19. **N.Shanthi**
K.Duraiswamy K.S.Rangasamy College of Technology, Tiruchengode, Tamil Nadu, India

20. **Dr. T. Ravi**
KCG College of Technology, Chennai.

Prof. R. Velayutham
Einstein College of Engineering, Tirunelveli.

21. **Seima Saki S**
ECE, Sabita Devi D, Sri Krishna College of Engineering and Tech., Coimbatore

Manoj S
Computer Technology, PSG College of Technology, Coimbatore

Mr.R.Vimalathithan
Sri Krishna College of Engineering and Tech, Coimbatore

22. **Sowmiya Dharmalingam and Madhan Karky**
Department of Computer Science and Engineering, College of Engineering Guindy, Anna University

23. **D. Mahendran, S. Gunasundari, Prof. B. Rajalakshmi**
Department of CSE, Velammal Engineering College, Chennai

24. **G.V. Uma**
Assistant Professor, Dept. of Computer Science Engineering, Anna University Chennai, Chennai.

25. **Mahalakshmi G.S, Sendhilkumar S, Shankar B.**
Department of Computer Science and Engineering, Anna University, Chennai 600025, India

26. **D. Narashiman, Dr.T. Mala**
Anna University, Chennai-600 025

27. **Uma Maheshwar Rao G, Christopher M, Parameswari K.**
Centre for Applied Linguistics and Translation Studies, University of Hyderabad, Hyderabad – 500046.

1

Face Waves

2D-Facial Expressions Based on Tamil Emotion Descriptors

—Sabitha Tammaneni
—Madhan Karky

ABSTRACT

This chapter aims at recognizing human emotions from textual descriptors and expressing the emotion in a 2 dimensional computer generated face for the Face Waves framework. The main objective of this chapter is to map facial expressions for the basic six emotions (Love, Joy, Fear, Anger, Surprise, and Sadness), 27 second level derived emotions, and a third level 79 emotions. Apart from hierarchically classifying these 112 emotions in Tamil, this chapter presents an object oriented emotion model, where the emotions at lower levels inherit properties from emotions at higher levels. The chapter also describes an 'expression index' built for efficiently storing and retrieving the facial features for corresponding expressions for every emotion. The 'expression index' plays a vital role in mapping the expression on a computer generated face with time efficiency. Discussing the results of mapping and efficiency of the index, the chapter concludes with open questions and future enhancements.

Introduction

Since Charles Darwin's early work on 'The Expression of Emotions in Man and Animals', there have been various proposals to classify human emotions. A few researches have been carried out in mapping expressions to emotions. The expressions to emotion mapping cannot be generalized as every individual has his or her own way of expressing various emotions. In many cases it will not be possible for one to distinguish extreme happiness from extreme sadness just by observing facial expression of a person. In this chapter we present a system that can identify emotions from textual descriptions and try to map a corresponding expression on a 2D computer generated face.

The primary aim of this chapter is to present an object model for all possible human emotions and their corresponding Tamil textual descriptors. The secondary aim is to map the action units of various parts of a human face to express the emotion. To best of our knowledge, this is the first time that such a work is presented in Tamil and first time an object-oriented model is proposed for representing emotions and their expressions.

This chapter is organized into five sections. The second section provides some background information and discusses literature related to this work. The third section presents the classification tree for human emotions in Tamil. The fourth section describes the system design and explains the action units for every expression. The fifth section presents the results and discusses the advantages of an expression index based on the object-oriented emotion tree to increase the time efficiency of expressing emotions on a 2D face for a text-to-video system.

Background

'Facial expression' has drawn interest to a few researchers around the world. Most of the research focuses on expressing emotions in a 3D face. Paul Ekman and Wallace F introduced a system called FACS,where each facial expression is described in terms of Action Units (AU's)[1]. Irfan A. Essa and Alex P. Pentland implemented a computer vision system which is developed by using mathematical formulation which is used for detailed analysis of facial expressions[3]. Prem Kalra, Angelo Mangili,Nadia Magnenat Thalmann and Daniel Thalmann made every expression from one or more MPA's(Minimum Perceptible Action),One or several simulated muscle actions constitute a MPA[2]. Praseeda Lekshmi.V And Dr.M.Sasikumar used multicast Support Vector Machine for Classification of different kinds of facial expressions belonging to the face image, they also used Gabor filters for image processing[4]. Hadi Seyedarabi, Ali Aghagolzadeh, and Sohrab Khanmohammadi developed a deformable muscle-based face model that tracks some FCP's in the real face image sequences and shows the same expressions[5]. Robert Plutchik created a wheel of emotions, which forms the base to this paper[6]. The emotions provided in English are translated in Tamil to present the emotion tree.

Classification of Human Emotions

As explained in section 1, there have been various proposals to classify human emotions. Many classifications do not recognize love as a basic human emotion. We have achived our classification of emotions based on Robert Plutchik's classification[6]. The first level of tree is provided in figure 1.1. Happiness, Fear, Love, Sadness, Anger and Surprise form the first level of emotions. All other emotions are derived from these basic emotions according to Robert.

Fig. 1.1 : Emotion Tree: Level 1

Each of these basic emotions in the first level of tree has sub-emotions as shown in figure 1.2. Figure 1.2 gives the second level emotions for two of the basic emotions happiness and sadness.

Fig. 1.2 : Emotion Tree: Level 2

The classification of these emotions runs down to a third level where each of the sub-emotions have subsub- emotions with the same base emotion. Figure 1.3 gives the third level emotions for happiness and sadness. The sub emotion shame(avamaanam) gives raise to four third level emotions. Similarly the subemotion cheerfulness (uRsaagam) gives raise to eight third level emotions.

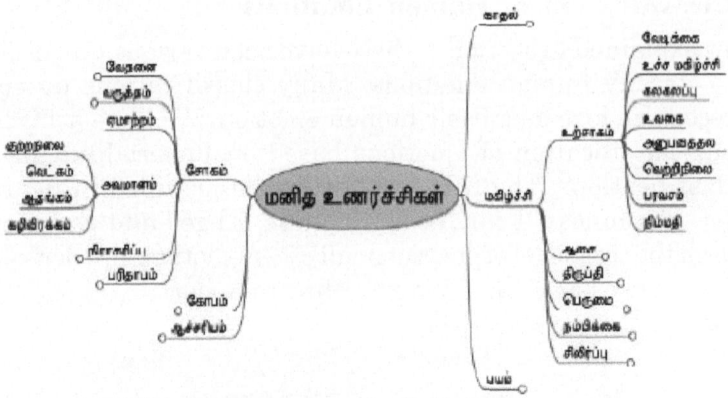

Fig. 1.3 : Emotion Tree: Level 3

The complete tree consisting of 112 emotions is not provided in this chapter owing to space considerations.

System Design

The design of our emotion processor is given in figure 1.4. Face Generator will accept the input (face description) from the user, which will analyze the input and then distributes the corresponding characteristics for each part of the face. The character Engine will construct the Human face, which is a 2D computer generated face.

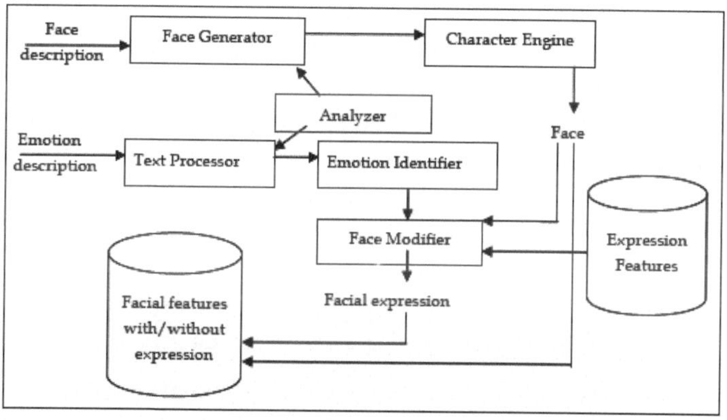

Fig. 1.4 : Emotion Processor System Design

The Text Processor processes a given text document for emotional descriptors. The text lines corresponding to the emotional descriptors are analysed using a morphological analyzer and the output of the analyzer is fed to the Emotion Identifier. Emotion identifier using the emotion model explained in section 3, identifies the emotion and sends the emotion tag to Face Modifier. The Face Modifier module uses an expression index to modify every part of the face according to the expression. Each part of face is modeled as an object and the face modifier based on the emotion tag controls the attributes of the object. Thus the emotion is mapped to the face that comes as input from the character engine as a set of feature changes termed as an expression of the emotion. The modified face can now be stored as text. in a database for efficient retrieval for the Text-to-Video system. It is to be noted that the Face Generator may generate any type of a face based on the descriptions it gets. The pre-generated face is given as input to the Face modifier along with the emotion descriptors.

Emotion to Expression

We use Ekman's FACS Action Units(AU)[1] to describe the transformations on a 2D computer generated face. The action units specify pull, raise like actions for every part of the face. Those Aus corresponding to 2D face alone have been used to represent the emotion on the face as an expression. The following are examples of two basic emotions and their corresponding action units.

Table 1.1 : Action Units for Joy

"மகிழ்ச்சி"(Joy):

AU	Description
12	Lip comer puller
5	Upperlid raiser

Table 1.2 : Action Units for Fear

"பயம்"(Fear):

AU	Description
1	Inner brow raiser
2	Outer brow raiser
3	Upper lid raiser
7	Lid tightenes
20	Lip stretches

Emotions in the second and third levels of the emotion tree inherit the action units from their parent emotion and have their own action units along with the inherited units.

Results

A simple face generated by the Face Generator module and a few samples of the faces modified by our Face Modifier for different emotions are given in figure 5. The features of the face are given as input to the Face Modifier. Emotion descriptors can be natural language text describing the state of the person.

அவன் சோகமாக காணப்பட்டான்

He looked sad

அவன் அப்போது பயந்துபோய் கிடந்தான்

He looked scared at that moment

The above given sentences can be examples of emotion descriptors. Our analyzer breaks the words to identify the root and when the emotion is identified, the corresponding features are retrieved from the expression index. The features are applied over the 2D face that was received as input for modification.

Fig. 1.5 : Original Face and Modified Faces

The face in the center of figure 1.5 is the original face generated by our face generator surrounded by the corresponding faces modified for six different emotions. Similarly any generated face is modified for one of the 112 emotional descriptors.

Conclusion and Future Work

This chapter proposes an object-oriented model for representing emotions hierarchically and proposes a system for applying emotions on a 2D computer generated face using Ekman's FACS action units. Improving the index for minimizing the number of changes from original face to modified face will be our immediate research that follows. Such an index will improve the time efficiency of creating text-tovideo. Applying these emotions for a 3D face can aid to generating 3D animation videos.

REFERENCES

1. Ekman.P,W. V. Friesen, *"The Facial Action Coding System: A Technique for Measurement of Facial Movement".* 1978.
2. Prem Kalra, Angelo Mangili, Nadia Magnenat Thalmann and Daniel Thalmann, "3D Interactive Free Form Deformations for Facial Expressions", *First International Conference on Computational Graphics and Visualization Techniques,* Sesimbra, Portugal, 1993.
3. Irfan A. Essa, Alex P. Pentland, *"Coding, Analysis, Interpretation, and Recognition of Facial Expressions,"* IEEE Transactions on Pattern Analysis and Machine Intelligence, 1997.
4. Praseeda Lekshmi.V and Dr.M.Sasikumar, "Analysis of Facial Expression using Gabor and SVM", *Interntional Journal of Recent Trends in Engineering* 2009.
5. Hadi Seyedarabi, Ali Aghagolzadeh, and Sohrab Khanmohammadi, "Facial Expressions Animation and Lip Tracking Using Facial Characteristic Points and Deformable Model", *International Journal of Information Technology,* 2005
6. List of Human Emotions, http://en.wikipedia.org/wiki/List_of_emotions, Last Accessed 23/04/2010

2

Face Waves

Tamil Text-to-Speech with Lip Synchronisation for a 2D Computer Generated Face

—A.G. Tamilarasan
—Madhan Karky

ABSTRACT

This chapter presents a system for converting Tamil text to speech and synchronizes the lip movements of a 2D computer generated face to the generated speech. This chapter describes the components of the system such as, grapheme to phoneme converter, a rule-based phoneme-sound selector, wave merger, lipphoneme synchronizer and face animator. Presenting the grapheme to phoneme algorithm and the phoneme-sound selector rules, this chapter presents the results from the grapheme to phoneme converter and rule based-sound selector. The chapter concludes with future extensions of the presented work.

Introduction

Tamil language has strict phonetic rules defined many thousand years ago in the ancient grammar definition Tholkaappiyam. These rules have formed the basis of many text to speech systems that exist in Tamil today. This chapter proposes a Tamil text-to-speech and lip-synchronization system that takes Tamil text and a 2D computer generated face as input and converts the Text to speech waves and lip synchronize the face to speak the given text along with audio as an animated video.

The motivation behind this work is to provide such a subsystem for a pure text-to-video system where an entire video can be created purely using natural language. Such a system will be of immense use to physically challenged and also enables common people with very less computer knowledge to create and distribute animation video. One major advantage of having such a system would be to transfer such animation over Internet or mobile as a simple text and converting the text to video using a local client.

This chapter is organized into four sections. The second section discusses the background and literature closely related to this work. The third section provides the system architecture and discusses the different modules and their functions. The fourth section discusses the results and issues related to text-to-speech conversion and lip synchronization. The fifth section summarizes and concludes this chapter and discusses future research directions.

Background

There have been many research works related to Text-to-Speech and generally the text-to-speech systems fall in one of the two categories namely speech synthesis and phoneme concatenation. Sreekanth Majji and Ramakrishnan A. G. used a labeled database to make a system capable of producing a speech output[1]. John Lewis proposed Naive approach for automatic lip-sync to open the mouth in proportion to the loudness of the sound[3]. Keith Waters and Thomas M. Levergood demonstrated an automatic lips ynchronization algorithm for automatically synchronizing lip motion to a speech synthesizer in realtime[5]. Masatsune

Tamura, Shigekazu Kondo, Takashi Masuko, and Takao Kobayashi used parameter generation algorithm, which is used to generate an audio-visual speech parameter vector sequence[4]. Marc Schroder developed Modular Architecture (MARY) for speech synthesis and has the capability of parsing speech synthesis markup.[2]

The Text-to-Speech system proposed in this paper is based on the Tamil Voice Engine[6] proposed by Madhan Karky et al., The Tamil Voice Engine takes Tamil text as input and uses a phoneme database with over 4000 entries. The words are split into corresponding phonemes using rules and the appropriate phonemes are selected and concatenated. This paper uses a similar system for Text-to-Speech but incorporates more rules to improve the phoneme selection and thereby improves the correctness of generated speech.

System Design

The system proposed for text-to-speech and lip synchronization can be naturally split into two major components. The Text-to-speech component receives text as input and converts the graphemes to phonemes. The waves associated with the phonemes are concatenated along with pauses into a single audio wave as continuous speech. The Lip-Sync component of the system receives a 2D computer generated face with all parts of faces and their coordinates. The coordinates of lips are identified and they are modified for different lip positions for different phonemes. The system maintains a lip coordinate index for phonemes that require modifications. Figure 2.1 presents the overall design of the system.

Text-to-Speech: The Text-to-Speech component comprises of four modules. Text Processor, Grapheme to Phoneme Converter, Rule Based Phoneme Selector and Merger. The component also comprises of a phoneme database. These modules together convert a given text dialogue to speech.

• ***Text Processor:*** The Text processor processes raw input text and tags the text to appropriate tags as words and pauses. Inter-word pause, inter-sentence pause are tagged by the text processor. A document is thus converted to a set of ordered word and pause tags.

• ***Grapheme to Phoneme Converter:*** Grapheme to Phoneme converter takes the ordered set from Text Processor as input and processes the word tags and splits them further into phonemes. The grapheme to phoneme conversion is based on an algorithm provided in[6] that uses consonant-vowel combinations of letters in a word. An example of such a grapheme to phoneme conversion is provided below.

தமிழுக்கு அமுதென்று பேர் | thamizhukku amudhenru paer

த-மி-ழுக்-கு அ-மு-தென்-று பேர்

Will be split into the following phoneme combinations separated by hyphen:

• ***Phoneme Merger:*** The phoneme database stores 4646 phonemes and based on the split provided by Will be split into the following phoneme combinations separated by hyphen:

• ***Phoneme Merger:*** The phoneme database stores 4646 phonemes and based on the split provided by the grapheme to phoneme converter, Phoneme merger applies certain rules to identify the right set of phonemes for the current split. <tha+mi+zhuk+ku> <a+mu+dhen+dru> <paer>

The selection of 'dhen' in the above example instead of 'then' is based on the rule that the sound of the phoneme changes based on where it occurs in a sentence. Similar rules are applied for the hard consonants (ka/ga sa/cha da/ta tha/dha pa/ba Ra/tra) based on their occurrences. 'kutriyalukaram' a property that states that words that end with 'u' have their meter length cut short by half a meter.

This rule is also being handled as a rule for selecting appropriate phoneme. Phoneme merger then chooses the appropriate waves from the phoneme database for the phonemes selected by the Phoneme Selector. The selected phonemes are then merged along with the appropriate pauses. The phoneme merger creates a single wave file that can be attached to a video or used for any text-tospeech application. In this framework, it sends the wave to animator and the phoneme and duration information to lip synchronization modules respectively.

• ***Lip Synchronization:*** The Lip Synchronization component comprises of a Face Generator, Face Animator and Lip Synchronizer. These modules together generate a video of a speaking face whose lip movements are synchronized to the speech generated by the Text-to-Speech component.

• ***Face Generator:*** The face generator module developed as part of the FaceWaves framework, receives textual description of facial features in Tamil. The descriptions are converted to coordinates and dimensions of various parts of the face. The coordinates of the face are used as input for the lip synchronizer

• ***Lip Synchronizer:*** Lip synchronizer receives temporal information about the generated wave such as the phonemes, the start and end time of every phoneme and pauses. Lip Synchronizer uses this information to suggest the lip positions for the face animation at every time instance. An example sentence and how it is converted to a phoneme-pause temporal information is given below:

Table 2.1 : Duration of Phonomes

Phoneme	From(Sec)	To(Sec)
நான் | naan	0.0	0.445
Pause	0.446	0.696
இங்| ing	0.697	0.931
கு | ku	0.932	1.207
Pause	1.208	1.457
வந் | van	1.458	1.707
தேன் | thaen	1.708	2.083

Table 2.2 : Lip Position

Lip Position	From(Sec)	To(Sec)
2	0.0	0.445
1	0.446	0.696
3	0.697	0.931
5	0.932	1.207
1	1.208	1.457
13	1.458	1.707
6	1.708	2.083

Face Animator: Face Animator uses the temporal information provided by the lip synchronizer to modify the lip coordinates of the face provided by the Face Generator. Face Animator uses the speech wave provided by the Phoneme Merger and creates frames of faces with varying lip coordinates over the same timeline. As the wave timeline and animation frame timeline are one and the same, the animation video has 100 per cent synchronization accuracy.

நான் இங்கு வந்தேன் | naan ingu vandhaen

Results

Text-to-speech system was tested over a dictionary[7] of 2,00,000 root words. Text was converted to speech with 92 per cent accuracy. Words with non-Tamil characters and missing phonemes can be attributed to the 8% results were the right phonemes were not selected. The same system when tested with 200 named entities (person names and organization names) gives 98 per cent accuracy.

Fig. 2.2 : Lip Positions

The Lip Synchronizer and Face Animator use a phoneme to lip-coordinate mapping. The mapping provides information as lip positions. Figure 2 provides the lip positions for various phonemes. The faces in Figure 1.2 were generated by the Face animator with input from Lip Synchronizer. As mentioned in the previous section the lip synchronization has 100 per cent accuracy as the same timeline is considered for the wave and for the animation.

Conclusion and Future Work

The current system has certain limitations such as the phoneme recordings are not normalized and the merged phonemes are not smoothened. Wave smoothening and professionally recording the sounds and mastering the waves will be essential to improve the quality of the audio. Secondly, the face animation is currently done for a 2D face. If the similar system can be extended to animate 3D faces the animation would look more realistic. This system we believe would be of immense use to common people with very little computer knowledge to create and distribute 2D animations. Creating mobile agents to communicate text messages or creating automatic news reporters with these animated faces will take this project to the next level.

REFERENCES

1. Sreekanth Majji, *Festival Based Maiden TTS System for Tamil, Language Research Paper,* Indian Institute of Science, Bangalore,2007.
2. Marc Schroder and Jurgen Trouvain, *German Text-to-Speech Synthesis System,* Institute of Phonetics, University of the Saarland, Germany,2008.
3. John Lewis, Automated Lip-Sync: *Background and Techniques, Computer Graphics Laboratory,* New York Institute of Technology, 1991.
4. Masatsune Tamura, Shigekazu Kondo, Takashi Masuko, and Takao Kobayashi, *Text-to-audio visual speech synthesis based on parameter generation from HMM,* Interdisciplinary Graduate School of Science and Engineering Tokyo Institute of Technology, Yokohama, 2007.

5. Keith Waters and Thomas M. Levergood, *DECface: An Automatic Lip-Synchronization Algorithm for Synthetic Faces,* Digital Equipment Corporation Cambridge Research Lab, 1993.

6. Madhan Karky V, Sudarsanan N, Thiyagarajan R, Manoj Annadurai, Dr.Ranjani Parthasarathi and Dr.T.V.Geetha: *Tamil Voice Engine, Tamil Internet Conference,* Malaysia, 2001.

7. *Agaraadhi Online Tamil Dictionary,* www.agaraadhi.com, last accessed 20/04/2010.

3

Statistical Analysis and Visualization of Tamil Usage in Live Text Streams

—J. Jai Hari Raju
—P. IndhuReka
—Dr. Madhan Karky

ABSTRACT

Tamil is slowly gaining popularity as an active language in social networking on the Internet. This chapter aims at statistically analyzing the usage of Tamil words in text streaming social networking sites. This chapter proposes an active Tamil text stream reader designed to obtain live usage statistics of Tamil words in Twitter, a text based social networking service. A spatio-temporal dynamic index is maintained by the text stream reader and the word usage and the geo-tags are recorded along with a time stamp. The chapter also presents a visualization tool where the data captured in the spatio-temporal dynamic index can be visualized graphically to show what topics are gaining and losing popularity over time and space. The results from the analysis are discussed along with snapshots from the visualization tool. The chapter concludes with open questions for future research in active text stream analysis for Tamil language.

Introduction

The number of text streaming social networking sites has increased drastically and the usage of Tamil in these sites has reached considerable proportions. The analysis of which will reflect the current scenario of Tamil usage among web users. These text streams can be analyzed to obtain the usage statistics of words over time and geographic location. This analysis requires a tool which will collect data pertaining to a given Tamil word, analyze it then index it. This chapter proposes an overall architecture of such a frame work.

The proposed framework contains a text stream retriever which interacts with the site in order to obtain the text stream units for analysis. The obtained data is parsed based on various constraints and the information retrieved is stored in an index. This information is then subjected to analysis. The results from such an analysis reflect various aspects of Tamil's web usage. When the results are visualized with respect to time, they depict how the usage frequencies of words vary. This data can also be used to find which topics are gaining and loosing importance. When the results are analyzed with respect to geographic location they provide insights into the global scenario of Tamil. In section 2 we provide an overview of the literature survey conducted. In section 3 we discuss the design of the various modules of the framework which provides us an overview of the spatio temporal properties of Tamil text streams. In section 4 we discuss the implementation of the proposed framework and the results obtained from the analysis. Finally we conclude in section 5 with directions for further studies in the field of text stream analysis for Tamil language.

Background

In the literature there are existing works on text stream analysis. Qiankun Zhao *et al.* explored the temporal and social information of text streams in order to achieve better results in event detection[1]. Jon Kleinberg analyzed the various techniques for Topic Detection and Tracking and also the various information visualization techniques for interpreting data from a temporal dimension[2]. Nilesh Bansal et al. developed a system called BlogScope[3]. BlogScope is an information discovery and text stream analysis system which follows blogs and analyses their content. Danyel Fisher et al. developed a visualization to track narrative events as they develop in text streams[4]. Le Wang *et al.* proposed a double time window algorithm for conversation extraction in dynamic text message streams[5]. Vagelis Hristidis et al. explored the techniques for extracting useful information from a collection of text streams and proposed a system for keyword search on textual streams[6].

Design of Tamil Text Stream Analyzer

The Tamil Text Stream Analyzer consists of the following major components:

- Text Stream Retriever
- Analyzer
- Indexer

Figure (3.1) given below depicts the architecture of the framework.

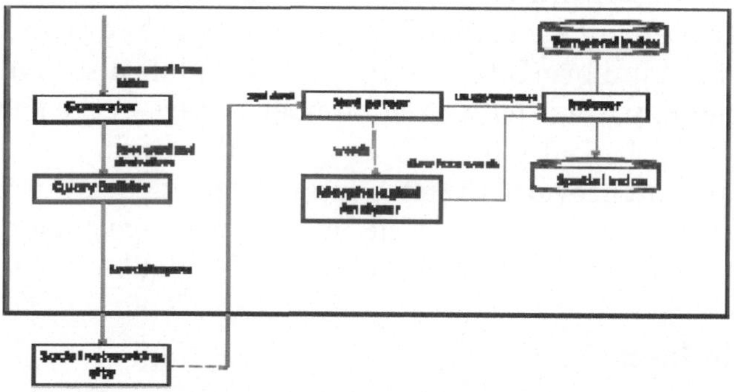

Fig. 3.1 : Tamil Text Stream Analysis Framework

(a) Text Stream Retriever

This module is responsible for retrieving the text stream usage instances for a given word. The initial input for this module is obtained from a list of predefined popular root words. In order to prevent the overhead of storing a very large search list comprising of both the root words and their derivatives only the root words are stored and their corresponding derivatives are obtained using a generator. The search query is constructed using the OR operator so that the occurrence of even one of the forms is taken in to account. Storing of only the root words in order to increase the memory efficiency is an important design decision. The query is targeted towards the particular site's Search API. The search results returned by the APIs which are generally XML files are in turn handed over to the analyzer module.

(b) Analyzer

The analyzer module is responsible for analyzing the raw data retrieved by the reader. The analyzer parses the given XML data in order to extract the required statistics. Predefined tags containing the required information are identified. The total number of entries for the given word is counted. As the amount of usage history maintained by the Social Networking sites is found to vary for each word, this parameter will not suffice for a conclusion to be drawn. So to provide a uniform interpretation, this module also analyses the per day usage for a fixed number of days in the past for all words. It is also possible to record the origin of the text stream unit provided the sites support geotagging. Currently Twitter, a Social networking site supports geotagging by allowing queries based on the origin of a text stream unit.

(c) Indexer

As the usage statistics of words are determined for two parameters namely time and geographic location, spatiotemporal indices are used to store the data. The decision to store, search and update a fixed list of words would result in a static application which cannot be scaled. Hence a dynamic approach is chosen, wherein the text stream instances returned for a keyword are parsed to obtain new words whose root words do not exist in the search list currently. Those words are added to the search list and are analyzed in the future searches.

Index Structure: As text streams are analyzed in a spatio temporal manner, two indices are maintained. The temporal index stores the usage statistics of words with respect to time. The spatial index stores the usage statistics of words with respect to geographic location. A Hashtable data structure is used for the indices. The temporal index is built with the temporal component (Date) as the key.

Implementation

In order to implement the proposed framework, Twitter a prominent Social Networking Site is chosen as the source for text stream. The root word to be searched is taken from the index and the word's derivatives are found using a generator. The search query for the temporal analysis is constructed from those words and is posted to the Twitter Search API. In order to analyze the word usage spatially we count the number of times the word originates inside TamilNadu. The search API responds with XML data. The analyzer module parses this data and populates the statistical and temporal indices maintained. The text stream units are parsed and the words are subjected to morphological analysis and the resulting root words if not already present, are added to the index.

Results

As the source of the text streams is a social networking site (Twitter), they contain conversations which have many stop words. These stop words are not excluded from the search.

The search for stop words yields many other words which accompany them in conversations. The analysis also shows that a considerable proportion of the text streams originate outside Tamil Nadu. The user interface is designed with options for the users to visualize the results in various aspects. Options for viewing the results for the top 5 words of the week, Comparing the usage statistics of the given words and analyzing the spatial usage distribution of a given word are provided. Figure (3.2) given below is a screen shot of the text stream analysis system. The bar graph depicts the usage statistics of the top 5 words for a time span of 7 days from 18th of April 2010. The line graph below compares the occurrence count for a given word originating within TamilNadu against the total occurrence count.

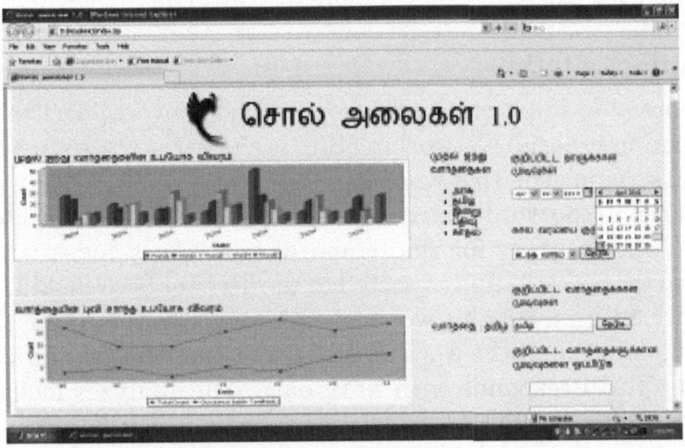

Fig. 3.3 : Screenshot of the Text Streams Analysis System

Conclusion and Future Work

In this chapter we have proposed a framework for spatiotemporal analysis of Tamil text streams. The performance of the current system can be improved by adapting a more efficient indexing mechanism. As a next level of analysis, Topic Detection and Tracking (TDT) and prediction of evolving topics can be applied for Tamil text streams. The usage of Tamil in blogs and search engine queries is on the rise. Blogs and search engine queries have inherent temporal properties, hence this analysis can be extended to these areas also. Related work has been carried out for text streams in English. But Tamil being a highly inflectional language, requires customized searching and indexing mechanisms for efficient analysis.

REFERENCES

1. Q. Zhao, P. Mitra and B.Chen, *"Temporal and Information Flow-based Event Detection from Social Text Streams,"* 22nd AAAI Conference on Artificial Intelligence, (AAAI'07), Vancouver, Canada.
2. J. Kleinberg, *"Temporal Dynamics of On-line Information Streams,"* In Data Stream Management: Processing High-speed Data Streams, (M. Garofalakis, J. Gehrke, R. Rastogi, eds.), Springer, 2004.
3. N. Bansal and N. Koudas, *"Blogscope: A System for Online Analysis of High Volume Text Streams,"* In VLDB, pp. 1410–1413, 2007.
4. D. Fisher, A.Hoff, G.Robertson and M. Hurst, *"Narratives: A Visualization to Track Narrative Events as They Develop,"* In IEEE Symposium on Visual Analytics and Technology(VAST 2007).
5. L. Wang, Y. Jia and Y. Chen.(2008,Oct). Conversation Extraction in Dynamic Text Message Stream. *Journal of Computers* (JCP). 3(10).
6. V. Hristidis, O. Valdivia, M. Vlachos, P.S. Yu, "A System for Keyword Search on Textual Streams," *Proceedings of the Seventh SIAM International Conference on Data Mining,* Minnesota, USA, April 26-28,2007.

4

An Analysis of Various Types of Distortions of Tamil Scripts

—R. Indra Gandhi
—Dr. K. Iyakutti
—Dr. C. Jothi Venkateswaran

ABSTRACT

While reading old documents, it is difficult to read the content if the pages or print found to be in poor condition. The damage might be because of poor maintenance, poor paper quality, prolonged disturbances like blurring of ink and damages done by bookworms like silverfish and booklouse. The objective of this study is to ascertain the distortions on Tamil scripts by various sources. The factors that cause each kind of distortion, the problems associated with them and the possible solutions for the identification of each kind of distorted text have been discussed in detail. This is extremely useful for researchers engaged in recognizing the distorted documents in any script as same kind of distortion can be found in most of the scripts used globally.

Introduction

The progress of any OCR recognition, which registers the

efforts of researches of the last six decades, can lead to the accuracy of 99.90 per cent obtained with the help of any commercial OCR system when the document images are sharp, clear and noiseless. Still, there are several applications were the recognition process miserably fails when a poor image source is used. In addition, even a slight distortion of the image quality can make the accuracy of document recognition fall flat. The occurrences of distortions in scanned images are affected by various factors, which are categorized into four areas[1,2]. Distorted documents do not include all the ideal properties of a document. Even a slight deter in the quality of source documents results in a downfall in the entire recognition process. Some well-known causes for deterioration on document images include:

(*a*) Natural calamities

(*b*) Vertical cuts caused paper folding

(*c*) Usage of poor quality of ink

(*d*) Excessive dusty noise

(*e*) Large ink-blobs merging the disjoint characters or components

(*f*) Disconnection of arbitrary direction due to paper quality or the presence of foreign material

(*g*) Floating of ink to the opposite pages or the next pages etc.,

(*h*) Defects caused during printing

(*i*) Defects introduced during digitization through camera, copying through photocopier and fax machines

General ink-blobs are nothing but the random occurrence of black or white pixels at or about a coordinate point. Even the spread of normal distribution (essentially the standard deviation) is also variable. Disconnection of characters is caused by the white blobs whereas black blobs results in merged characters. Keeping above in mind different kinds of distortions have been observed in Tamil document scripts.

Review of Literature over Different Type of Distortion

In order to reach the goal, an ample study of research outcome in several related areas were surveyed. Touching characters: Segmentation is a major problem during recognizing touching characters. Utilizing projection profiles and topographic method features extracted by Lee *et al*[3] have dealt with segmenting the touching characters. Bose and Kuo[4] used a robust structural analysis technique. Tsujimoto and Asada's[5] constructed segmentation method by several candidates for break positions. Casey and Nagy[6] utilized recursive procedure to decompose all blocks wider than a certain adaptive threshold. Hong[7] endorse the focus on segmentation of Roman script characters. Kahan *et al*[8] made an attempt on double differential function. A wide-ranging study of research outcomes in touching characters in Indian scripts is seen in[9-17].

Broken: Whichello and Yan[17] introduced a reconstruct method. Bern and Goldberg[19] advocates a scanning process adopting a probabilistic model. Akiyama *et al*[20] has taken their methods absorbed multi resolutions pyramid and fuzzy edge detectors. Lu *et al*[21] proposed an algorithm based on estimation procedure and a sequential merging procedure. Nakamura *et al*[22] and Okamoto *et al*[23] in-took the propagation and shrinking in vertical and horizontal directions. The estimation of the pitch and location of pitch window helped Yanikoglu[24]. To rejoin the appropriate connected components Droettboom[25] used a technique based on graph combinatory.

Heavily Printed: Even advanced OCR of Roman script stands a failure to recognise the heavily printed characters[26].

Double-sided: Leedham *et al*[27] attempted the recognition process with the introduction of binarization methods with bleed through defects. Anna Tonazzini *et al*[28] have drawn more general approaches and statistical methods such as Independent Component Analysis (ICA) and Bline Source Operation (BSS). Dubois and Pathak[29] real samples are used for various distortion models. Like[30] more information regarding this can be accessed using[30]. Gang Zi and Doermann[31] and Gang Zi[32] proposed types of defects taking the base of blurring and mixing techniques.

Faxed document: Bloomberg[33] delivered his message as storing the fax as an electronic image. Oguro *et al*[34] gave a proposal of three-step solution for restoring fax documents. Randolph and Smith[35] comprised of directional components developed a binary Directional Filter Bank (DFB). The recognition accuracy has gained better percentage by the hands of Hobby and Ho[36]. Natarajan *et al*[37] have trained the system on distorted documents and then adapted to adjust the parameters of the trained model.

Type written document: Cannon *et al*[38,39] have advanced an automatic quality improvement technique for recognition of distorted typewritten images. A new cost function was formulated by Rodriguez *et al*[40] to segment degraded typewritten digits.

Different kinds of distortion in Tamil scripts

A careful scanning of 200 Tamil documents resulted in the following discussion on the causes of each kind of distortion, the problems associated with them and the immediate need of analyzing the solution to overcome those problems that are obstacles of character recognition. The following enlists the various kinds of distortion:

1. Merging Characters (Touching)
2. Fragmented Characters (Broken)
3. Over Imprinted Characters (Heavily Printed)
4. Electronically Shared documents (Fax etc.,)

5. Double-sided Documents (Bleed Through)
6. Type Written Documents

1. Touching Characters

This is the most commonly found distortion in hand-written and printed Tamil scripts. It happens due to overlapping of parts of two characters in one or more places in different zones. Segmentation is a process involved in recognition. As OCR depends heavily on the accuracy of the segmentation process, each OCR system has to perform well to maximize the result of segmentation. Documents containing touching characters are magazines with heavy printing, hand written documents and Photostatted documents copied on low quality machines.

A careful analysis and investigation help to classify the touching characters into three types:

(*a*) Single touching

(*b*) Multiple touching

(*c*) Long touching

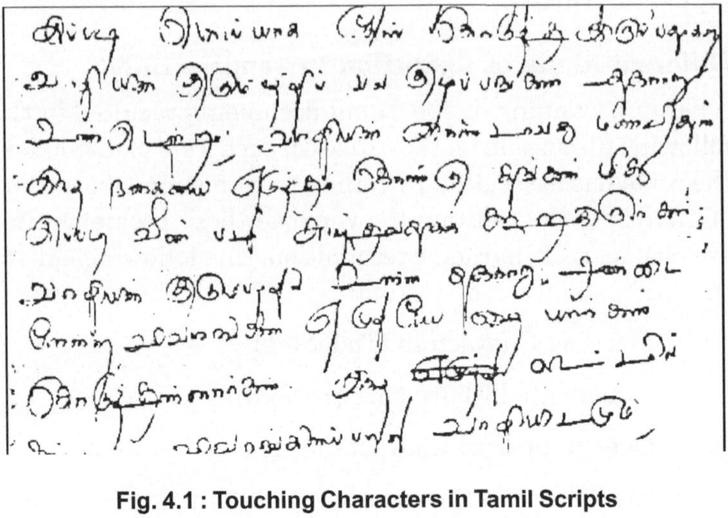

Fig. 4.1 : Touching Characters in Tamil Scripts

In the first case, the neighbouring characters touch each other in only one place, in the second case the merging occurs in more than one place and in the third, the characters merge with each other as hardly separable components. The OCR meets with a drastic decrease in accuracy when touching characters are involved.

A statistical analysis enlists the following observations:

(*a*) Probability is more for the merging of characters at the middle zone rather than upper or lower zones;

(*b*) In most cases, touching characters in Tamil script either closely resemble some other character or totally differ from valid characters;

(*c*) Most of the images encounter a single black run at the touching position;

(*d*) Image characters, which are taken for treatment, are generally of two characters. Merging with one another and overlapping of three or more characters takes rare occasions;

(*e*) The aspect ratio (width divided by height) clearly distinguishes the touching characters from the usual and isolated characters, which are comparatively smaller than that of the merged ones;

(*f*) In fact, the identification of vertical thick ink blob differentiates the touching characters that possess the abnormal thickness in it;

(*g*) From a series of analysis of touching characters, it has been noted that generally a word may contain only a pair of characters touching each other;

(*h*) Possibility of more than two characters touching is very feeble;

(*i*) Obviously, the characters of many Indian scripts contain a sidebar at the right end, which is absent in Tamil scripts. Hence, ambiguity is comparatively the least in that particular position.

2. Broken Characters

Resembling the touching characters, the broken characters also cause some obstruction in the character recognition of Tamil scripts.

The following observations have been made on the statistical analysis of broken Tamil characters :

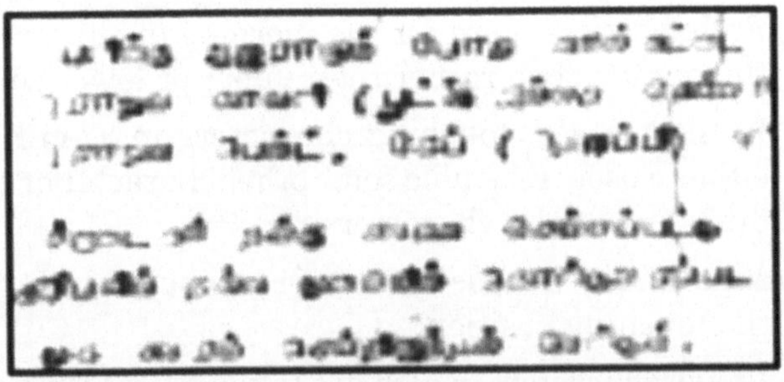

Fig. 4.2 : Broken Characters in Tamil Script

(*a*) Broken characters have common occurrence more in lower zones rather than upper and middle zones;

(*b*) The appearance of a character is generally not similar in shape like other individual characters. In some cases it may be same in shape of some other character;

(*c*) Despite the distinct shapes of each character, some resemble other, causing complexity of conception;

(*d*) Generally, there is a heavy loss of information in Tamil when compared with headline-based characters;

(*e*) Broken characters generally adhere to the aspect ratio (width divided by height) lesser than other single isolated characters;

(*f*) The segmentation of vertical and horizontal break of the characters has added one more problem of diagonally broken characters;

(*g*) The improper spacing of character causes overlapping lines producing difficulty in understanding.

3. *Heavily Printed*

Characters

Sometimes isolated characters turn out to be unidentifiable due to heavy printing, equally significant problem like touching characters. So the problem of heavily printed character of Indian language still posses a need for an innovative solution. This kind of distortion takes the same sources as the touching characters.

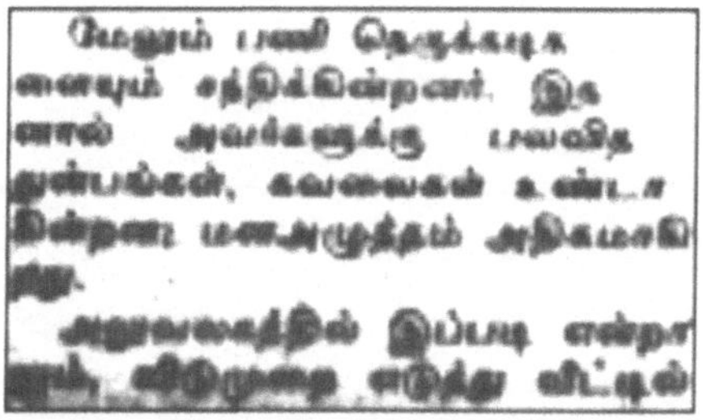

Fig. 4.3 : Heavily Printed Characters in Tamil Script

Observations after statistical analyses are enlisted below:

(*a*) Generally, the shape of a heavily printed character may look like some other character;

(*b*) In most of the characters, when printed heavily, there is a gain of a loop in their structure;

(*c*) Heavy prints cause damages in almost all zones. Even in clean documents heavy printing sometimes heavily influence the character recognition;

(*d*) Extending the problem, heavy printing leads to merging of characters, which fall into the touching character category;

(*e*) Unfortunately the heavily printed characters also occupy the same space as the original characters and hence maintain the same aspect ratio;

(*f*) Practically, it is difficult to extract the features of heavily printed characters due to their likeness with the originals. They take just a blob of the pixels with height and width of the original characters with no ascenders or descenders to help distinguish them;

(*g*) The reasons of production of heavily printed characters are as same as that of touching characters.

4. Double-sided Documents

This is a kind of distortion found generally in very old documents were a text on a side is visible on the other side, which is technically called as show- through or bleeds-through problem. This is one of the most challenging one in distortion problems.

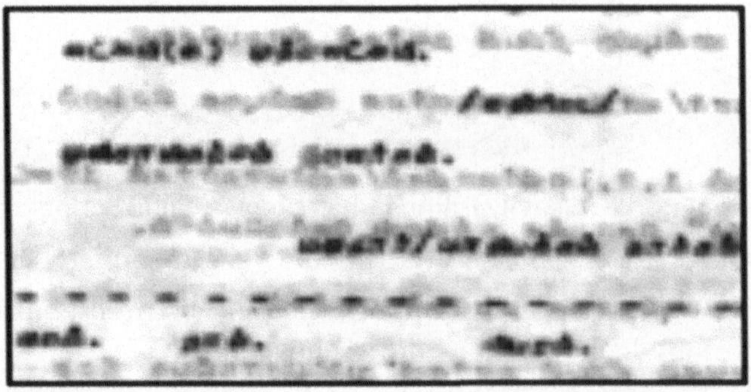

Fig. 4.4 : Back-sided Text Visible in Tamil Script

The following observations have been made on Backside Text visible documents in Tamil script:

(*a*) This problem is quite common when papers are thin or poor in quality;

(*b*) Deep dark printing on pages resulting in bleed through;

(*c*) Due to the partial appearance of backside characters the original characters on the front are misunderstood;

(*d*) Binarization processes of these documents have registered a lot of noise pixels;

(*e*) All segmentation processes prove to be failure in front of this distortion at most of the places.

5. *Faxed Documents*

Fax machines are considered one of the major sources of text distortion, when they create the problems in recognition of their own. This distortion is very apparently visible in the form of spurious point noise and ragged edges. Fax involving light printing, produces a huge number of broken characters, few touching characters and sometimes only a few pixels of characters. Distortions of fax are listed out as salt and pepper noise, the thickening or the partial omission of figures cause inappropriate threshold sensor outputs, which adds random noise and ill balanced bias that should be overcome.

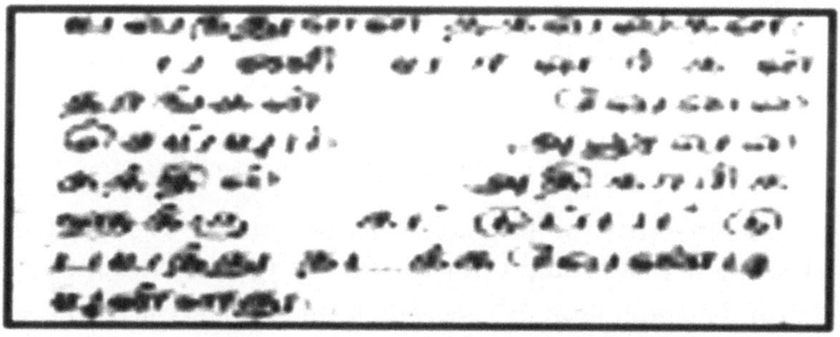

Fig. 4.5 : Faxed Documents in Tamil Script

However, generally it is difficult to restore distorted fax images of fax, as almost all the gray scale information of the output image is lost when using the binarization process. Even the human beings sometimes do not recognize distorted images.

The observation read as the list follows:

(*a*) The width of the stroke is not constant over the document;

(*b*) Entire document is found with all types of distortions at all the zones;

(*c*) The quality of the fax document depends upon the fax machine.

6. Type Written Documents

Typewritten documents also encounter the problem of distortion. Typewriters are widely used in Government offices of India. As far as Tamil scripts are concerned, 80 per cent of official works are processed by means of type written documents only.

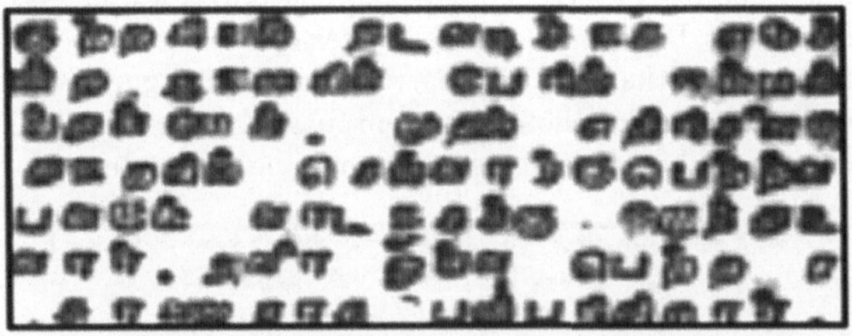

Fig. 4.6 : Type Written Documents in Tamil Script

A sequence of statistical analysis of typewritten characters has brought out the following observation:

(*a*) The middle zone is terribly influenced by the distortion in the form of merged characters;

(*b*) Lower zone characters, almost every time merge with the previous upper zone characters complicating the segmentation of lower zone from the middle zone;

(*c*) Unequal spacing between lines, words and characters has been observed;

(*d*) There is a significant change in the shape of upper zone and lower zone characters;

(*e*) Some times the characters are broken into many parts placed at various base lines. Usually most of the difficult algorithms have been designed on the basis of headline and baseline;

(*f*) Extra force applied during typing leads to character distortion of heavy printing;

(*g*) The technical inability of the typewriter with fixed width or variable grid produces characters of the same horizontal shape irrespective of the actual shape of the characters.

Conclusion

On the whole, this study has shouldered the task of venturing into the treatment of distorted characters of Tamil scripts. Aiming at the maximization of the recovery rate of damaged or dilapidated documents of various Indian languages with special highlights on Tamil scripts was covered under different headings viz., touching characters, broken characters, heavily printed documents, faxed documents, typewritten documents and the like. This study not only probes into the character recognition process that deals with so many problems of distorted Tamil characters, the kinds of distortions on it and the possible solutions to overcome those stumbling blocks, but also wide spreads ample of opportunities and scope for further researches in the same field of character recognition. Though researches enlist a range of character distorters like spray marks, curved base lines, blurred images, presence of punctuation marks and so on, this study pacts the treatment of only a handful initiation to the researches in the field of character recognition of Indian scripts in general and Tamil scripts in particular.

REFERENCES

1. Y. Li, D. Lopresti, G. Nagy and A. Tomkins, "Validation of Image Defect Models for Optical Character Recognition", *IEEE Transactions on PAMI*, Vol. 18(2), pp. 99-108, 1996.
2. H. S. Baird, "The state of the Art of Document Image Degradation Modelling", Invited Talk, in the *Proceedings of Int., Workshop on Document Analysis Systems*, Rio de Janeiro, Brazil, pp. 10-13, 2000.
3. S. W. Lee, D. J. Lee and H. S. Park, "A New Methodology for Gray-scale Character Segmentation and Recognition", *IEEE Trans., on PAMI*, Vol. 18(10), pp. 1045-1050, 1996.

4. C. B. Bose and S. S. Kuo, "*Connected and Degraded Text Recognition Using Hidden Markov Model*", Pattern Recognition, Vol. 27(10), pp. 1345-1363, 1994.
5. S. Tsujimoto and H. Asada, "Resolving Ambiguity in Segmenting Touching Characters," *1st Int., Conf., on Document Analysis and Recognition*, pp. 701-709, Saint-Marlo, France, Sept. 1991.
6. R.G. Casey and G. Nagy, "Recursive Segmentation and Classification of Composite Character Patterns," *Proc. 6th Int., Conf., on Pattern Recognition*, pp. 1023-1026, Munich, 1982.
7. T. Hong, Degraded Text Recognition Using Visual and Linguistic Context, Ph. D. Thesis, Computer Science Dept., of SUNY at Buffalo, 1995.
8. S. Kahan, T. Pavlidis and H. S. Baird, "On the Recognition of Printed Characters of Any Font and Size", *IEEE Trans.Pattern Anal.* Mach. Intell. 9, 274 288 (March 1987).
9. Y. Lu, "On the Segmentation of Touching Characters," in Proc. Int. Conf. Document Anal. Recognition, Tsukuba Science City, Japan, 1993, pp. 440–443.
10. U. Garain and B. B. Chaudhuri, "*Compound Character Recognition by Run Number-based Metric Distance*", SPIE Proc., Vol. 3305, pp. 90-97, 1998.
11. B. B. Chaudhuri, U. Pal and M. Mitra, "Automatic Recognition of Printed Oriya Script", in the *Proceedings of 6th ICDAR*, pp. 795-799, 2001.
12. M. K. Jindal, G. S. Lehal and R. K. Sharma, "Segmentation of Touching Characters of Indian Scripts—An Overview", in the *Proceedings of National Conference on Recent Advances and Future Trends in IT* (RAFIT 2005), Punjabi University Patiala, pp. 74-77, 2005.
13. G. S. Lehal and C. Singh, "*Text Segmentation of Machine-printed Gurmukhi Script*", Document
14. Recognition and Retrieval VIII, *Proceedings SPIE*, USA, Vol. 4307, pp. 223-231, 2001.
15. G. S. Lehal and C. Singh, "A Technique for Segmentation of Gurmukhi Text", Computer Analysis of Images and Patterns, Proc. CAIP 2001, W. Skarbek (Ed.), *Lecture Notes in Computer Science*, Vol. 2124, Springer-Verlag, Germany, pp. 191-200, 2001.
16. V. Bansal, *Integrating Knowledge Sources in Devanagari Text Recognition*, Ph. D. thesis, IIT Kanpur, India, 1999.

17. R.M.K.Sinha and H.Mahabala, "*Machine Recognition of Devanagari Script*", IEEE Trans. Syst. Man Cybern. Vol. 9, 1979.

18. A. Whichello and H. Yan, *Linking Broken Character Borders with Variable Sized Masks to Improve Recognition*, PR, Vol. 29, pp. 1429. 1435, August 1996.

19. M. Bern and D. Goldberg, *Scanner-model-based Document Image Improvement*, in ICIP00, pp. Vol II: 582.585, 2000.

20. T. Akiyama, N. Miyamoto, *M. Oguro, and K. Ogura, Faxed Document Image Restoration Method-based on Local Pixel Patterns*, in SPIE98, vol. 3305, pp. 253.262, Apr. 1998.

21. Y. Lu, B. Haist, L. Harmon, J. Trenkle and R. Vogi, "*An Accurate and Efficient System for Segmenting Machine-printed Text*", U.S.Postal Service 5th Advan., Tech., Conf., Washington, Vol.3, pp.A93-A105, 1992.

22. O. Nakamura, M.Ujiie, N.Okamoto and T. Minami, "*A Character Segmentation Algorithm for Mixedmode Communication*", Trans. IEICE, (D) 167-D, 11, pp. 1277- 1285, 1984.

23. N. Okamoto, O. Nakamura and T. Minami, "*Character Segmentation for Mixed-mode Communication*", IFIP'83, pp.681-685, 1983.

24. B.A.Yanikoglu, "Pitch-based Segmentation and Recognition of Dot-matrix text", Int., *Journal of Doc.,t Analysis and Recognition* (IJDAR), Vol.3, pp.34- 39, 2000.

25. M. Droettboom, "Correcting Broken Characters in the Recognition of Historical Printed Documents", in the *Proceedings of the 3rd ACM/IEEE-CS Joint Conference on Digital libraries* (JCDL), Houston, Texas, USA, pp. 364-366, 2003.

26. Stephen V. Rice, George Nagy and Thomas A. Nartker, Optical Character Recognition: An Illust., *Guide to the Frontier*, Kluwer Academic Pub., 1999.

27. G. Leedham, S. Varma, A. Patankar, and V. Govindaraju, "Separating Text and Background in Degraded Document Images—A Comparison of Global Thresholding Techniques for Multi-stage thresholding," *Proc. 8th IWFHR*, Aug-2002, pp.244–249.

28. Anna Tonazzini, Emanuele Salerno, and Luigi Bedini, "*Fast Correction of Bleed-through Distortion in Grayscale Documents by a Blind Source Separation Technique,*" *IJDAR*, Vol. 10, no. 1, pp.17–25, 2007.

29. E. Dubois and A. Pathak, "Reduction of Bleed-through in Scanned Manuscript Documents," in Proc. IS&T Image Processing, Image Quality, *Image Capture Systems Conference* (PICS2001), Montreal, Canada, April 2001, pp. 177–180.
30. Google, *Book Search Dataset, Version vs.* Edition, 2007.
31. Gang Zi and D. Doermann, "Document Image Ground Truth Generation from Electronic Text," in Pattern Recognition, 2004. ICPR 2004. *Proceedings of the 17th Int.,Conference on, D. Doermann*, Ed., 2004, vol. 2, pp. 663–666 Vol.2.
32. Gang Zi, "*Ground Truth Generation and Document Image Degradation*," Tech. Rep. LAMP-TR- 121/CARTR- 1008/CS-TR-4699/UMIACS-TR-2005-08, University of Maryland, College Park, 2005.
33. Dan S. Bloomberg, "*Determining the Resolution of Scanned Document Images*", Presented at IS&T/SPIE EI'99, Conf.,ce 3651, Doc., Recognition and Retrieval VI, Jan 26-28, San Jose, CA.
34. M. Oguro, T. Akiyama and K. Ogura, "Faxed Document Image Restoration Using Gray Level Representation", in the *Proc., of 4th ICDAR*, Vol. 2, pp. 679-683, 1997.
35. T.R. Randolph and M.J.T. Smith, "*Enhancement of Fax Documents Using a Binary Angular Representation*", in the Proc., of Int., l Symp., on Intelligent Multimedia, Video and Speech Processing, Hong Kong, pp.125-128, 2001.
36. J. D. Hobby and T. K. Ho, "*Enhancing Degraded Documents Images via Bitmap Clustering and Averaging*", in the Proc., 4th ICDAR, pp.394-400, 1997.
37. P. Natarajan, I. Bazzi, Z. Lu, J. Makhoul and R. Scwhartz, "Robust OCR of Degraded Documents", in the *Proceedings of 5th ICDAR*, pp. 357-361, 1999.
38. M. Cannon, J. Hochberg and P. Kelly, "QUARC: A Remarkably Effective Method for Increasing the OCR Accuracy of Degraded Typewritten Documents", *in the Proc., of the 1999 Symposium on Doc., Image Understanding Tech., (SDIUT'99),* Annapolis, MD, pp. 154-158, May 1999.
39. M. Cannon, J. Hochberg and P. Kelly, "Quality Assessment and Restoration of Typewritten Document Images", *IJDAR*, Vol. 2(2-3), pp. 80-89, 1999.
40. C. Rodriguez, J. Muguerza, M. Navarro, A. Zarate, J.I. Martin and J.M. Perez, "Segmentation of Low Quality Typewritten Digits", in the *Proc., 14th ICPR*, pp. 1106.

5

Development of Tamil Digital Libraries

Advances and Challenges

—Dr. K. Kalyanasundaram

Introduction

Computers and Internet possibly are the two most important technological innovations of the last century that had a pronounced impact on the humanity. Together they have changed dramatically the way people store information and exchange them with others. On the educational front, the impact in the Indian subcontinent is more pronounced. Ways and means by which information (knowledge?) has been stored and transferred from generation to generation has been evolving over many centuries: from 'gurukulam' system[1] (direct largely vocal transmission of knowledge from the teacher to the student) to inscriptions in caves, copper plates to written texts as in palm-leaf manuscripts to printed books. The contents of 26-volume summary—a systematic collection of inscriptions of south India compiled by Prof. Hultzsch, published by the Archeological Survey of India is available online[2]. At the dawn of the 21st C, information storage and exchange is moving to electronic form. Net-based information interchange available widely and at low cost has shrunk the distance barriers that exist amongst friends and relatives living in far off places. Growing number of educational tools are produced in electronic form as e-Books, multimedia-based teaching software and even distance/remote education through online portals. In this chapter we focus on one important component in distance education and information sharing through the net, viz., digital libraries with exclusive focus for Tamil language.

For any society or community, its cultural heritage is measured by the variety and level of content available in key areas such as literature and performing arts (music, dance and drama). Tamil is one of the oldest and living languages of the Indian sub-continent, with a vibrant history that dates back at least to 2000 years. Tamils have a remarkable cultural heritage, evidenced by huge and rich repertoire in all the key areas mentioned above. Preservation and propagation of this rich cultural heritage in a form compatible with contemporary trend and usage mode is essential. For many reasons, Tamil heritage information is largely preserved in forms that are at great risk. There are thousands of works in science and literature still in palm leaf manuscripts, not yet published in printed book form. With poor storage conditions, existing collection of palm leaf manuscripts and printed books is degrading rapidly. In the case of Sri Lanka, huge and precious collections of literary works of Tamils for several centuries simply vanished when the Jaffna Library got burnt in a major fire incident[3]. Anthropologists are concerned about rapid changes in the life-style of Tamils with a rapid decline in the practice of rich 'folklore arts' that are unique. Even in areas such as archeology, Tamils are proud to have a vast collection of temples of varying sizes and artistic features, each with its own unique mural paintings and other treasures[4]. Sadly these are also not being preserved in a form that can guarantee posterity. In view of this Tamil Diaspora have an important moral obligation to start e-preservation efforts in the areas outlined above.

Objectives of Digital Libraries

It is useful to start with the simple question, 'what is a digital library'. Widely accepted definition of a digital library is one of "a comprehensive « networked » information environment, a seamless rich set of tools and resources for the user community, accessible round the clock across the globe with the power of the Net. Digital resources can be in different formats and for different purposes, different target audience(s), accessible online or offline and derived from various « primary, existing » resources in different formats (books, audio/video recordings, manuscripts and photographs). Of late many information sources are produced directly in digital or e-form.

Digital Catalogue of Tamil Materials and Digital Dictionaries

A first step in any digitization effort is assessment (stock-taking) of diverse form of cultural heritage materials that are still available, a catalogue of 'who has what and where?' While a catalogue of the library holdings in digital form 'searchable' remotely is routine and exists for nearly all the libraries in the west, the same cannot be said about major libraries of Tamilnadu. There is no central inventory of public and private collections of cultural heritage related materials of Tamils within and outside India. Tamil Diaspora has migrated in large numbers to several far-off places (e.g., Sri Lanka, Malaysia, Singapore, Fiji and Mauritius to name the major ones) and developed their own local 'identity' over the years.

Academic Institutions of North America and Western Europe have been working together to build 'union catalogue', a central inventory of "who has what and where?" Many countries are building 'union catalogue' of regional collections. Two notable ones are i) CRL (Center for Research Libraries, an international consortium of university, college, and independent research libraries[5]; ii) 'Worldcat', sponsored and run by OCLC (Online Computer Library) a nonprofit, membership, computer library service and research organization dedicated to the public purposes of furthering access to the world's information and reducing the rate of rise of library costs[6]. More than 72,000 libraries in 171 countries and territories around the world use OCLC services. Nearly 1.5 billion items in all world languages held in different libraries worldwide are catalogued here. A notable feature of the Worldcat is that their database can be searched directly in Tamil script in Unicode.

For languages of south India, Digital South Asia Library (DSAL) is a major initiative of CRL managed by the University of Chicago[7]. An important component of the DSAL is their Digital Dictionaries of South Asia[8]. In addition to the classic Madras University Tamil Lexicon, digital searchable versions of important Tamil dictionaries of Fabricius, Kadirvelu_Pillai, McAlpin and Winslow are available online. The South Asia Union Catalogue, initiated by CRC and managed by DSAL, intends to become an historical bibliography comprehensively describing books and periodicals published in South Asia from 1556 through the present[9]. In addition, it will become a union catalog in which libraries throughout the world owning copies of those imprints may register their holdings. For an overview of some of the digital south asia library efforts, see the special issue of Focus, Vol. 24, number 3 (spring 2005), PDF downloadable from CRL website[10]. Roja Muthiah Research Library based in Chennai is an important and modern library for Tamils with over 100,000 volumes of books, journals, and newspapers in their shelves[11]. A digital catalogue of RMRL library is available via the DSAL gateway.

INFLIBNET is a Government of India UGC supported consortium network and is slowly evolving as the major information gateway on the holdings of Indian Universities[12]. Vidyanidhi is another Digital library initiative of India to facilitate the creation, archiving and accessing of doctoral theses[13]. Vidyanidhi is envisioned to evolve as a national repository and a consortium for e-theses through participation and partnership with universities, academic institutions and other stakeholders. 'Indcat' project of INFLIBNET is unified Online Library Catalogues of books, theses and journals available in major university libraries in India[14]. Over 11 million books and twenty thousand doctoral theses are included in the 'indcat' database.

Digital Preservation of Tamil Literary Works

One of the earliest preservation modes for printed books, still widely in use, is to take microfilm copies of the work. Three main advantages of preservation as microfilm are compact size, long bench life of microfilms (at least 75 years) and facile browsing the content using a microfilm reader. Modern version of the microfilm readers permits even digital capturing of pages of the microfilm or print out the page. University libraries of major institutions in north America and Europe still prefer microfilm form of preservation. Roja Muthiah Research library of Chennai has been making microfilm editions of Tamil works for more than a decade—possibly the only organized effort for Tamil literary works.

The second popular method of digital preservation of works is in the form of image files scanned at high resolution. The main advantage of this approach is that the digital image preserves all the presentation details (layout, artistic drawings, calligraphy used to present the work). Disadvantages are that the file size are huge and the content of the image files not easily searchable. Digital Library of India initiative, launched as part of a larger 'million ebooks' project of the Carnegie-Mellon University focused on the digitization of works in various languages of India. Image files in the form of 'tiff' format have been made for several thousand works. Tamil books available in e-form at DLI is only few percent, many duplicate files of the same work scanned at different scanning centers.

Recent initiative of Google to digitize collections of major university libraries of US falls in the same category – eBooks in the form of scanned image files[15]. Interestingly for many European languages, good OCR (optical character recognition) software's exist and they can be used on the scanned image files of printed books to generate a machine-readable version. Google's online ebooks interface for browsing the content of their eBook collections in fact has enabled this OCR processing to export the equivalent text of a text page displayed as an image file. Unfortunately for Tamil we do not have high performing OCR software for direct use on the image file version of eBooks.

In the last decade several initiatives have been launched for digital preservation of Tamil works. Mention here must be made of Tamil Heritage Foundation[16], Noolaham.net[17] and that of Pollacchi Nesan[18]. All of them produce etexts as image files in tiff or jpg format. Noolaham focuses on the works (books and newspapers) of Tamil authors of Sri Lankan origin. An urgent need in the digital preservation exercise of Tamil Heritage related materials is a central database (union catalogue) of what has been generated as of date. Without a union catalogue, precious human and machine resources are being wasted in digitization of the same work/object by several initiatives.

Machine Readable Version of eTexts

There have been several projects to prepare machine-readable version of ancient works (those in public domain) for free distribution on the Net. Pioneering effort has been Project Gutenberg[19], where over 30000 free eBooks are made available to read on the PC and in a number of portable devices such as iPhone and dedicated ebook readers[20] such as Kindle and Sony eBook Reader. Dr. Thomas Malten of the Institute of Indology and Tamil Studies of the Univ. of Koeln, Germany possibly was the first person to take initiative to digitize Tamil works in machine-readable form in early nineties[21]. Supported by grants from the German Government, he prepared electronic texts in Romanized (transliterated) format of Tamil works of first sangam period and few major works such as Kamba Ramayanam. The etexts used a simple plain ASCII based transliteration scheme so that the etexts can be readily searched. An online search interface was made available to search the entire collections free of cost, an extraordinary feat at a time where the computer usage by the linguists and Tamil Diaspora was not wide, as it happened after the arrival of low cost personal computers. In the early nineties, free Tamil fonts started appearing and also software such as Adami that permitted text input in Romanized format with the option to display the equivalent text natively in Tamil script form. Parthasarathy Dileepan of Tennesse US led a maiden initiative to produce e-version of the entire 4000 verses of nalayira divya pirapandam. Using Adhawin (windows version of Adami) software, it was now possible to view and print the etext verses in Tamil script form. Then came Project Madurai devoted to preparation of etexts directly in Tamil script format. Tamil Virtual University, launched in 2001 has included a digital library section which carries etexts of several Tamil works as web-pages[22].

Project Madurai

Project Madurai (PM) was launched in 1998 as a voluntary Net-based initiative for the digital preservation and propagation of Tamil literary works through Internet, natively in Tamil script form[23]. Volunteers from all four corners of the world use their spare time and personal computer equipment to prepare etexts of Tamil literary works natively in Tamil script form. During the past ten years, over 400 Tamil works, big and small, have been digitized and distributed through a dedicated web-server. The eTexts are distributed FREE as formatted text in HTML and PDF formats. Anyone can download for personal use and forward to others. Only requirement for reproduction is that the credit acknowledgement lines included in the header part of the etext be preserved.

The coverage is very broad in scope, spanning a wide time period and include works from early Sangam period to contemporary literature: pattuppATTu, eTTuttokai, patinenkIzkaNakku, epics, religious works of saivaite, vaishnavite canon, Old and new Testament of Bible in Tamil, ciRappuRaNam, saiva siddhanatha works, works of Bharathi, Bharathidasan and Kalki and works of Sri Lankan and Malaysian Tamil authors to mention broad cateogories. Only condition is that the covered Tamil work should be free of copyrights (work of 'public domain') or the author, their legal heirs give permission for royaltyfree reproduction of the work and free distribution of the eText worldwide. The coverage includes all 'genre'—poetry, prose and drama, English translations of important Tamil works as well Tamil translation of key literature of other world languages.

Challenges faced by PM during the past decade

Project Madurai is the only initiative devoted to preparing machine-readable (searchable) form of eTexts. Nearly all other initiatives of digitization store the etexts in the form of image files in tiff, jpg and other formats. For web-delivery of Tamil eTexts in a form usable by any average user of Tamil worldwide, several conditions are to be met. For machine-readable texts, important question is the font encoding to be used. Unlike most of the languages of the west, for Tamil, there has not been universal agreement on the font encoding to be used for electronic version of digital data. If the encoding used is not a standard for use in all computer platforms, then suitable Tamil fonts that work flawlessly in all platforms are to be made available free and the font encoding used should be such that there is no corruption of the data during transfer across platforms. When Project Madurai was launched in 1998, we had only two Tamil fonts (Inaimathi and Mylai) were available that satisfied above requirements. Hence eTexts were prepared in these two font encodings. Soon there was a Net-based encoding TSCII (Tamil script code for Information Processing) evolved as a popular encoding for Tamil and Project Madurai started releasing eTexts in this 8-bit bilingual encoding. It may worth pointing out here that flawless delivery and processing of Tamil digital materials require use a bilingual 8-bit scheme with standard ASCII scheme as part of the scheme. Around 2000 windows PC started supporting Tamil in the multilingual Unicode encoding scheme. As a consequence, Project Madurai started distributing eTexts in Unicode format as well. As of date, PM etext collections are available in two encodings TSCII and Unicode.

Project Madurai has been fortunate to have a steady team (small, max 20. at a time but fully committed) of volunteers who contribute hours in the preparation of the eTexts. They are Tamil enthusiasts keen to see our literary heritage preserved in e-form but are based in various far-off places without access to a good collection of printed copies of the Tami literary works. Persons who had time to key-in the work or to proof-read the work typed by other (PM works are proof-read at least once independently by a second volunteer) do not have access to printed books and those who have a good personal collection do not have time to contribute to the project. As Project Managers we have to go periodically to different bookshops in Chennai to procure target books for digitization. Sadly Tamil books covering good part of Grammar, prose and poetry are no longer reprinted due to pronounced shift in the interests of Tamils towards novels in late 20th C. So we are obliged to depend on the precious collections still preserved in major public libraries of Tamilnadu. Janet Library of the Univ. of Koeln, Germany is unique in this context to host possibly the biggest collection of Tamil books outside India, with collections over 60,000. Unfortunately financial resources available to the Indology Institute IITS there (where Prof. U Niklas and Dr. T Malten are associated) are extremely limited and the Institute even had passed through total shut down few years ago.

In order to improve the accessibility of books to our volunteers willing to type in the text, PM adopted the 'distributed proof-reading (DP)' approach developed by Project Gutenburg. In DP, scanned image files of printed books are collected and stored in a web-server. Volunteers willing to participate in the eBook preparation access these image files, one page at a time, either for key-in or proof-reading. Using special software, the image of a printed page is displayed on the left in a split-screen window with a text-editor on the right to key in (or proof-read) equivalent text. Using this distributed proof.-reading implementation at PM (DP-PM)[24] we have been able to produce nearly 100 eBooks during the past few years wherein a single eBook was produced as a joint effort by a group of volunteers based in different parts of the globe.

Digital Library of India initiative[25] has been very useful to us in supplying image files of several Tamil literary works and we are very grateful to them for this wonderful effort. Unfortunately funding for the DLI project has ceased, though the collections are still available on the Net. One serious limitation of the DLI collections is that the integrity of the text cannot be guaranteed. The image files have been not systematically checked with the source after editing of the graphic files. For several works often few lines at the top or bottom of the page are missing or words clipped on the right or excessive cleaning of the contrast resulting in pure consonants and akara-varisai abugida characters appear in the same manner (as is the case with palm-leaf manuscripts). With such pitfalls, we are obliged to consult the original printed version to ensure textual accuracy of the eText being produced.

Another important factor to consider is the selection of an 'authentic' edition of a given work for the eText preparation. Some works have ancient works reproduced without much of sandi/word splitting so as to make the work more understandable to the lay public. For many ancient works there are textual variants (pATa pEdam). One key decisive factor at least for works of poetry in nature is the compliance to the grammar rules (metrics). Checking of a given work for metric accuracy requires a higher level of linguistic expertise, not often available with the volunteers who help us produce the eTexts. In this context it is preferable that the entire collection of PM eText collections are vetted by a team of language experts, possibly by a team of university level researchers. Tamil scholars like UVeCa compared several editions of ancient Tamil works to compile 'authentic' or 'critical' editions.

Project Madurai eText collections at best are raw texts as they were written. In his presentation at the last year's Tamil Internet 2009 conference, Dr. Jean-Luc Chevillard proposed creation of a second generation of etexts for scholarly research[26]. Suggestion was to produce 'critical' editions where individual words of verses are 'tagged' with indication of the ciir for each word of the verse. Dr. Chevillard pointed out 'Text Encoding Initiative (TEI)' provides a number of modules which can be applied (or adapted) to the Tamil case. An eText can be 'metric compliant' or 'sandi-split'. Since the meaning of verse can vary with the words, contemporary 'sandi-split' versions are in reality an interpretation of a literary work. In principle, with the knowledge of the 'sandi-splitting' rules and information on the metrics of a given work, sandi-split versions can be converted to metric compliant versions with the use of a software. In fact In the last TIC 2009 conference, Balasundararaman presented a model software that permit checking of poetic works for their metric compliance (venba metrics). Project Madurai just started extending the coverage of Tamil works with the inclusion of commentaries of works.

There are 'classical' commentaries by scholars such as parimelazhakar, naccinarkiniyar that must be preserved in digital form.

The advantage of a machine-readable version of an eText is that all the words of the work can be indexed in a database in several ways, permitting facile search on the occurrence of a given word or a string of words (word sequence) in one or more literary works. With a vast collection of etexts of Project Madurai covering Tamil works spanning a wide time frame over two thousand years, such database-driven search for specific words can be very useful in etymology studies by the language experts. We have provided prototypes of such searchable online interfaces for Tamil works, using databases based on MySQL and php query calls. Dr. Vasu Renganathan of the Univ. of Pennsylvania for example, has undertaken such systematic studies of etymology using etext collections of Tamil literary works.

The digital edition of 'tEvAram' published by the Pondicherry Institute of Indology is an excellent example of combining multimedia tools with machine-readable text to bring an ebook of the next generation. For each tEvAram verse, in addition to the text, audio version of the verse and graphic (map showing the location of the town where the temple/deity referenced in the text is given) files are added to enhance the utility of the electronic version. Online websites for the teaching of Tamil of the Tamil Virtual University and of Univ. of Pennsylvania Tamil web have nicely integrated multimedia tools to the electronic text of the Tamil work taken up for detailed study.

Concluding Remarks

There are areas such as computer-aided teaching of Tamil online or off-line need a comprehensive digital library. In pioneering efforts, Tamil Virtual University and Tamil Web of the University of Pennsylvania have put together a number of educational tools—lessons as web pages with a number of audio-and video clips integrated. The Ministry of Education of Ithe Singaporean Government also has been supporting development of numerous multimedia tools to aid teaching of Tamil at the primary and secondary school level. Throughout this article we have indicated numerous public-funded and voluntary efforts working in the area of Tamil digitization. An umbrella organization that can interface all these isolated efforts can go a long way in reducing redundancies and accelerate output. In addition to the governmental agencies, academics and IT/ICT professionals have important role to play in this key area of academic and public interest.

REFERENCES

1. http://www.lifesciencefoundation.org.in/page6.html
2. http://www.whatisindia.com/inscriptions/
3. http://en.wikipedia.org/wiki/Burning_of_Jaffna_library
4. http://www.tamilartsacademy.com/articles/list_of_articles.html
5. http://catalog.crl.edu/
6. http://www.worldcat.org
7. http://dsal.uchicago.edu/
8. http://www.crl.edu/focus/article/509;
9. http://sauc.uchicago.edu/
10. http://www.crl.edu/focus/spring-2005
11. http://www.lib.uchicago.edu/e/su/southasia/about-rmrl.html
12. http://www.inflibnet.ac.in/
13. http://www.vidyanidhi.org.in/
14. http://indcat.inflibnet.ac.in/indcat/
15. http://www.tamilheritage.org/
16. http://www.noolaham.net/
17. http://www.thamizham.net
18. http://ebook-reader-review.toptenreviews.com/
19. http://www.uni-koeln.de/phil-fak/indologie2/
20. http://webapps.uni-koeln.de/tamil/

21. http://www.tamilvu.org
22. http://www.projectmadurai.org
23. http://www.new.dli.ernet.in
24. http://www.linguist.univ-paris-diderot.fr/~chevilla/
25. http://www.infitt.org/ti2010/
26. http://www.ifpindia.org/Tamil-Saiva-Hymns.html

6

Reducing Digital Divide in Tamilnadu Using Data Mining Techniques for better e-Governance

—R. Jayabrabu
—Prof. (Dr). V. Saravanan

ABSTRACT

The term digital divide refers to the gap between people with effective access to digital and information technology and those with very limited access. In other words it is closely related to the knowledge divide or knowledge share due to the lack of technology and knowledge. The extraction of useful and non-trivial information from the huge amount of data available in many and diverse fields of science, business and engineering is called as Data Mining. Data Mining techniques and algorithms are the actual tools that analysts have at their disposal to find unknown patterns and correlation in the data. For effective use of e-Governance in Tamil Nadu, the digital divide to be reduced. Most of the Government departments are already using e-Governance in Tamil Nadu. This is the appropriate time for us to analyze the effectiveness and reach ability of technology to all sectors of peoples. Even the most learned peoples are reluctant in using the technology. This digital divide gap leads to improper usage of Information and Communication technologies. The objective of this chapter is to analyze the following two important digital divide issues using data mining and present recommendations for better e-Governance in Tamil Nadu.

Improving Quality of Bandwidth/Parameters

Since, the information and communication technologies are being implemented in the Government at different levels; good bandwidth is needed for constant transformation of knowledge in a proper format. For the better usage of e-Governance, the quality and performance of bandwidth performance has to be increased. In Tamil Nadu, there are so many service providers available for connectivity. But, the expected quality of bandwidth is less than the assured bandwidth. This chapter analyses the bandwidth parameters using data mining techniques and suggest a better framework for improving bandwidth across Tamil Nadu.

Taking Technology to Reduce the Gap

Now a day, many new information and communication technologies are introduced. The urban sector is reluctant in using the technology due to the fear of using the technology and also thinking communication/network failure, which occurs frequently. The middle age person still thinks that the technology is very far from them and also is very costlier. The rural sector is unaware of these technologies and they need to be provided infrastructure and training. With the increase usage of mobile phones; convergence of technologies also need to be thought of. This chapter analyses the need of urban and rural sector people for the effective reach of technology. Data Mining Techniques are used for data analysis, which leads creation of to better e-Governance standards.

The above mentioned parameters are studied by applying data mining techniques such as Association rule mining (determine implication rules for a subset of record attributes, Classification (assign each record of a database to one of a predefined set of classes analysis and Clustering Techniques (find groups of records that are close according to some user defined metrics) and a suitable framework is proposed for better e-Governance.

Introduction

When the IT industry increased globally in the 19th century, simultaneously the Internet and the Mobile technologies are also emerged into the world and ruled majority of the people. With this, e-Governance also booms out with the help of some Government Departments around the world. In India, National Informatics Center (NIC) played a vital role for the development of e-Governance in which they incorporate some of the Government related activated like Tax payment, Census Generation, Election Management, Disaster Management,[1] etc.,

In Tamil Nadu, some of the successful e-Governance projects are land registration, call for tender, issue of birth/death certificates, agriculture, e-Transaction, RTO, tourism, infrastructure, land/local tax, local body election details, e-Ticket etc.,[1]. The major scenario in the above-mentioned successful e-Governance is heterogeneous based System. The entire activities of each Government related activities posses a unique database to store their respective data. This technique is followed in our state and also other states too[2]. As a fact, each Government department maintains their own database as unique and there is no interlinking between various departments/databases. When, the land registration department needs some information about agriculture data, they are not able to access the agriculture database. This leads to minimum usage of the e-governance projects by the citizens. The digital gap increases due to the issue and the important e-Governance projects fails after implementation. This chapter proposes the use of data mining techniques and a better framework to reduce the digital gap and to interlink the heterogeneous databases. This chapter proposed two stages to reduce the digital gap:

(*a*) Improving Quality of Bandwidth/Parameters;

(*b*) Taking Technology to reduce the gap;

Using Data Mining Techniques to Reduce the Digital Gap

Data Mining is the technique to explore and analyze the large data sets, in order to discover meaningful patterns and rules[6]. The evaluation of data mining techniques began when the business data are stored in the database and the technologies were generated to allow the user to navigate the data in the real time.

Recently, the ICT made a proposal for all the state and central Government for the betterment of database maintenance in the near future generation[3]. As we know, now-a-days, all the Government departments utilizes huge amount of data in their day-to-day work, which leads to maximize the access of current or history of datasets from the database[4]. But, it is not possible to fetch the datasets when they need. This is because of insufficient data, improper format, duplicated data, and some technical problems etc.,; When we discuss on other side, it is also due to less bandwidth, natural disaster, network failure, and loss of data during data transmission and collision of packet with one another etc. As a result of this, the end user cannot able to perform the operation with in the time and also little afraid to continue the e-Governance system. Since, a gap is generated between user and existing e-Governance systems. As a result, the Government should concentrate on above set problems for the betterment of e-Governance. By considering these issues, this chapter proposes the use of data mining techniques to reduce the digital gap. The major data mining techniques considered in this chapter are[6]:

(*a*) Association Techniques;

(*b*) Classification techniques;

(*c*) Clustering Techniques.

Association: It is method for discovering interesting relations between the variables in the large database. There are different types of algorithm for association rule. They are Apriori algorithm, éclat algorithm, FP-growth algorithm, One-attribute-rule algorithm, Opus search algorithms, and Zero-attribute-rule algorithm[6]. Let us consider the existing e-Governance agriculture database as an example. Suppose, when a user needs a land for the cultivation process with the following features, i.e, good water, larger area, good manpower, and good soil. Based on the above features, the end user can easily search the availability of lands form the existing database with the help of some association algorithm. The one of the best algorithm for technique is Apriori Algorithm.

Classification

It is one of the data mining techniques used to predict the group for data instance. Some of the popular classification techniques are decision trees and neural networks[6]. From the existing database, the end user can classify the land with required parameters like state wise, of district wise, area wise and etc by means of tree like structure. By this classification technique, the user can easily classify the required data from the existing database using some protocols. Based on this, the user can identify the locations and nature of the land with a faster manner. Some of the best and easiest algorithms are decision tree and nearest neighbor algorithm that is available in data mining techniques for better classification.

Clustering

It defined as collection of data object that are similar to one another within the same cluster and dissimilar to the objects in the other cluster. Clustering algorithms are broadly classified into hierarchical and partitioning clustering algorithm (Jain and Dubes, 1988). Again, the Hierarchical algorithm are Agglomerative and Divisive algorithm and the Partitioning Algorithms are k-means, kmediod, DBSCAN, CLARA, CLARANS, BIRCH CLIQUE, OPTICS etc[6]. When a person is willing to find the group of land for cultivation respective of location, the user can apply the clustering techniques with the existing e-Governance database to form a new groups based upon the user requirement. Thus the user may satisfy.

This is the appropriate time for us to discuss the effectiveness and reachability of technology to all sectors of people. Even the most learned people are reluctant in using the E-Governance technology. This digital divide gap leads to improper usage of Information and Communication technologies. By using the above specified data mining techniques, the digital gap is reduced which in turn help the state to move towards implementing better and quality of e-Governance projects.

Improving Quality of Bandwidth/Parameters for Better e-Governance

In general, some of the service providers like BSNL, AIRTEL, etc., are available for network connectivity in Tamil Nadu for good quality of Bandwidth. Bandwidth is defined as amount of data transferred in a given period of time [8]. Since, each service providers are having different qualities of bandwidth. But the expected quality of bandwidth is less than the assured bandwidth. As result the network connectivity in Tamil Nadu reached towards down state. Due to this, the successful e-Governance projects get failed while performing data transactions. By considering the above facts, the quality of service (QoS) need to be improved and also all the service provides are expected to provide guarantees for constant network connections. Bandwidth is one of the major constrain for better e-Governance. Some of the parameters are identified to rectify the poor bandwidth problem. For constant connectivity and the better usage of e-Governance, the identified parameters are as follows:[8]

(*a*) Availability

(*b*) Throughput

(*c*) Data latency
(*d*) Error rate
(*e*) Network Traffic
(*f*) Routing Performance.

Availability

It is defined as the probability that a device will perform a required function without failure under defined conditions for a defined period of time. In most of the case, availability is an important characteristic of system but it becomes more critical and complex issues on networks. With the help of Data Mining technique the network availability are classified with various parameters and helps the service provided for better network availability. Thus, by applying the classification techniques in network database, availability problem will be rectified.

Throughput

It is defined as the rate of communication links or network access. The Throughput is generally measured in bits per second, and sometimes in data packets per second or data packet per time slot. By applying the data mining association algorithm, the service provided will come to normalize the size of the packet for data transformation from one place to another with respect to time and network availability. Based on the mining techniques, the problems are identified and help in future that is not repeated.

Data Latency

It is defined as how much time it takes for a packet of data to transfer form one destination point to another destination. The latency mainly depends on the nature of the electromagnetic signal. Thus the latency may be differing from device to device. Hence, data mining association techniques are applied on the history dataset to identify when the problem happens and how the problem happens; Is it happen previously? If yes, what actions are taken to solve the problem?

Error Rate

It is defined as the number of received bits that have been altered due to noise and interference while during digital data transmission. The error rate may vary from device to device and software application to application. Thus by applying clustering techniques, the service provider can mine the error rate with respect to the hardware and application software from the previous data. Based on this method, the service provider knows which application software Vs hardware device suppose to minimize the error rate.

Network Traffic

It is defined as the data in a network, where the network traffic controller controls the traffic, bandwidth, prioritizing the data packet while during transformation form one point to another. The major part is to measure the network traffic like where the network congestion happens, with this, the classification techniques are applied and the same issue was happened in the previous days or not. Based on the result, the identified problems are rectified.

Routing Performance

It is defined as measuring the performance of the router depends upon the load offered of it, i.e. by means of heavy load of test traffic will reveal the performance. Based on the traffic and load the performance may vary. For better performance, the traffic should be shaped and the packet size should be constant throughout the entire process. With the help of data mining classification techniques, the provider can mine the lesser traffic network for better routing performance.

Network problem happens not only due to technical side but also due to natural calamities, breaking of cable, etc. From the above scenario, the Central or State Government has to rework on the abovementioned areas to improve the bandwidth performance by means of advanced networking technology, Fiber Optic and recent computing technologies will acted as catalyst for improving bandwidths.

In this chapter, bandwidth parameters are analyzed with the help of few data mining techniques for network connectivity to improve the bandwidth. The framework is developed to provide better network connectivity for e-Governance. This chapter analyses the bandwidth parameters using data mining techniques and suggest a better framework for improving bandwidth across Tamil Nadu.

Proposed Framework for Reducing the Digital Gap

In Tamil Nadu, there are more successful e-Governance projects being implemented. But, all the implemented applications are heterogeneous in nature i.e. the databases are not linked for effective usage. Due to the non-linking of databases and availability in different geographical locations, there exist a digital gap. In the proposed framework, a new concept is introduced to reduce this digital gap, instead of storing the data in different location. This chapter proposes the creation of data warehouse, which is a subject-oriented, integrated, time-varying, non-volatile collection of data[5,7].

All the existing and emerging E-Governance databases which is heterogeneous in nature and available in geographical locations are combined and get stored in a common place called 'Data Warehouse'. It may be called as state data warehouse or data repository. The users using a particular e-Governance application is able to use the other application also effectively thereby the usage of e-Governance applications are increased. Thus, digital gap is also reduced.

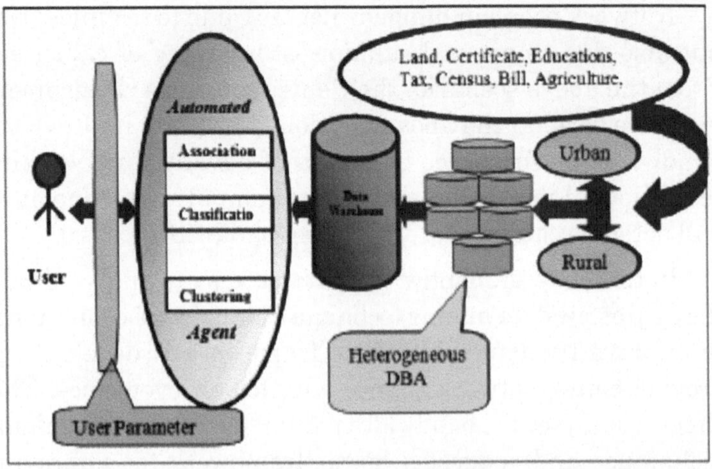

Fig. 6.1. Framework for the Betterment of e-Governance

From the above figure, the e-Governance technology/ applications data are collected from different locations and get stored in different database. This chapter proposed a framework in which all the heterogeneous databases are combined and stored in one common place called data warehouse[5]. It contains the summary of all the data, which are made available in a day today process. As per this concept, any one can access any kinds of data at any time by the data warehouse with a faster way. Different data mining techniques are also made available in the proposed framework. By applying these data mining techniques based on the user requirement, the user can mine the data with meaningful order, proper format and in time[7]. Hence, the Tamil Nadu Government e-Governance projects are used more effectively than other State Government projects. With this work, the technology gap is also reduced and the users may utilize the e-Governance by higher level.

Conclusion

In this chapter, the importance of digital gaps and the parameters for reducing the digital gap with the e-Governance in Tamilnadu are discussed using different data mining techniques for the better performance. Various network Quality of Services(QOS) parameters such as availability, throughput, data latency, error rate, network traffic and routing performance are considered in data mining perspective to increase the available bandwidth. With the help of proposed framework, the gap also gets reduced between the user and the e-governance systems which enable the Tamilnadu government to implement successful projects.

REFERENCES

1. Prof. T.P. Rama Rao, "ICT and e-Governance for Rural Development", Governance in Development: Issues, Challenges and Strategies organized by Institute of Rural Management, Anand, Gujarat, December, 2004.
2. Bhatnagar S.C., "e-Government : From Vision to Implementation—A Practical Guide with Case Studies", Sage Publications Pvt. Ltd., New Delhi, 2004.
3. Rama Rao, T.P., Venkata Rao, V., Bhatnagar S.C., and Satyanarayana J., "e-Governance Assessment Frameworks", http://egov.mit.gov.in, e-Governance Division, Department of Information Technology, May 2004.
4. Lee, C.-H., Lee, G.-G., Leu, Y. "Application of Automatically Constructed Concept Map of Learning to Conceptual Diagnosis of e-Learning", (2009) Expert Systems with Applications, 36 (2 Part 1), pp. 1675-1684.
5. Bai, S.-M., Chen, S.-M. "A New Method for Automatically Constructing Concept Maps based on Data Mining Techniques (2008) "Proceedings of the 7th International Conference on Machine Learning and Cybernetics, ICMLC, 6, Art. No. 4620937, pp. 3078-3083.
6. Witten I.H., Frank E. "Data Mining: Practical Machine Learning Tools and Techniques". 2nd ed., Elsevier, Morgan Kaufmann Publishers, (2005).
7. Piatetsky- Shapiro, G and Frawley, W.J, "Knowledge Discovery in Database," AAAI/ MIT Press, 2000.
8. WWW.compnetworking.about.com, April 2010.

7

An Extended Cross Lingual Information Retrieval System for Agricultural Domain Using Statistical Document Translation for Tamil Farmers

—D. Thenmozhi
—Arun Balachandran Ganesan
—C. Aravindan

ABSTRACT

Cross Lingual Information Retrieval (CLIR) system allows a user to pose a query in one language and search documents in a different language. In this chapter, we extend the use of Tamil-English CLIR system for Tamil farmers by translating the English web pages to Tamil, through which the farmer can pose a query in Tamil and read the information in the same language. We have developed statistical English-Tamil translation engine to translate the English documents that are retrieved from CLIR system to Tamil. The parallel corpus for this statistical engine was built using the text in the domain of Agriculture for Tamil and English languages. The translation model is then trained with this sentence aligned domainspecific corpus. Also a text corpus for Tamil has been built and used in building and training the language model. A Statistical Machine Translation Decoder tool has been used to perform the decoding as the final step.

Introduction

The world of information is huge and expanding; also most of the information is available in English. The non-English speaking users still find it a major problem in utilizing this vast resource of information. Accessing this information through queries written in Indian languages is still more difficult. CLIR systems solves this problem by allowing the non-English user to specify their information need in their native language and accessing rich information that are available in English. We have developed a Tamil-English CLIR system for Agriculture society[1] which allows the Tamil farmers to pose Tamil queries and retrieves information from English corpus. The CLIR systems generally display the search result in English. It is appropriate, if the results are displayed in their own language for the users who do not know how to give query in English.

In this chapter, we extend the CLIR system by translating the retrieved English documents to Tamil in the domain of Agriculture through which Tamil farmers can enter their query in Tamil, retrieves relevant pages from English corpus and read the information in Tamil. Machine translation is a sub-field of computational linguistics that investigates the use of computer software to translate text from one language to another. It can use a method based on linguistic rules, when the content to be translated is simple, for example short queries. When the content to be translated is complex in structure, machine translation requires the problem of natural language understanding to be solved first. Statistical machine translation solves this problem with a probabilistic approach based on bilingual text corpora.

We have built English-Tamil parallel corpus in the domain of Agriculture to train the statistical translation system for translating the retrieved documents in English to Tamil. Our translation system may contribute in developing Tamil Wikipedia by translating the Wikipedia content that are available in English in the domain of Agriculture to Tamil. Literature Survey.

Cross Lingual Information Retrieval System

The Advanced Cross Lingual Information Access (ACLIA) currently works on two tasks Information Retrieval and Question Answering[7]. For both these tasks, they work for cross-lingual and mono-lingual topics for the languages English (EN), Simplified Chinese (CS), Traditional Chinese (CT), and Japanese (JA) for the tracks EN-CS, EN-CT, EN-JA (cross-lingual) and CS-CS, CT-CT, JA-JA (mono-lingual)[7] created the Evaluation Package for ACLIA and NTCIR (EPAN). The EPAN toolkit contains a web interface, a set of utilities and a backend database for persistent storage of evaluation topics, gold standard nuggets, submitted runs, and evaluation results for training and formal run datasets[4]. Developed a Question Answering system that answers complex questions from multilingual sources.

They improved the performance of Chinese-to-Chinese and Japanese-to-Japanese subtasks of NTCIR7 IR4QA by means of Mean Average Precision. ACLIA presently not working on the document translation of cross-lingual track. Many research groups are working on the CLIR system for Indian Languages[6,5] developed a Tamil-English CLIR system that uses Tamil morphological analyzer for language analysis. A named entity recognizer is used to identify the named entities in the document for indexing and ranking. They used a bi-lingual dictionary approach for translation. A statistical engine based on n-gram approach is used for transliteration. A simple ontology is used for query expansion. Ranking is based on term frequency. They evaluated the system for the news domain by collecting the English corpus from the magazine 'The Telegraph'.

We differ from the above works by extending Tamil-English CLIR system with document translation in the domain of Agriculture which helps Tamil farmers who have English as a language barrier.

Machine Translation System

Developed a English to Tamil translation system using statistical approach. SRILM toolkit it used for language modeling[1]. Translation model is trained using the parallel corpus in the News domain. They learnt Named entities from this statistical machine translation system. Phrase-based decoder is used to translate the English sentences to Tamil[3]. Used the same phrase based approach of statistical machine translation to transliterate word from English to Hindi, Tamil and Kannada languages for the Named-entities. They used GIZA++ for word alignment and Moses for decoding.

Improved the English-Hindi statistical machine translation system by considering the case markers and morphology of Hindi language[2]. They used factored based translation model instead of phrase based model. We also developed a similar kind of statistical machine translation system that translates English sentences to Tamil by using SRILM toolkit for the language modeling of Tamil and Moses for translation modelling and decoding.

System Architecture

The extended CLIR system uses a three phase model that accepts the query from the user in Tamil extracts the documents from English corpus and translates them to Tamil in the domain of Agriculture. This is illustrated in the figure 7.1. (*See on next page*)

Tamil-to-English Query Translation

A rule based Tamil-to-English translation engine is developed through which the query is entered in Tamil and translates to English. It uses morphological analyzer to split the query into individual words. These words are translated to English using a Tamil-English bilingual dictionary. When Tamil words gets ambiguous meaning, the correct meaning is obtained based on the context using word sense disambiquater. The obtained English words are re-ordered based on the syntactic structure of English language (Subject-Verb-Object pattern).

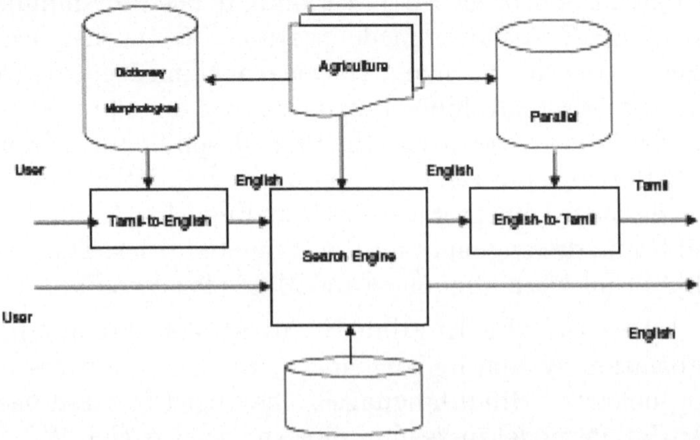

Fig. 7.1 : System Architecture

Searching and Retrieval

The translated English query is given to the existing search engines like Google, AltaVista, etc that retrieves the English documents. We considered top twenty pages that are retrieved by the search engine for statistical document translation. The documents with the extension doc, html and pdf are converted to plain text before given to the English-to-Tamil translation Engine.

English-Tamil Document Translation

A statistical English-Tamil document translation engine is developed with the phases namely constructing English-Tamil parallel corpus, training the translation model with the parallel corpus, training the language model for Tamil language and decoding. Tamil Wikipedia, and the Tamil Nadu Agricultural University websites have been identified as excellent sources that would help in providing the data needed for corpus building. Information in documents has been extracted/retrieved using a semi-automated text extractor and unnecessary attributes to the data is removed either by automation or human intervention depending on the type of attribute. The encoding of the content in Tamil language is converted to Unicode standard. The aligned parallel corpora that is built follows Unicode standard.

Moses toolkit is used to train the translation model using the parallel corpus based on phrase based approach. This model works on the principle of Baye's rule

$$P(t \mid e) = P(e \mid t)^{*}P(t)/P(e)$$

$$T = argmax\ P(e \mid t)^{*}P(t)$$

where T is the translation probability.

SRILM toolkit is used to build tri-gram language model for Tamil language. Tamil sentences extracted for building parallel corpus in the domain of Agriculture is used to build this model. A beam search decoder of Moses toolkit for phrase-based statistical machine translation model is used to translate the sentences of English documents to Tamil.

Experimental Evaluation

Agriculture Corpus

We extracted the parallel sentences from Tamil Nadu Agriculture University (TNAU) website and Wikipedia content in the domain of Agriculture. Some additional sentences in Tamil from the TNAU website is used to train the language model. The number of sentences used to train the translation model and language model are given the table.

	Number of Sentences	
	TNU Site	Wilapedia
Translation model	6133	226
Language model	6900	—

Comparison with Google Translation System

We compared the performance of our extended system with the Google translation system by various measures that are listed in the following table:

	Google Translation System	CLIR system
Tamil Queries	Trans-lateraled Approach	Machine Translation Approach
Document Retrieval for Tamil Queries	From Tamil Corpus	From English Corpus
Recall value for Tamil Queries	Less	More
Translation	Available for many Asian/European languages, Tamil is not available	Translates English documents to Tamil

Conclusion

This extended CLIR system helps the Tamil farmers to look for rich information available in English corpus by specifying their need in Tamil and view the results also in Tamil language. This system uses a rule based approach for query translation and statistical based approach for document translation. With the available parallel corpus, query translation also can be done statistically in future. Factored based translation model can be used for improving document translation. Query also can be enriched with more semantics by using Agriculture ontology.

REFERENCES

1. Amrita Vishwa Vidyapeetham, "Valluvan-English to Tamil Statistical Machine Translation", Center for Excellence in Computational Engineering and Networking (CEN), 2005
2. Ananthakrishnan Ramanathan, Hansraj Choudhary, Avishek Ghosh, Pushpak Bhattacharyya, Case Markers and Morphology:

Addressing the Crux of the Fluency Problem in English-Hindi SMT, Proceedings of the 47th Annual Meeting of the ACL and the 4th IJCNLP of the AFNLP, pp 800–808

3. Manoj Kumar Chinnakotla and Om P. Damani, Experiences with English-Hindi, English-Tamil and English-Kannada Transliteration Tasks at NEWS 2009, Proceedings of the 2009 Named Entities Workshop, ACL-IJCNLP 2009, pp. 44-47

4. Ni Lao, Hideki Shima, Teruko Mitamura, and Eric Nyberg, "Query Expansion and Machine Translation for Robust Cross-Lingual Information Retrieval", Proceedings of NTCIR-7 Workshop, 2008, Japan

5. Pattabhi R.K Rao and Sobha. L, "AU-KBC FIRE2008 Submission - Cross Lingual Information Retrieval Track: Tamil- English", First Workshop of the Forum for Information Retrieval Evaluation (FIRE), pp 1-5, 2008

6. Prasenjit Majumder, Mandar Mitra Swapan Parui and Pushpak Bhattacharyya,"Initiative for Indian Language IR Evaluation", Invited paper in EVIA 2007 Online Proceedings.

7. Teruko Mitamura, Eric Nyberg, Hideki Shima, Tsuneaki Kato, "Overview of the NTCIR-7 ACLIA Tasks: Advanced Cross-Lingual Information Access", Proceedings of NTCIR-7 Workshop, 2008, Japan.

8

Tamil e-Archives Management

—B. Asadullah

ABSTRACT

From the year 2000 onwards, we had noticed that new innovations were made enormously to serve the human needs in every core area from Agriculture to Engineering, Medical, and Automobile etc., from every corner of the universe in every language of the world, and more especially by Tamil Literature. This has compelled us to tap all these new findings and old traditional findings in a secure way so that these resources can be better utilized in future by our new generation peoples. In keeping these concerns in mind, I am trying to explain how we can secure all these findings in a secure way using the suitable technology by applying possible low cost of implementation and maintenance. This chapter will explain the way, on how to manage the archives of new findings and old traditional findings of Tamil languages in electronic format using pictorial images and formal text format utilizing the best technology at low cost using best available free of cost Open Source Software.

Introduction

Tamil language is spoken and widely used by over 66 million peoples across the world in particular in three countries as official language and in six countries as monitories, where our state of India Tamil Nadu is the largest user of Tamil in every aspect of life. Tamil scripts are preserved in different format from palm leaf to paper, due to accessibility and timely availability. But this preservation does not last for number of years as every functional item has a stop point that is everything has a counted life span. This chapter will help in preserving archive in computer using latest and freely available licensed open source software.

Electronic Preservation

Due to moderate and vast development of Computer Technology, preservation has become reliable, secure and durable. Here preservation means not only documents, but for vast range of items in electronic format like running text, document, book, journal, pictorial, audio, video and animated format etc., all these above said format are also known as e-Achieves.

Preservation in computer is also a big question, but the answer to this question is having backup of all thing in a compact format, or having a mirror storage which can be made possible using the RAID technology while storing the data in computers. In case of one's end of life, another mirror image can be utilized in less effort, instead of building whole thing from scratch.

From the above last two clause, we come to know that preservation in computer is possible, durable and securable. But maintenance of unlimited e-archives in a computer is not so simple and easily accessible for all end-users. For this purpose, after wide consultation and analysis, it was concluded that there were a suitable software which fit for the chosen topic, and it is available free of cost in different users operating environment also known as operating system like Microsoft Windows, Linux, under the Open Source Software GNU licence.

Institutional Repository

An Institutional Repository is an online locus for collecting, preserving, and disseminating in digital form. (Also known as Digital Library). The main objectives for an institutional repository are to create global visibility for an institution's scholarly research and to collect content in a single location, to provide open access to institutional research output by self-archiving it and to store and preserve other institutional digital assets, including unpublished works. Some examples are Fedora, e-Print, IR+, and dSpace, Green Stone.

dSpace is developed by HP Lab and MIT Libraries of US. At the time of writing this article for presentation at the 9th Tamil Internet Conference held at Coimbatore, Tamil Nadu (India) 2010, dSpace 1.6.2 is available for utilization. DSpace is widely accepted and used by different educational institutions across the world. DSpace is open source software based on BSD Licence, it is an digital object/assets management system to create, store, search and retrieve digital objects. It allows open access to digital objects and building institutional repositories and the collections are searchable and retrievable on the web. Since it is open source technology platform which can be customized and its capabilities can be extended.

Main features of dSpace are it is a low cost, including all hardware and software components. Technically simple to install and manage, robust, scalable, open and inter-operable, it is modular and user friendly with multi user environment (including both searching and maintenance), it is multimedia digital object enabled and platform independent interoperable. dSpace stores all data as a digital object, which has the following standard model.

Objects in the dSpace Data Model

Object	Example
Community	Like Deaprtment/Section
Collection	Report, Statistical Data
Item	Technical report, A data set with accompanying description
Bundle	A group of HTML, image bitstream
Bitstream	A single HTML file, a image file or a text file
Bitstream format	MS Word Document, IPEC image format

dSpace has its own Ingest Process and Workflow Steps in three stage, which verifies all type of documents with their corresponding information, then only it accept the document to be stored in the repository. This method helps in gathering authenticated Tamil document for building a healthy achieve. dSpace uses the CNRI Handle System for creating identifier, which is required by dSpace to store and locate the independent mechanism for creating and maintaining digital objects. dSpace uses the Lucene Search algorithm, which helps in searching the tamil text using Fielded search, Boolean, Exact term, proximity and wild cards, fuzzy and range, boosting terms search techniques.

Content Management System

A content management system is a collection of procedures used to manage work flow in a collaborative environment. These procedures can be manual or computer based. The procedures are designed to allow for a large number of people to contribute to and share stored data with controlled access to data, based on user roles. User roles define what information each user can view or edit and aid in easy storage and retrieval of data by reducing repetitive duplicate input with improving the ease of report writing and improved communication between users.

In a content management system, data can be defined

as nearly anything documents, movies, pictures, phone numbers, scientific data, etc. These are frequently used for storing, controlling, revising, semantically enriching, and publishing documentation. Examples are web content management, digital asset management, digital records management and electronic content management. Synchronization of intermediate steps, and collation into a final product are common goals of each. The features of content management systems are, it can structure the document repository as per requirements and automatic document versioning control with content categorization and role-based access control. Using varied content types, it can be managed like HTML, Unicode Tamil text, PDF, Documents of different standard of any language, image files, video clips etc., Document can be accessed through web-browser and network drive mapping with full text searching facility in txt, doc, pdf, odt, sxw, html, xls, sxc, ods etc.,

Document Repository System

A document repository system is a systematic way of storing documents along with a set of user defined attributes that need to be filled in at the time of storage. Documents can be searched based on these attributes or on their content. Every organization needs a good planned Document repository system in their specific official language like in our case Tamil language.

Owl is one of the best examples for document repository system, Owl is a powerful system, full of use full features, it allows defining personal sets of attributes for documents. MS-Word of Tamil language, PDF, Unicode TEXT of Tamil, can be word indexed and searched. However documents and files of any type can be stored. Owl has security model for document access. The documents are uploaded and stored in a folder, uploaded files can be stored in tables in the open source database like RDBMS, MySQL, PostgreSQL for storing file / folder related information.

Conclusion

Managing achieve is not the easy task, when large numbers are being created day to day because of vast development of Tamil language and literature. In this context managing archive has become easy with the help of computers using proper software depending on our usage and requirement. From the above article, we come to conclusion that dSpace is good digital library software, which helps in managing the vast digital objects of Tamil literature by giving good retrieval facility with modern technology.

Content management system, also helps in managing e-Archive, but its method is different when compare with Institutional repositories software. Document repository system, help in storing e-Achieves systematically.

REFERENCES

1. Wilson Katie : *Computers in Libraries*, New Delhi, New Age International Publications., 2006.
2. Bhatt, R K : March *Towards Digitations of Information Resource in India*.
3. Sreekumar MG and Others Ed., *Digital Libraries in Knowledge Management*, New Delhi, ESS ESS Publishers, 2006.
4. http://www.unesco.org/
5. http://ta.wikipedia.org/wiki/
6. http://www.eprints.org/
7. http://www.irplus.org/
8. http://www.dspace.org/
9. http://www.greenstone.org/
10. http://www.infitt.org/ti2010/register/papersubmission.php

9

Very Long-term Digital Preservation and Archival Strategies for Tamil Documents

—Mani M. Manivannan

ABSTRACT

The decipherment of Indus script remains controversial. For several years, the inscriptions in Tamil Brahmi script weren't recognized as Tamil. The inscriptions in Vateḻuttu, Pallava grantha, and evolving Tamil Brahmi scripts required careful analysis to decipher. Probable errors in inscriptions and reading of the inscriptions have led to multiple interpretations. As writing instruments and technology changed, Tamils have lost valuable literature and public documents. In the short duration that digital Tamil has existed, we are already finding it difficult to retrieve early Tamil writings on the internet. As we embark on the e-Governance and digital archival of precious documents, we have to remember that unless we are careful, we may find it difficult to preserve these documents for the long duration of centuries. In this chapter, we will explore some of the strategies to minimize the loss of valuable documents.

Background and Overview

Tamils have been creating digital documents in Tamil since the mid 1980s[1] using MS-DOS based editors. Since the early 1990s Tamils have been privately exchanging e-mails in Tamil and with the advent of tamil.net mailing list in 1996, Tamils worldwide started to communicate with each other in Tamil script. Since then there have been multiple Tamil mailing lists, web pages, webzines, blogs that added Tamil digital content. Project Madurai, a community project has been digitizing classical Tamil literature and Tamil books in the public domain and creating a major Tamil corpus with its digital documents since January 1998. Though the Tamils of the diaspora were instrumental in creating a lot of the early Tamil digital content on the web, the mainland Tamil Nadu media have taken to the web and nearly all the Tamil news media have Tamil content on the web. Tamil Nadu government departments have been creating Tamil digital documents in various encodings including TAB, TAM and Baamini.

With a nation-wide push for e-Governance in India, the Tamil Nadu government is about to embark on one of the largest Tamil digitization efforts. Before the advent of the standardization efforts to unify the multiple encodings after the TamilNet'97 conference in Singapore, there were multiple fonts each with its proprietary encoding. These discussions led to the TSCII encoding, the first open, non-proprietary Tamil encoding specification in 1998. At the TamilNet'99 conference in Chennai, the Government of Tamil Nadu formally declared two encoding standards TAB and TAM. During this period, neither ISCII, the Indian national standard and Unicode the global standard based on ISCII, had much support among the Tamil developers. However the standards TSCII, TAB and TAM did not stop others from creating fonts based on proprietary encodings.

Baamini has been popular among the Eezham Tamil diaspora before TSCII and it is still used by some in the

Government of Tamil Nadu. Other encodings that were used to create Tamil digital documents include Vanavil, Indoweb, Murasoli, Webulagam, Thinathanthi, Dinamani, Thinaboomi, Murasu Anjal, Mylai, Thatstamil, ShreeLipi, Amudham (Dinakaran), Vikatan, Anu Graphics (Pallavar), and Senthamizh (Nakkeeran). These encodings are popular enough that some converters recognize all of these. With strong support for the Unicode encoding in Microsoft Windows and Apple platforms as well as Google's search and e-mail applications, use of Unicode has started to spread. Tamil Wikipedia is a popular site that uses Unicode as does the Tamil Lexicon at Chicago University. With the National e-Governance plan of Government of India notifying Unicode as the standard for e-Governance applications, creation of Tamil digital documents in Unicode encoding is expected to increase substantially.

INFITT has recognized Unicode as the main standard for Tamil computing. INFITT has also acknowledged that there are commercial applications that don't yet support Unicode, such as those used in publishing and other industries. For these applications that are not Unicode-ready, INFITT has recognized Tamil All Character Encoding TACE-16 as the only Alternate Standard for Tamil Computing. Since high-end publications are expected to create PDF documents such as Government notifications, text books, etc., along with books published by vendors in Tamil using TACE-16 encoding, this will form part of the Tamil digital document collection.

In this chapter, we will review the impact of technological obsolescence on the Tamil digital documents created in the past 25 years and compare it to the impact on English language digital documents. We will also study the preservation and archival strategies that are evolving in the rest of the world to address the threats to the stability of digital documents. Drawing inspiration from the seminal paper by Paul Convey[3], we hope that this chapter will stimulate in-depth discussions among the technical specialists and the broader audiences interested in preserving not only the historical and cultural heritage of Tamils but also the more mundane public records that the government and the citizens depend on across generations.

What is the Problem? Digital Dilemma!

All current digital storage media are ephemeral. As Conway's graph demonstrates the millennia-old Indus valley signs and the ancient Tamil inscriptions, while fragile, are still legible[2]. Even the palm manuscripts have managed to survive long enough to transfer information to the future generations.

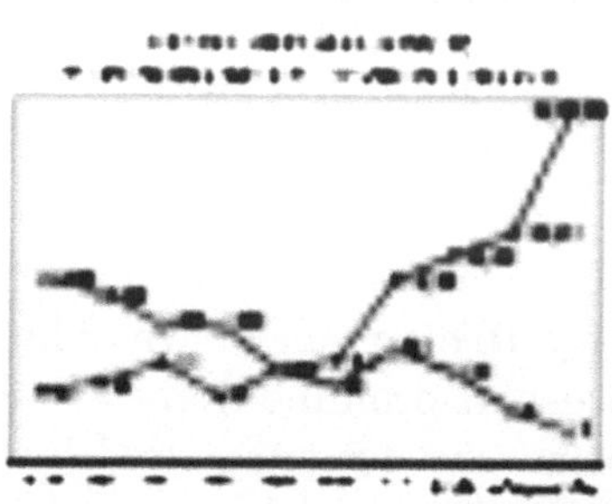

Fig. 9.1 : Information Density *vs.* Life Expectancy[2]

Books printed on acidic paper have lasted more than a century. While the newer recording media allow us to pack enormous information in much smaller area, the shelf-lives of the media, the machines that read them and the applications that render them are all very short (*see Figure 9.1*).

Threats to the Digital Storage

Researchers have identified several threats to the longevity, integrity, access and quality of the digital information storage. Some of these are Media decay and failure, Bit rot, Outdated media, Massive storage failures, Network failure, Access component obsolescence, Outdated formats, Applications and systems failure, Natural Disasters, Human and Software errors, External attacks, Insider attacks,

Economic failure, Organizational failure, Politics and Censorship.

In the Tamil context, we can cite some prominent examples. Ambalam.com, a webzine that was launched before Tamil Internet 2000, with a pre-eminent Tamil writer 'Sujatha' Rangarajan at the helm, is no longer online. The TamilNation.org site, a veritable encyclopedia of Tamil themed collections shut down once, was resurrected later only to shut down recently for reasons unknown (*see Figure 9.2*).

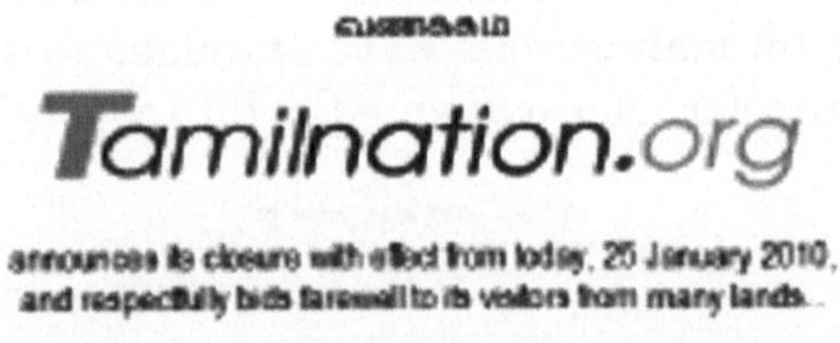

Fig. 9.2 : A Major Tamil website disappears

The status of the archives of Tamil digital data from the late 1980s to early 1990s is unknown. The data formats of the old word processors prominent in the MS-DOS and early Windows platforms are not supported by the vendors. In some cases the vendors are no longer around.

The mail archives of one of the first public mailing lists in Tamil (tamil@tamil.net) do not have its oldest archives (starting from October 1996 to September 1998) online. If a researcher were to look for the email where Kōmakaṉ (aka Rajakumaran, the editor of the Malaysian Tamil weekly 'Nayanam') proposed the word iṇaiyam (இணையம்), it will be difficult to get an authentic version of that e-mail from the tamil.net archives.

The encoding and format changes have impacted Tamil digital information in a major way as well. Several early Tamil mailing lists such as tamil.net, agathiyar@ yahoogroups.com, tamilulagam@ yahoogroups.com, had to switch Tamil encoding from Anjal to TSCII and then recently to Unicode. The archives were however left in their original encoding. ForumHub.com, a pioneer in the web based, public bulletin board successfully migrated from TSCII encoding to Unicode including its archives. Similarly, the webzine Thinnai.com switched from TAB encoding to Unicode successfully including its archives. Project Madurai started with TSCII encoding and it now has files both in TSCII and Unicode encodings. Major encoding conversions seldom go without errors. Initial conversions from TSCII to Unicode at the Project Madurai site had some minor errors (orphaned characters with dotted circle) which appear to have been cleaned up after user feedback.

The founder of the Agathiyar e-mail group, Dr. Jayabharathi, a Tamil scholar and an author from Malaysia, chose to convert all of the Agathiyar postings in the YahooGroups to Unicode and host them separately at his personal site treasurehouseofagathiyar.net. However, he lost most of the articles that he had hosted at various URLs at the geocities.com site when Yahoo shut down Geocities. Several of the pioneering Tamil mailing lists including Agathiyar were once hosted at the hosting site coollist.com and lost their archives when coollist.com folded. The hosting site eGroups.com was acquired by Yahoo and redesigned as YahooGroups.com. Without Yahoo's rescue, the pioneering Tamil mailings all would have lost all of their archives had eGroups.com folded like coollist.

Of equal concern is the information deluge[3]. With the advent of Twitter and Facebook, there is an explosion of public digital content that is rich with information. However, our ability to create digital information far outstrips our capacity and infrastructure to store, manage and preserve it over time.

Why is Preservation Important?

Tamil scholars know very well the importance of preservation of manuscripts and inscriptions in the service of cultural heritage. In the 19th century, critical works of Tamil literature were saved from certain destruction just in time by U. Vē. Cāminātaiyer and Ci. Vai. Tāmōtaranār. And yet, they were unable to recover some major works such as Valaiyāpati and Kuntalakēci.

The examples cited for preserving the Tamil digital documents are not unique. This experience is common to English language based sites as well. The shutdown of GeoCities.com did bring down a major collection of articles in English. The U.S. Library of Congress reports that 44 per cent of the sites available on the Internet in 1998 had vanished one year later. Another study says that 27 months after publication, up to 13 per cent of online cited sources are irretrievable[4] leading to link rot, the process by which the collection of links on a website gradually point to web pages that have become permanently unavailable.

Some of the U.S. Census data are reported to be inaccessible due to rapid obsolescence of hardware and software formats. The data recorded by two Viking space probes sent to Mars on magnetic tapes got corrupted despite being kept in a climate controlled environment. Individual consumers are not immune either. Their personal collection of digital photos, documents, e-mails on their floppy disks, portable drives, backup tapes, etc., are equally vulnerable. A lot of consumers have audio cassettes, video tapes in BetaMax and VHS formats that are becoming unusable as machines needed to play them are no longer available.

As the examples cited demonstrate even in the short duration of Tamil digital information's existence, it has experienced the challenges forecast for global digital information storage. This is only going to get more challenging when e-Governance projects are executed in Tamil and millions of Tamil users access e-Governance kiosks to create Tamil documents. The need for planning digital preservation is great.

Long-term Digital Preservation

What is long-term digital preservation? And how long is 'long-term'? "Long-Term Digital Preservation (LTDP) is a means of keeping digital information such that the same information can be used at some point in the future in spite of obsolescence of everything: hardware, software, processes, format, people, etc."[5] 'Long-term' is taken to be the case where it is impossible for a writer to converse with an eventual reader and impossible for the reader to clarify uncertainties by asking the writer or the writer's contemporaries[6]. In other words, if you write a will bequeathing your wealth to your grandchild and save it in a CD, your grandchild should be able to read what you wrote and prove it to others when you are no more. Your grandchild should do so even if the CD drive, the PC, the Windows operating system, CD driver, the software that reads the contents of the CD and the computer monitor all familiar to you are no longer available and even the CD media itself may have failed. It is not easy. It is not cheap. It will require a lot of organization. And in the end, in spite of best efforts it may not be possible to satisfy all the requirements.

Challenges of Digital Preservation

Unlike analog data like an old black and white photo, digital data does not degrade gracefully. It requires a specific environment, if not an exact one, to be accessible. Digital files on a medium need specific device drivers to access the medium, specific operating systems to understand the file system and launch a specific application program that knows how to interpret the content of the file. These further depend on specific hardware. If any of these fail, the digital data are not accessible. Digital Preservation aims at packaging the digital objects such that their authenticity is provable and the data are accessible as long as there is a need to read that object. Three main methods of digital preservation are technology preservation, technology emulation and information migration.

Technology Preservation

This is the 'computer museum' solution that assumes that the computer/equipment, operating systems, original application software, media drives, etc., all can be preserved, and maintained and that the media is readable. This is the method that was used to recover the pictures taken in 1966 by NASA's robotic probe Lunar Orbiter 1 and stored on 2500 tapes that needed a specialty FR-900 Ampex tape drive, very few of which were made and sold at the cost of $330,000. It took considerable effort by the very few technicians who had the special skills to work with the reader, a lot of salvaged parts and some good luck. Since there is no commercial or practical interest in such equipment, it is impossible to keep such obsolete equipment functional forever. It worked in this case because of the rarity of the digital object that people were trying to retrieve.[7]

Technology Emulation

Emulation uses a special type of software, called an emulator or virtual machine, to translate instructions from original software to execute on new platforms. This is a fairly well understood technology and practical applications do exist. For example, the popular software VMware offers legacy emulation mode to read DVD-ROM or CD-ROM drives. However, it is difficult to predict how many generations of such emulation will be possible. And for very long-term preservation of the order of several decades to a century or more, technology emulation is yet to be proven.

Information Migration

Information migration requires periodic transfer of digital objects from one system software configuration to another or from one generation of computer technology to a subsequent generation with no loss in content or context and little or no loss in structure. This may require that encrypted digital objects be decrypted. Careful processes need to be evolved to guarantee object authenticity and integrity with this method.

Some of the early creators of Tamil digital objects used a migration method to transfer digital data from MS-DOS based applications and file formats across multiple generations of Windows operating system releases and several versions of applications. Even on the web, users migrated data from one provider to another, as well as from one encoding to another using the conversion tools available. As the Government of Tamil Nadu embarks on the e-Governance program, its offices across the state will be migrating their existing digital data files from various encodings such as TAB, TAM, Baamini, Vanavil etc., to Unicode. This migration of information avoids obsolescence not only of the physical storage medium, but of the encoding and format of the data.

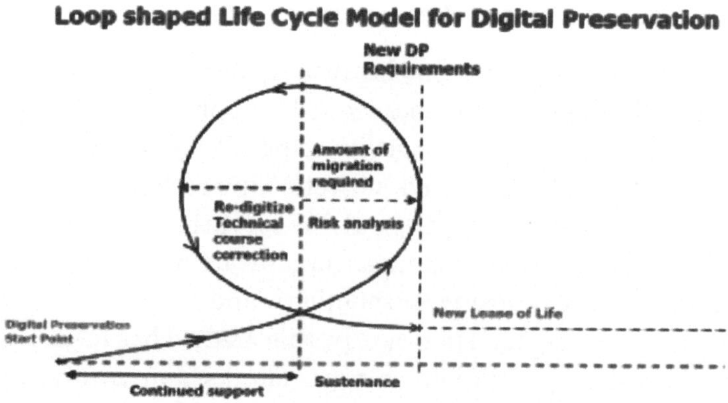

Fig. 9.3 : CDAC-Katre Loop shaped life cycle model

In a sense, the Tamil scribes who have been migrating palm manuscripts in Tamil across the centuries have been doing precisely that and have been largely successful in transmitting heritage information to later generations. While this is still error-prone across very long time scale, it is a proven method. This requires that digital objects be constantly migrated to use new storage media, software and computers whenever a current system is in danger of obsolescence.

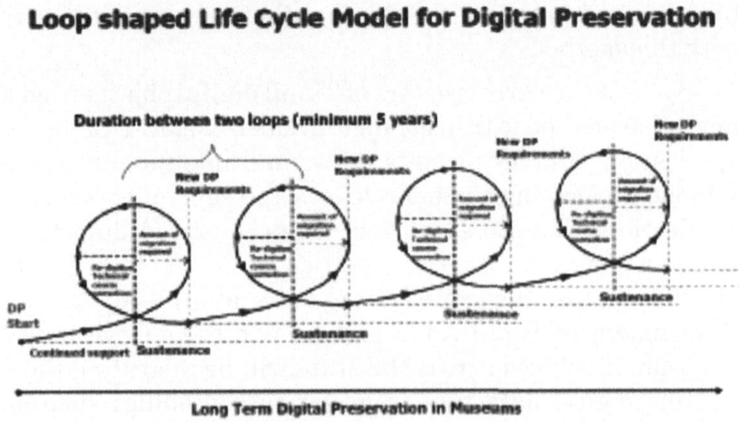

Fig. 9.4 : CDAC-Katre Multi-Loop life cycle model

Distributed Digital Preservation

One of the ways in which the authenticity and integrity of digital objects can be preserved is by Replication. Multiple copies also improve the longevity of digital objects if multiple storage locations are used as well. This technique is also known as Distributed Digital Preservation (DDP). This requires extreme discipline, high organization and dedication while the risk of losing authenticity and integrity is high unless one is careful. Historically, this method has been used successfully by religious orders, monks and traditional scholarly communities dedicated to transmitting specialized knowledge across generations. It is noteworthy that a lot of the Tamil palm manuscripts were found in Saiva and Vaishnava mutts, traditional medicinal families, and traditional Tamil scholar families. A classic example of DDP is the LOCKSS (Lots of Copies Keeps Stuff Safe)[8] technology used by a consortium of publishers, librarians, and learned societies to support a community-managed failsafe repository for scholarly content (http://lockss.stanford.edu/).

Metadata and Digital Preservation

Metadata (data about data) is critical to the authenticity and integrity of digital preservation. Metadata is concerned with content, context, and structure of the digital data. Content is intrinsic to the digital information and refers to what the object contains. Context indicates who, what, why, where, how and other data associated with the object's creation and is extrinsic to the object. Structure describes the associations within or among individual objects and can be either intrinsic or extrinsic.

The key to successful implementation of a digital preservation effort are metadata. There are three different types of metadata, all essential to ensure the usability and preservation of the collection over time.

***Descriptive Metadata*:** convey some sense of intellectual content and context.

***Structural Metadata*:** describe the attributes of an object, such as size, electronic format etc.

***Administrative Metadata*:** information related to rights management, creation date of digital resource, hardware configuration etc.[10]

Current Standards and Best Practices

There are several standards that address digital preservation that are of interest to us. The Open Archival Information System (OAIS) was initiated by Consultative Committee for Space Data System (CCSDS) in 2002 and became an international standard with ISO 14721: 2003.

This is the reference model for several other standards. LOCKSS and CLOCKSS comply with the OASIS model and are popular with digital librarians and research publications. The Victorian Electronic Record Strategy (VERS) is a practical specification that addresses the immediate problems of handling large digital documents in popular formats. The National Electronic Records Archive (NARA) consolidates several models with an aim to preserve government records. There are several digital preservation initiatives in India as well, with Digital Library of India (DLI) being the one that digitizes books in Indian languages. There doesn't appear to be any special program anywhere in the world that addresses the unique challenges of Tamil digital documents.

Issues of Interest for Tamil Documents

Tamil digital documents are constantly being created not only in mainland Tamil Nadu but also in Eezham and the vast Tamil diaspora. While the diaspora largely shares common interests in classical Tamil, when it comes to modern culture, literature, politics, cinema, lifestyle etc., it is quite diverse and differs significantly from the mainland Tamils. Not all of the political opinions of the diaspora are appreciated or even tolerated everywhere. As a result, unpalatable opinions or culturally variant expressions of the diaspora are likely to be ignored if not outright censored by a conservative digital librarian. Selection of the digital content to be preserved is a matter of judgment and since it is expensive to preserve digital content for a long time, it would be tempting to reject the content that one disagrees with regardless of how representative such content may be of contemporary Tamil culture. The digital librarians need only to look at the anthologists that put together the Cañkam anthologies that have stood the test of time as a guide for selection.

There are some interesting lessons to learn from the fact that the Indus Civilization seals are yet to be satisfactorily decoded and how the Rosetta Stone helped decode Egyptian hieroglyphic writings. The Rosetta Stone had carved text made up of three translations of a single passage: two in Egyptian language scripts (hieroglyphic and Demotic) and one in classical Greek. This is a classic example where Arthur C. Clarke's Rule of Three worked. As interpreted by Mike Shea (mikeshea.net) this rule becomes "preserve in three formats on three media types in three places". Extending this to Tamil documents, one could save important Tamil documents in three different encodings (Unicode, TACE-16 and ISO-15919), in three different formats (PDF/A, XML, HTML) in three different places (Tamil Nadu, Malaysia and Canada). Since the Unicode Tamil block could be used to encode texts in Sanskrit and Saurastri and ISO-15919 could be used to encode all Indic languages, only TACE-16 encoding exclusively encodes Tamil.

The subscript/superscript modifiers to indicate varga sounds of other Indic languages do not mix well with TACE-16. So, this could serve as the Rosetta stone for a future researcher if there is any doubt as to the identity of the language of a Tamil digital document. Since the Māṉkuḷam 7 Tamil brahmi inscriptions were thought to be a prakrit inscription for a long time, this is not an idle speculation. The metadata also should be used to clearly identify the language and encodings used to avoid any misidentification. Since such triple encoding preservation is expensive this should be considered only for important documents.

Conclusion

The reality is that solution to the LTDP problem is a work in progress. Some acceptable solutions exist for static data such as documents where the current process is to store in standard encapsulated formats such as PDF/A, wrap with metadata as defined by OAIS and migrate when necessary to address media obsolescence and technology following the CDAC-Katre multi-loop life cycle model. Even here, critics are unsure of the selection of PDF/A for an encapsulated model, preferring HTML or XML. More research is being done to understand the preservation requirements for dynamic data.

We hope that this chapter sparks an interest in the long-term preservation and archival challenges to preserve Tamil digital information. The Tamil Virtual University could be one of the best Digital Librarians for preserving all Tamil and Tamil related digital documents and could be one of the nodes of a distributed archival center, perhaps using the LOCKSS technology. Since large numbers of Tamil digital documents exist with multiple data formats and encoding, it is hoped that accurate metadata is specified to encapsulate these documents in their original format before migrating them to one standard encoding or three standard encodings (Unicode, TACE-16 and ISO 15919) as discussed earlier. We hope that this paper would spark an interest in and stimulate in-depth discussions among those interested in very long-term preservation of Tamil digital documents.

REFERENCES

1. Muracu Ne_uma_a_, 2007. Maleciyat Tami_arum Tami_um. *International Institute of Tamil Studies*. pp 250-264.
2. Conway, P. 1996. Preservation in the Digital World , CLIR Reports, Pub 62, 24 pp. ISBN 1-887334-49- (http://www.clir.org/pubs/reports/conway2/index.html)
3. Hey, T. and Trefethen, A., 2002. The Data Deluge: An e-Science Perspective. In: Berman, Fran (Ed.), 2003, *Grid Computing: Making the Global Infrastructure a Reality*, (John Wiley and Sons).
4. Dellavalle, R. P. *et. al. Information Science: Going, Going, Gone*. Science302, no. 5646 (Oct. 31, 2003), pp. 787-788.
5. Factor, M. 2010. *Long-term Digital Preservation: A View from IBM Research*. The Irish Universities Information Services Colloquium, March 2010. http://www.iuisc.ie/2010/Micheal_Factor.ppt
6. Gladney, H. M., 2009. *Critique of Architectures for Long-Term Digital Preservation*. (Draft). http://eprints.erpanet.org/162/01/LDPcrit.pdf
7. Johnson Jr. J. 2009. *NASA's Early Lunar Images, in a New Light*. The Los Angeles Times, March 22, 2009. http://articles.latimes.com/2009/mar/22/nation/na-lunar22
8. *A Guide to Distributed Digital Preservation*. K. Skinner and M. Schultz, Eds. (Atlanta, GA: Educopia Institute, 2010).
9. Katre, D. 2008. *Imperatives for Survival of Digital Preservation in Indian Museums* (A Case Study), National Workshop on Digital Preservation in India, November 7, 2008

10

Fostering Tamil Web Communities for Mining Tamil Web Pages

—Dr. A. Vijaya Kathiravan, R. Vidhya

ABSTRACT

"There are three popular qualities identified with Tamil people in 20th century: Creativity, intelligence and artistic thinking". With the growing Tamil interest and Internet, the amount of Tamil data doubles every 12-14 months and will increase even more dramatically in the coming year. With an enormous amount of Tamil data stored in web databases and warehouses, it is increasingly important to develop powerful tools for analysis of such Tamil data and mining interesting patterns from it. There is a strong interest in employing methods of data mining to generate models of Tamil related web pages forming web communities. The main intention of this chapter is to establish cyber community mining technique for Tamil domain and to identify the Tamil resources available in the free web. This chapter proposes a new initiative for forming Tamil web communities with concise introduction about community mining.

It also groups research publications and literatures in Tamil using bibliometric analysis. This community mining will yield benefits to all Tamil lovers, who want to be well-versed in a Tamil domain of his own interest. By forming people communities (i.e., people belonging to similar interest) using social network analysis, the domain knowledge in Tamil can be shared. Hence, web community mining may play an important role in forming Tamil Web Communities for gathering Tamil resources and documents of similar interest.

Keywords: *Web communities, Tamil communities, social network analysis, community mining, web mining, web structure mining, citation, co-citation and bibliometric coupling.*

Introduction

The ability to train computers to predict properties based upon knowledge of Tamil computing for Tamil data offers the prospect of automatically screening massive libraries of other language information to produce prediction. Tamil computing is an application of information technology in Tamil to the storage, management and analysis of Tamil information. Tamil information consists of Tamil databases, Tamil articles, Tamil publications, Tamil literatures, Tamil news, agricultural, health care, scientific information and other Tamil related information. With the increase in Tamil interest in web, computer-based Tamil databases, operating systems, hardware, software, tools, search engines and mining techniques have become very essential. Now-a-days, web mining outperforms a significant position in information retrieval process using search engines, in which the main ingredients are web content mining, web structure mining and web usage mining. About 40 per cent of the people are likely to surf the web using hyperlinks. Community mining is transpired from web structure mining that aims to utilize the hyperlinked structural pattern available in web provided that it has some meaningful information hidden inside. A web community refers to group of web pages sharing a common interest like Tamil implicitly or explicitly. Using people communities, people in similar profession can group together as virtual teams to accomplish their tasks.

Tamil Community Mining

A Tamil web community is a set of Tamil web pages that provide resources on a specific topic in Tamil. By modeling the Web as a graph and performing several operations on it, it was able to separate the Web in sets of related items in which Tamil community is extracted. The different types of association relationship existing in a community are citation, co-citation and bibliographic coupling. Those have been described in fig. 10.1.

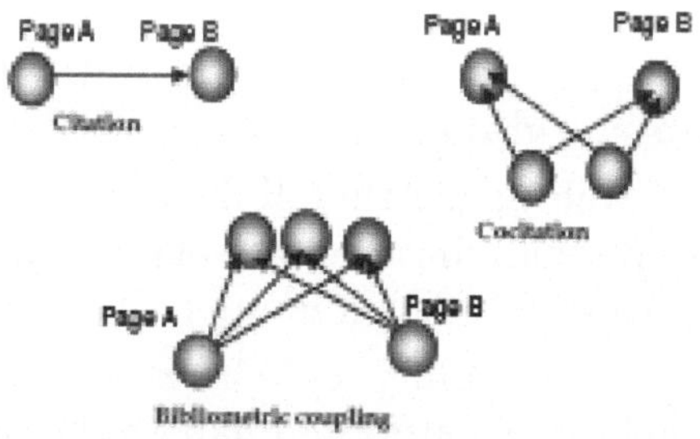

Fig. 10.1 : Types of Associations in Community

Using the above associations, bibliometric coupling finds patterns in citation graphs; sociometric finds patterns in social networks; collaborative filtering finds patterns in rank graphs; webometric finds patterns in web page links. The main scope of community mining is to measure the similarity of web pages on the web graph and to extract the meaningful communities through the link structure pattern.

Definitions of Community

Several different definitions of community were also raised in the literature that has been explained in:

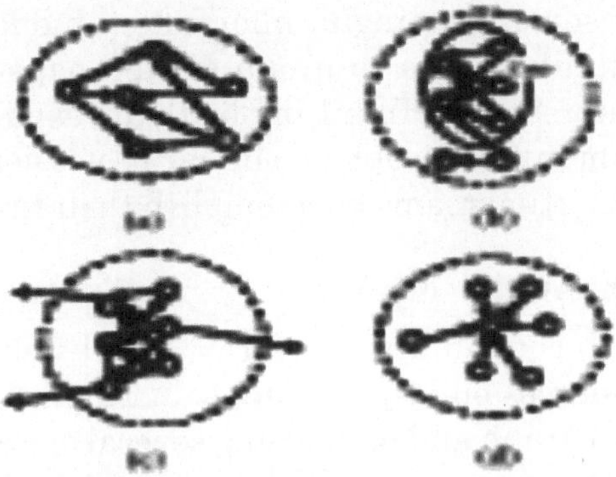

Fig. 10.2 : Several Different Definitions of Community

(*a*) A web community is a number of representative authority web pages linked by important hub pages that share a common topic.

(*b*) A web community is a highly linked bipartite sub-graph and has at least one core containing complete bipartite sub graph.

(*c*) A set of web pages that linked more pages in the community than those outside of the community could be defined as a web community.

(*d*) A research community could be based on a single most cited paper and contain all papers that cite it. While each of the above definition characterizes some essential properties of a community, it makes the community mining task rather difficult because of a lack of uniform definition.

Discovering Communities

In this chapter, a community on the web is defined as a cluster of web pages, which share common topics. However, there are many ways to detect the clusters of web communities. One of the key distinguishing features of the algorithms has to do with the degree of locality used for assessing whether or not a page should be considered a community member. On the one extreme are purely local methods, which consider only the properties of the local neighborhood around two vertices to decide if the two are in the same community. Global methods operate at the other extreme, and essentially demand that every edge in a Web graph be considered in order to decide if two vertices are members of the same community. Broder *et al.*[1] reported on an algorithm of clustering web pages based on the contents. This approach can be applied not only to hypertext but also plaintext. However, indexing web pages accurately is difficult because the contents of web pages are not always meaningful. In contrast to the content-based approach, links in web pages can be reliable information because they reflect human judgment. Botafogo and Shneiderman[2] proposed an idea for abstraction called aggregate based on graph theory.

Their algorithm removes 'indics' (nodes with high number of out-links) and 'references' (nodes with high number of in-links) iteratively to clear the graph. However, removed nodes often become very important elements to understand the web. On the other hand, Kumar *et.al,*[3] defined a community on the web as a dense directed bipartite subgraph, and discovered over 100,000 communities. However, the scale of subgraphs depends on its parameters. This implies the difficulty in detecting communities from the web, since the communities are often somewhat related with each other. As another use of links, Kleinberg[4] and Brin and Page[5] used the link structures for ranking web pages. Their main idea was based on mutually reinforcing that the more a web page is referred, the more authoritative the web page becomes, and the higher the web page ranks. The highly ranked web pages tend to be the representative web pages of communities. There are several data structures such as biconnected components, strongly connected components, bipartite graph (BG), dense bipartite graph (DBG) and complete bipartite graph or bipartite core (CBG) employed for forming communities.

Terminologies in Web Community

Bipartite graph (BG). A bipartite graph BG (*T,I*) is a graph, whose node-set can be partitioned into two non-empty sets *T* and *I*. Every directed edge of BG joins a node in *T* to a node in I2 Dense bipartite graph (DBG). Let *p* and *q* be nonzero integer variables and tc and ic be the number of nodes in *T* and *I*, respectively. A DBG (*T, I, p, q*) is a BG (*T,I*), where (*i*) each node of *T* establishes an edge with at least *p* (*1<=p<=ic*) nodes of *T*, and (*ii*) at least *q* (*1<=q<=tc*) nodes of *T* establish an edge with each node of *I*.

Complete Bipartite Graph (CBG)

A CBG (*T,I, p, q*) is a DBG (*T,I, p, q*), where *p* = *ic* and *q* = *tc*. K L M K L M

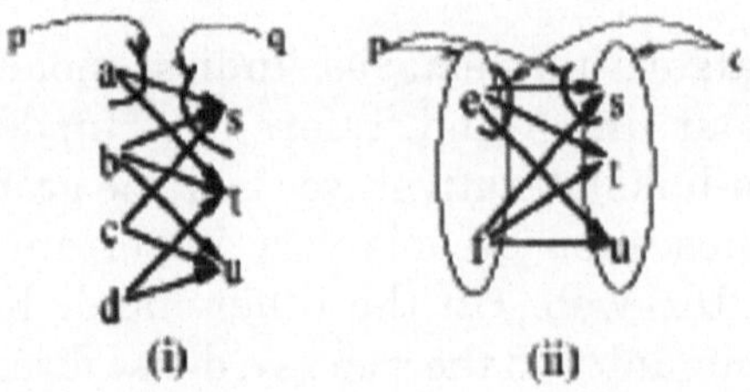

Fig. 10.3 : (i) DBG (*T, I, p, q*) (ii) CBG (*p, q*)

Fig. 10.3 shows the difference between a DBG(*T,I, p, q*) and a CBG (*p,q*).

Community Hierarchy

Let the variable num_levels denote the number of levels in a hierarchy for a given data set. A community is denoted with C(*i,j*) , where *i* (1 <= I <= num_levels) is a nonzero integer value that denotes the level and *j* is an integer value which denotes unique community identifier at level *i*. Then, If *i* = 1, members of C(*i,j*) are the web pages. If *i* > 1, members of C(*i,j*) are the communities at level "*i*-1".

Community [C(*i,j*)] Let *pi* and *qi* be integer variables that represent threshold values. The community C(*i,j*) = *T*, if there exist a DBG(*T, I, p, q*) over a set of nodes at level "*i-1*" with *p* >= *pi* and *q* >= *qi*. Cocite Let *pi* and *pj* be pages.

Cocite(*pi, pj*)=true, if | child(*pi*) - child(*pj*) | >= cocite_factor, where cocote_factor represents a non-zero integer value.

Relax cocite Let *T* be the set of pages and *Pj* be another page (*Pj-T*). For any page *Pi*-, if relax_cocite (*Ti, Tj*) = true if | child (*Pj*) -child (*T*) | >= relax_cocite_factor. Here, relax_cocite_factor is nonzero integer variable and child(*T*) contains the children of the pages of *T*.

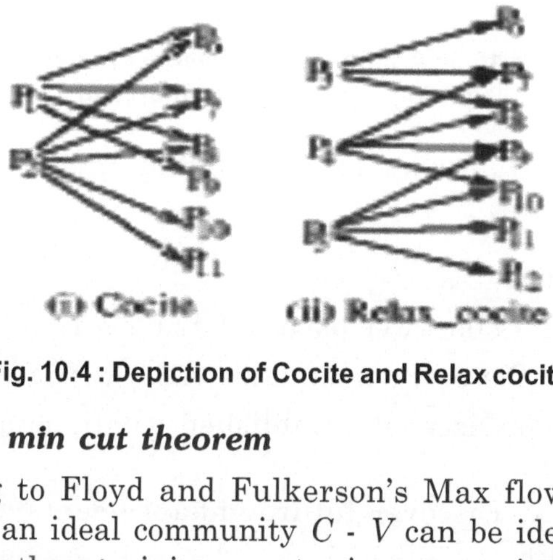

Fig. 10.4 : Depiction of Cocite and Relax cocite

Max flow min cut theorem

According to Floyd and Fulkerson's Max flow min cut Theorem, an ideal community *C* - *V* can be identified by calculating the *s-t* minimum cut using appropriately chosen source and sink nodes. In recurse over algorithm, community obtained in one iteration is used as input to next iteration. Finally, mirroring pages in the community are eliminated using 'shingling' method. Quite a lot of work has been done in mining the implicit communities of users, web pages or scientific literature from the Web or document citation database using content or link analysis. Forming Communities among users is called as people community. Using bibliographic references in scientific literatures and document citations, scientific literature community can also be formed, which are described in detail.

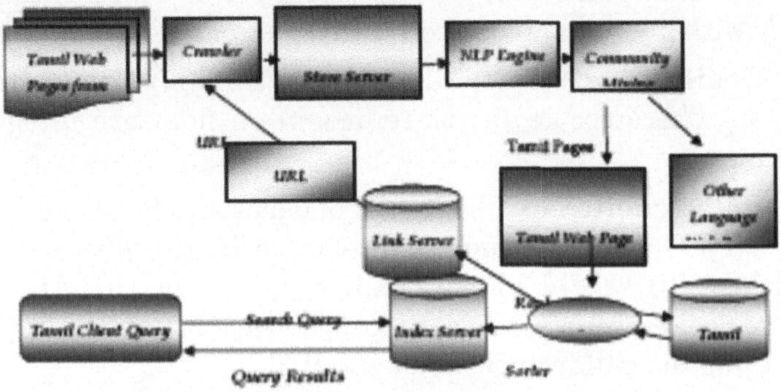

Fig. 10.5 : Architecture of Search Engine for mining Tamil Web Communities

Proposed Algorithm for Evaluating Tamil Communities

Main Phases

Phase 1. Collect web pages related to a Tamil domain.

Phase 2. Discover communities on the web for all domains.

Phase 3. Discover established relations among the communities.

Phase 4. Discover future enhancements among the communities.

Phase 5. Visualize inter and intra relationship of communities.

The Detailed Process

Phase 1. Preparations: First of all, let a user decide a Tamil domain, which she/he wants to explore thoroughly. Then, source web pages *D* are collected by using any conventional search engine like Google. Here, web pages of Google's output for the query are downloaded.

Phase 2. Discover Communities: Use community trawling algorithm or *s-t* max flow min cut algorithm for community mining. For surveying the picture of communities with future enhancements among communities, only centered web pages in communities are used instead of all the web pages. The centered web page named as core-page is extracted as follows:

1. Count the frequency of links included in *D*.
2. Regard the top *N1* links *C* as the 'core-pages' of communities.

Phase 3. Discover Established Relations: Measure the relations among core pages by counting the number of co-citations, and regard strong relations as established links. The process is as follows:

1. For every pair of two core-pages in *C*, count the number of links included in both the core-pages.
2. Regard the top N2 pairs as established links *L1* (solid lines in Fig. 10.6).

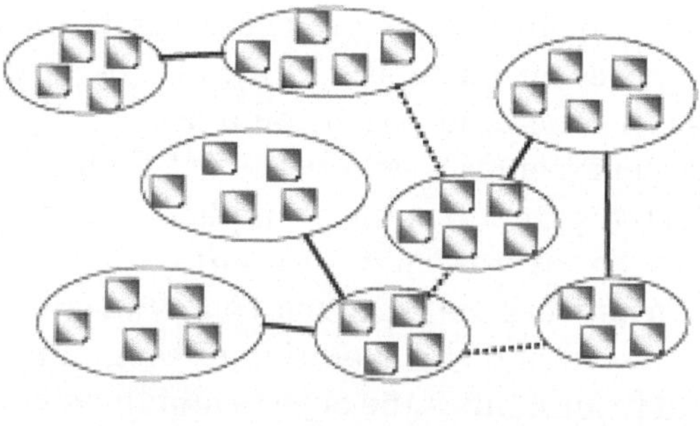

Fig. 10.6 : Visualization of established and future links in Tamil communities

Phase 4. **Discover Future Enhancements:** Measure the relations among core-pages by counting the number of co-citations, and regard weak relations as future links. The process is as follows:

1. For every pair of two cores in *C* except for *L1*, count the number of links included in both the cores.
2. Regard the top *N3* pairs as future links *L2* (dotted lines in Fig. 10.6).

The movement of communities is shown by established and future links. Therefore, future enhancements are expressed by the combination of these two kinds of relations.

Phase 5. **Visualization:** Core-pages and its relations (*C,L1,* and *L2*) are visualized into 2-dimensional interface to piece out the connections of communities and to understand the potential needs or demands.

Conclusion and Future Work

In this chapter, the importance of discovering communities in Tamil for gathering resources has been strongly insisted. Using visualization, an idea for discovering established web pages in a Tamil community is mined by chaining primitive communities to understand potential needs or demands. It could find communities of adaptive granularity. By using techniques such as community clustering, social network analysis and bibliometric analysis, the Tamil world can get more benefits in future. For efficient community mining, algorithms based on machine learning may be used in future. Since this is a general ides that could potentially be used in any application scenarios, where the data can be abstracted to a graph structure, this may be applied to any domain. Its usefulness in other environments such as human relationship network, newsgroups, communication network, etc can be tested and the evolution of communities can be analyzed in future. Since the objects and links in a network are usually dynamic, changes of communities in a time series manner can be observed. From this idea of implementing community mining in Tamil, it has been confirmed that communities are the useful means to share resources and knowledge among people from different community domains.

People community and scientific literature community may act as a powerful knowledge acquisition tool for the Tamil community. The ideas and methods presented in this study can be proved useful by analyzing more domain communities. Future research in community mining focuses on generalizing the notion of community parameterized with coupling factor low for weakly connected communities, high for highly connected communities and optimal for ideal community. Co-boosting is a method for information retrieval from an unlabelled data. By combining this technique with community mining in Tamil, variety of Tamil-based community like social community, literature community, political community, student community, Tamil cinema and songs community, research community and other Tamil related communities may be formed in future.

Acknowledgement

"Thou art the real goal of human life, we are yet but slaves of wishes putting bar to our advancement. Thou art the only God and Power to bring us upto that stage". I sincerely thank INFITT-2010 Conference Selection Committee for having given us this opportunity. My extended gratitude goes to our college superiors, colleagues, friends and family members.

REFERENCES

1. Broder, A. Z., Glassman, S.C., Manasse, M. S., "*Syntactic Clustering of the Web*", Proc.World Wide Web Conference, 1997.
2. Botafogo, R. A., Shneiderman, B, "*Identifying Aggregates in Hypertext Structures*", Proc.ACM Conference on Hypertext, p.63-74, 1991.
3. Kumar. R., Raghavan, P. Rajagopalan. S., Tomkins, A., "*Trawling the Web for Emerging Cyber-Communities*", Proc. World Wide Web Conference, 1999.
4. Kleinberg, J. M., "*Authoritative Sources in a Hyperlinked Environment*", Proc. ACM- SIAM Symposium on Discrete Algorithm, pp. 668-677, 1998.
5. Brin, S., Page, L., "*The Anatomy of a Large-scale Hypertextual Web Search Engine*", Proc. World Wide Web Conference, 1998.
6. Furen Lin, ChunHung Chen, KuoLung Tsai, "*Discovering Group Interaction Patterns in a Teachers Professional Community*", Proceedings of the 36th Hawaii International Conference on System Sciences (HICSS'03), IEEE, 2002.

7. Wen-Jun Zhou, Ji-Rong Wen, Wei-Ying Ma, Hong-Jiang Zhang, "*A Concentric-Circle Model for Community Mining in Graph Structures*", Technical Report in Microsoft Research, MSR-TR-2002- 123, Nov. 15, 2002.
8. P. Krishna Reddy and Masaru Kitsuregawa, "*An Approach to Relate the Web Communities through Bipartite Graphs*", Institute of Industrial Science, The University of Tokyo, Japan, 2001.
9. Naohiro, Matsumura1, Yukio Ohsawa, Mitsuru Ishizuka, "*Future Directions of Communities on the Web*", School of Engineering, University of Tokyo, Japan, 2000.
10. Alexandrin Popescul, Gary William Flake, Steve Lawrence, Lyle H. Ungar, C. Lee Giles, "*Clustering and Identifying Temporal Trends in Document Databases*", in IEEE Advances in Digital Libraries, ADL 2000.
11. Dmitry Zelenko, Chinatsu Aone, 2006, *Discriminative Methods for Transliteration*, Proceedings of the 2006 Conference on Empirical Methods in Natural Language Processing (EMNLP2006), pp. 612-617, 2006.
12. Surya Ganesh, Sree Harsha, Prasad Pingali, Vasudeva Varma, *Statistical Transliteration for CrossLangauge Information Retrieval using HMM alignment and CRF*, The Second International Workshop on Cross Lingual Information Access—Addressing the Informaion Need of Multilingual Socoeties, 2008.
13. Sathiya Keerthi S, Sundararajan S, CRF versus *SVM-struct for Sequence Labelling*, Yahoo Research Technical Report, 2007.
14. Taskar B, Lacoste-Julien S, and Klein D., *A Discriminative Matching Approach to Word*, 2005.

11

A Tamil Web Portal Development with Online Dictionary

—A. Parimaladevi
—A. Muthukumar

Introduction

Purpose

The purpose of this document is to present a detailed description of the mytamilthai.com which is a Tamil web portal development that includes all the details in Tamil. It will explain the purpose and features of the website. This document is intended for both developers and end-users of the system.

Scope of the Project

This site is going to develop mainly for the people who feel uncomfortable while browsing in English. This site includes the information about youth, jokes, sports, medicines and also information for women in Tamil. Instead of searching different sites user can search a single site for his/her entire requirement. This site also includes the English to Tamil dictionary. User who needs to search the Tamil meaning for a particular English word can effectively use this site. Also if the particular word is not found and if the user knows the meaning, then he/she can add the new word. Administrator who has the rights to see the words in temporary database and add to the existing database of the dictionary. Some pages of the site can be viewed by all people but certain pages are viewed by the user only after they register their name in this site. Also authorized user can advertise for the jobs they provide with admin assist. Also user can post their comments.

About Index Page

An index page is the first page of web portal system. The site mainly consists of four main divisions. The division at the top is Header with the title and division at the bottom with privacy policy and conditions are displayed in all pages of Tamil web portal system. The next division is for menus which will be displayed only in certain pages.

The menus includes the following.

இளமை — youth
பெண்கள் — women
நகைச்சுவை — jokes
விளையாட்டு — sports
மருந்தகம் — medicines

The last division will be content division. In this, there will be some sub-divisions. Left side which includes tabs like,

நடப்புச் செய்திகள் — recent news
என்னைப் பற்றி — about author
மக்கள்கருத்து — user comments

In recent news, daily news will be updated for eg. About stock market, gold rate, politics, sports, etc. All the details about author will be displayed in next tab and at last if any user posts comments about any particular topic then with admin assist, the comment will be displayed.

The middle sub-division will be the exact content of particular topic. And the last sub-division includes the tabs like

உள்ளே செல்ல — login
வேலை வாய்ப்பு — jobs available
கருத்தைச் சேர்க்க — post comments
விசைப்பலகை — keyboard

To login, user needs to register in the site. The information about the registration will be stored in the database. All the jobs advertised will be displayed here. Every one can see all the information about that particular job by just clicking it. User who needs to post the comments, can post here but it will be stored in the database for admin to approve it to display in the site.

Admin login

Administrator who has all the rights on the system. As admin login, all the tabs displayed in index will be displayed with some extra tabs which includes

அகராதி – dictionary
புதியசொல் சேர்க்க – add new word in dictionary
புதிய வேலை – new job advertising
வேலை வாய்ப்பு – advertised jobs
விசைபலகை – keyboard

The menu will be enabled once admin login. As the menu contains the topics, the information regarding the particular will be displayed in the content page once we select the particular topic in that menu.

Online dictionary is available here. Tamil to English and English to Tamil dictionary is available with the description in both the languages. Admin add words to dictionary and it will be stored in database in Unicode format. Admin who enters all the information about the job by the information provided by the job provider. Also already advertised jobs will be displayed.

User login

User after registering, user enters the site and views all the tabs displayed in index page with some extra tabs. User also can add words to dictionary but it will be stored in database. If admin find that word is irrelevant then he has the rights to remove the word from database so that, that word won't be displayed further unless again adding it properly. Users who wish to post comments can post here. This is also stored in database for admin use.

Online Dictionary

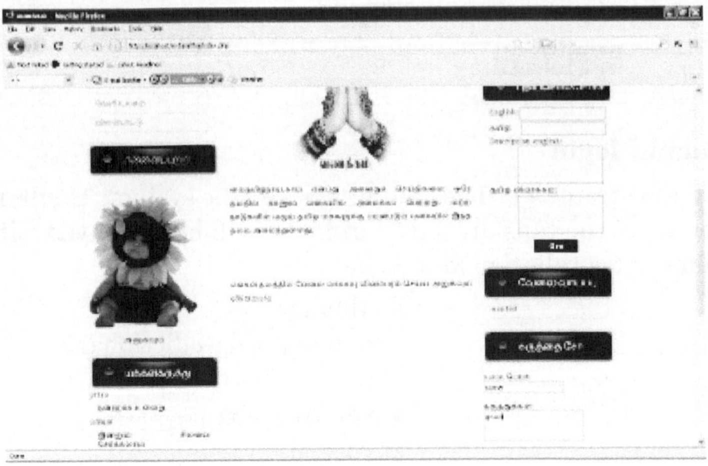

As described earlier, online dictionary will be displayed both in admin and users login. By typing English word we will get Tamil meaning as well as description in Tamil and the same way if we type in Tamil we will get English meaning with description in English.

Conclusion

Mytamilthai.com is developed to help all the people who need to know all the information at a single site. Here there is an availability of dictionary with English to Tamil as well as Tamil to English dictionary with glossary. So it is very useful for all people at different countries to the know the meaning for any word they wish. Recent updates are displayed and it will be updated daily. Future enhancement: This project has been developed as a Master's project and is constrained by time.

There is scope for extending the system as per the need. Job providers advertise for the job availability now. Job seekers at present can view just the job advertisement and need to contact separately by them selves with the information provided by the job provider. Further it is going to extend by job seekers to post their resume for the advertisement displayed in the site through this site directly.

Also now there is an availability of English to Tamil and Tamil to English dictionary only. Further it is going to enhance in different language according to users need. Also according to users authorized comments the site will be enhanced.

REFERENCES

1. PHP 6/MySQLR Programming for the Absolute Beginner – Andy Harris –
2. Course Technology, 2009.
3. http://www.w3schools.com/PHP
4. http://www.php.net/manual

5. http://www.actionscript.org
6. http://senthilvayal.wordpress.com
7. http://classroom2007.blogspot.com
8. http://www.webulagam.com
9. http://tamil.webdunia.com
10. http://www.thamilworld.com
11. http://www.adhikaalai.com

12

Methods and Options for Videoconferencing in Relation to the Tamil Language in 2010

—Eric Miller

On 21 February 2009, Chief Minister Kalaignar Karunanidhi in Chennai made a video call to launch the 3G (Third Generation) network services of BSNL, the Government-run telecommunications company. Today, video calls on mobile telephones using BSNL's 3G network are being routinely made by members of the public in Tamil Nadu. Airtel's 3G network is also expected to be operational soon.

At this moment in time, as we are on the verge of the Video Call Revolution, it may be useful to look both backward and forward. This might help us to decide what to do with our new videoconference capabilities, as we enter the Age of Videoconferencing in earnest. Previously, I have written three articles about videoconferencing for INFITT — in 2002, 2003, and 2004.[1] This article summarizes and adds to those. Videoconferencing, video calls, video chat, or simply, being able to see people as we speak with them through electronic devices, has been on the horizon for many years. Two major ways of videoconferencing are:

Through one's computer, and through one's mobile telephone. In both cases, the hardware is increasingly coming with a video camera built-in. The videoconference camera is generally above the screen. In the case of mobile telephones, there are usually two cameras, one facing the user (for videoconferencing), and one facing away from the user (for optional use for recording still-images and video). Actually, the computer and the mobile telephone are converging, to produce smart phones—and these are the mobile telephone models that tend to be videoconference-capable.

Skype is most commonly used on personal computers, but it can also be used through smart phones. Skype has brought videoconferencing to wider-than-ever-before public use. Other free video chat programs include those in Gmail and iGoogle, Microsoft's Windows Live Messenger, Yahoo! Messenger, and Apple's iChat. Among online social networks (also known as, social media), Orkut is one of the most advanced in offering the video chat option to users. How will people with similar interests find each other to videoconference with? They could join communities, or becomes friends, fans, or followers of others, as many people already do on social media.

There are also programs such as Webex, which, for a cost, enable videoconferencing over the Internet, with sharing of files—for text, electronic drawing, video, etc.— in various windows.[2] In the 2004 and 2005 Chennai-Philadelphia videoconferences I facilitated, we used a simpler (and lower-quality) method for showing Tamil text: we projected it onto the back wall of our room in Chennai (Figure 12.2). In other videoconferences, I have placed the Tamil text next to the image of the speaker, like in a comic book (Figure 12.1). The development of ways of producing instantaneous visual translation sub-titles, or captions, is going to be an important part of videoconferencing's future. This will require voice recognition technology (from spoken to printed words), and automatic translation technology (from one written language to another).

Microsoft's Natal system will feature motion-sensing technology—not just for game-playing, but for operating the computer in general. Thus, the Gesture Revolution is upon us, in which a crucial input device is a video camera.[3] Based on what I have seen in the college students I teach in Chennai, many young people today will not rest until they can play games via videoconference in social networks on mobile telephones. Regarding high-quality types of videoconferencing in Tamil Nadu, India, and beyond: Early videoconferencing in India (in the 1990s) tended to occur via dedicated non-Internet ISDN lines (three lines together yield 384kbps). However, ISDN lines cost by the minute, and are quite expensive to use—and are even more so when a bridge is needed, for connecting more than two partners in a videoconference.

The global development is now toward videoconferencing via very high-speed Internet. For example, Reliance—whose videoconference rooms in their over 200 Reliance World stores across India have led the way in making high-quality videoconferencing visible and available—previously offered only dedicated ISDN-line videoconferencing; now they also offer Internet videoconferencing. Access Grid is an 'ensemble of resources' that enables many sites—using interactive multimedia and appearing on multiple screens—to participate in a videoconference[4] (Figure 12.4). Polycom, Cisco, LifeSize, and Tandberg are among the videoconference companies that offer telepresence (presence, from a distance), which involves life-size high-definition images of people, simulated eye-contact, and minimum delay-time— replicating the experience of physically-present meetings as much as possible.

In India, three Governmental entities that are involved with developing videoconferencing—or the connectivity systems that enable videoconferencing— are: (1) ERNET (Education and Research Network)[5]; (2) NIC (National Informatics Centre)[6]; and (3) CDAC (Centre for Development of Advanced Computing).[7] NRENs (National Research and Education Networks) are playing increasingly important roles in Internet development in many developing countries. An NREN is a specialised internet service provider dedicated to supporting the needs of the research and education communities within a country. ERNET (Education and Research Network) is India's NREN.[8]

Internet2 is a USA-based networking consortium.[9] The technical standards and connectivity that Internet2 involves are very important factors in the global development of the Internet. Founded in 1996 by members of the education and research community, Internet2 provides both leading-edge network capabilities and unique partnership opportunities that together facilitate the development, deployment and use of revolutionary Internet technologies... Internet2 brings academia together with technology leaders from industry, government and the international community...and promotes collaboration and innovation...[10] Internet2 has a section relating to Emerging NRENs.[11] One of the Emerging NREN groups is the South Asia Special-Interest-Group (SA-SIG).[12] SA-SIG's mission is to help to facilitate high performance networking in South Asia. SA-SIG's e-mail list—<southasia-interest@internet2.edu>—is very much worth joining.

Two annual videoconference showcase events based in the Internet2 community are the Megaconference,[13] which began in 1999; and the Megaconference Jr,[14] which is especially for/by/with schoolchildren, and which began in 2004. Megaconferences are marathon events (up to 12 hours) that are webcast live to a global audience. They are composed of numerous brief videoconferences, each between up-to-six parties. I participated in the 2005 Megaconference, and in the 2006 Megaconference Jr (in both instances along with Tamil children, and exploring children's songs and language learning; from TENET's IIT-Madras facility). Reliance personnel have participated in a number of Megaconferences.

TEIN3 is another network that enables high-speed videoconferencing and assists in facilitating interesting collaborations.[15] TEIN3 is the third generation of the Trans-Eurasia Information Network. With direct connectivity to Europe's GEANT network, TEIN3 offers researchers and educators in Asia- Pacific a gateway for global collaboration with their peers in Europe and other parts of the world. India connected to TEIN3 in March 2010 (through ERNET). Sri Lanka connected to TEIN3 in April 2010 (through LEARN).[16]

An entity to keep in mind in relation to high-speed international videoconferencing for education and development is the Global Development Learning Network (GDLN).[17] The GDLN, which is coordinated by the World Bank, is "a partnership of over 120 institutions in over 80 countries that collaborate in the design of customized learning solutions for people working in development".[18] A regional association of GDLN, is GDLN Asia Pacific (GDLNAP).[19] Presently there is one GDLN site in India, in New Delhi.[20] It might be good to seek to have a GDLN site in Tamil Nadu also. A GDLN site typically features a large room equipped with top-notch videoconferencing facilities. Teaching Tamil language via videoconference—on computers and mobile telephones—could be a very important field. Tamil Nadu could be a world leader in developing language teaching in general by videoconference. These services should be available via Skype or similar programs, 24 hours a day.

At present, Tamil language-learning materials and instruction are available on webpages such as Web Assisted Learning and Teaching of Tamil.[21] Such asynchronous learning processes could also have an optional synchronous videoconference component. The videoconference language-practice lesson-plans could be coordinated with the lessons on the webpages. The on-line tutors—or language-practice partners—would need to be recruited, trained, and put in contact with clients. This would involve a lot of work. It could be done as a business, an NGO, and/or an educational project, possibly subsidized by a government. In any case, it should be done, as a way of preserving, developing, and globalising the Tamil language. The early pervasiveness of the English language on the Internet is fading. Other languages are now also entering cyberspace, especially as the audio and video options are becoming more available and convenient.

My dissertation[22] recommends three techniques for teaching language via videoconference: Question-and-Answer Routines, Repetition with Variation, and the Simultaneous Saying and Physical Enacting of Words. My research shows that these are prominent elements of Tamil children's songs/chants/dances/games—activities that very likely facilitate the acquisition of spoken language.

Question-and-Answer Routines place language-practice in the interactive context of human relationships, whether one participates in a routine as oneself or as role-playing other characters.

Repetition with Variation gives the learner a sense of control and competence. If only one aspect of a sentence is modified, the learner can still hold onto the grammatical structure of a sentence. Variations can include changes of tense, and substitutions of words (substitution drills); and going from a positive to a negative statement, or going from a command to a question (transformation drills). Repetition with variation is a key aspect of the modern language-teaching approach, the Audio-lingual Method. Systematic and methodical learners tend to especially enjoy this approach.

The Simultaneous Saying and Physical Enacting of Words utilises the entire body—not just the brain and mouth—in the language-learning process. The modern language-teaching method, Total Physical Response, is based on this idea. These three practices are especially good for videoconference language teaching-and-learning, because in the course of videoconference communication it may at times be difficult to make out what a distant person is saying, and these practices makes interpersonal verbal comprehension more likely.

We also found that playing with puppets can add fun to videoconference language-practice. This additional level of mediation and role-play, which enables people to interact with each other indirectly, seems to relax people and take some pressure off them (Figure 12.3). Tamil Nadu should take a leadership role in developing ways for many aspects of its culture to be shared via videoconferencing. Training, interactive performance, and discussion about the various aspects of culture could all occur via videoconference. This could be done in part in coordination with the State crafts organisation, Poompuhar; and the annual folk performing arts festival, Chennai Sangamam.

Videoconferencing in the classroom is a huge field in the USA and Europe, and students and teachers there are very eager to videoconference with their counterparts in exotic places like India.[23] Videoconference interviews with tradition-bearers are increasingly being held in Folklore and Social Studies classrooms.[24] Videoconference interviews for employment, and for admission to academic programs, are also becoming commonplace. Chennai and other cities in Tamil Nadu need teletoriums: halls equipped with large screens and videoconferencing facilities. Setting up videoconference systems in halls for single events is too timeconsuming and risky. A single teletorium could be used by numerous academic institutions and other groups.

A word should be said about a world-famous experiment in bringing videoconferencing (and general computer and Internet use) to the Tamil countryside, and to other rural areas in India. In the early 2000s, Dr. Ashok Jhunjhunwala — leader of TENET (Telecommunication and Computer Networking Group, Depts of Electrical Engineering, and Computer Science and Engineering, IIT Madras) — helped to develop SARI (Sustainable Access through Rural India),[25] which was serviced by n-Logue Communications Private Ltd and other companies. While it seems that this project has for the most part proved non-sustainable,[26] Dr. Ashok Jhunjhunwala continues to champion the idea of videoconferencing for people in the Indian countryside. It may well be that such people may achieve the ability to videoconference through mobile telephones before they achieve it through desktop computers. In any case, there remains a place and need for NGO and Government support for rural and economically-disadvantaged people to utilize videoconferencing for educational, employment, cultural, and other applications.

Apollo Hospitals is one among a number of hospitals in Tamil Nadu—private and public—that have strong telemedicine components, using videoconferencing in the diagnosis process, for staff training, and for other applications. Sad to say, but difficulties for the environment (such as the ash cloud that recently floated above Europe), and inconveniences for travel, tend to cause booms for videoconferencing. Videoconferencing can be thought of as a green activity, in that it can reduce the amount of petrol needed for travel, and it can make it unnecessary for people to travel through delicate natural environments. However, videoconferencing should not be seen as a substitute for physicallypresent communication—it is simply a different type of communication, with its own strong and weak points.

Years ago, people could often be heard in Tamil Nadu's browsing centres, singing Tamil cinema songs to distant others. Browsing centres have decreased, as Internet connectivity in the home, school, and office—and on portable communication devices—has increased. However, Tamil Nadu has been a world leader in bringing tribal, folk, and classical performing arts into the realm of cinema. Now these arts—along with the teaching-and-learning of the Tamil language itself—should be brought into the realm of videoconferencing, to further enable the sweet sound of Tamil to be heard and spoken around the globe.

Fig. 12.1 : A videoconference featuring electronic drawing and Tamil words (with transliteration and translation)

Fig. 12.2 : The words of a children's song are shown on the Chennai side of the Oct. 2004 Chennai—Philadelphia videoconference

Fig. 12.3 : A conservation through puppets. From the Oct. 2004 Chennai-Philadelphia videoconference

Fig. 12.4 : An Access Grid videoconference

Eric Miller <eric@storytellinginstitute.org> is Director of the World Storytelling Institute (based in Chennai); and is Assistant Professor of Story and Storytelling at ICAT, the Image College of Animation, Arts, and Technology (also based in Chennai).

REFERENCES

1. "*Videoconferencing and the Teaching of Tamil Language and Verbal Arts*", http://www.infitt.org /ti2002/papers/41EMILLE.PDF , presented at TI2002, San Francisco Area, California, September 2002.
2. "*Chennai and Videoconferencing: Videoconferencing for Performing, Teaching, and Discussing Tamil Language and Performing Arts*", http://infitt.org/ti2003/papers/50_emiller.pdf , presented at TI2003, Chennai, August 2003.
3. "*The 16 Oct. 2004, and 15 Oct. 2005, "Webcasted-video-Conferences for the Demonstration and Discussion of Children's Tamil (and Other) Songs/Chants/Dances/Games, and Methods of Teaching and Learning Spoken Tamil Language*", in Min Manjari, INFITT's e-Journal, December 2004.
4. http://www.webex.co.in
5. "*Now, Electronics That Obey Hand Gestures*", 12gesture. html , New York Times, 11 January 2010
6. http://www.accessgrid.org
7. http://www.eis.ernet.in
8. http://home.nic.in
9. http://www.cdac.in
10. http://www.eis.ernet.in .
11. http://www.internet2.edu .
12. http://www.internet2.edu/about .
13. http://www.internet2.edu/international/index.cfm .
14. http://southasia.indiana.edu .
15. http://www.megaconference.org .
16. http://www.megaconferencejr.org .
17. http://www.tein3.net .

18. Sri Lanka's NREN is LEARN (Lanka Education and Research Network), http://www.ac.lk .
19. http://www.gdln.org .
20. http://www.gdln.org/about .
21. http://www.gdlnap.org .
22. TERI Distance Learning Center, New Delhi. http://www.gdln.org/about/locations.
23. http://ccat.sas.upenn.edu/plc/tamilweb , by Dr. Vasu Renganathan.
24. "*Ethnographic Videoconferencing, as Applied to Songs/Chants/Dances/Games of South Indian Children, and Language Learning*", http://www.storytellingandvideoconferencing.com/280.html, PhD dissertation, Folklore Program, University of Pennsylvania, 2010.
25. *E-School News: Technology News for Today's K-20 Educator, expands-schools-possibilities*. The Education Initiative of Internet2,
26. "*Conducting Interviews via Videoconference*", Feature.html , in the Folklore and Education e-Newsletter of the American Folklore Society, Spring 2008.
27. "*Sustainability Failures of Rural Telecenters: Challenges from the Sustainable Access in Rural India* (SARI) Project.

13

Thin Client and Server-based Computing to Provide Integrated School and Classroom Management System in Malaysian Tamil Schools

—Saminatha Kumaran Veloo
—Saravanan Mariappan

ABSTRACT

Most of the educational institutions now have extensive information and communications technology (ICT) in place. The cost of supporting, upgrading and replacing this equipment to provide a robust infrastructure for teaching and learning is increasingly onerous. This brings into question whether alternative network architectures, such as Thin Client computing could provide the required level of functionality with lower long-term costs and/or other benefit.

This chapter addresses the use of thin client technology to provide optimum and cost effective solution for IT infrastructures which have the ability to integrate class room management application and school network management application with reliable and stable solution at minimum maintenance cost. The proposed thin client technology will be able to provide effective and secured centralized server-based solution of schools with class room management systems integrated.

Keyword: *Thin Client, school and classroom management, server based computing*

Introduction

This chapter addresses the key area of institutional concern for the education sector, that of delivering effective and efficient school and class room management system in a flexible, secure, and accessible way to students in Malaysian Tamil schools. The system will adopt the thin client technology linked with centralized server to implement school and classroom management. The proposed system will have secure integration with other key educational systems (e.g student records, module registration, and examination scheduling conducting trial exams and distribution of teaching materials), which will be delivered via network services and centralized server technology. Thin client technology offers major advantages over conventional PC-based class room systems in terms of scalability, economy and sustainability. It can also offer additional flexibility in the range of schoolteaching material and multimedia content that can be delivered without needing elaborate installation procedures or additional software to control the security, access and database.

Integration of the System

The system integration of Thin client based School and Class-room management system with open source technology consists of:

(*i*) School management System software designed to automate a school's diverse operations from classes, exam to school events, calender and to create powerful online community, by bringing parents, teachers, and students on the common interactive platform.

(*ii*) Local Centralized Server-based Technology that consists of storage Server well equipped with database using Linux Edubuntu server platform.

(*iii*) LAN/WAN network system which allows thin client terminals to access the centralized server remotely via

PXE LAN booting technology. This allows freedom for user to access their desktop from any thin client terminals within the network coverage.

(*iv*) Classroom management System provides teachers with ability to instruct, monitor and interact with the students either individually, as predefined group or to the overall class.

(*v*) Thin Client Server provides solutions for central deployment, configuration and management of thin clients and users connections.

(*vi*) Thin Client Terminals that consists of motherboard, display devices, keyboard and mouse, without any preinstalled operating system and hard disk.

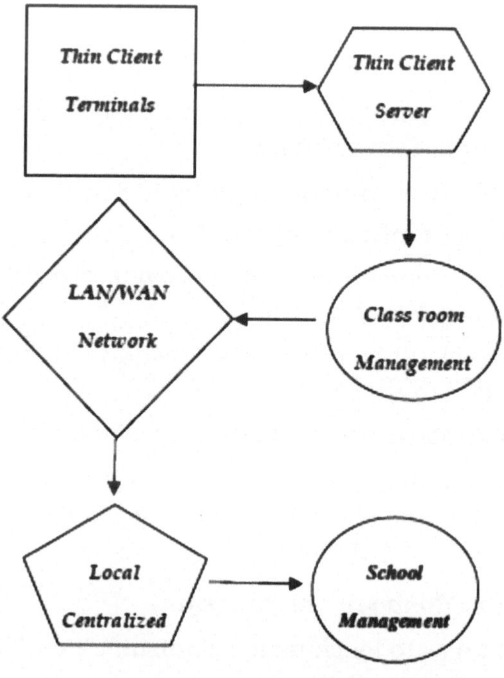

Fig. 13.1 : System Integration of classroom and school management system

School Management System

The school Management System has something for everyone related directly or indirectly with the school and teaching environment. Some of the key advantages to schools and educational institutions are:

- Easy performance monitoring of individual teaching modules.
- Automated and quick report generation along with process turn around time.
- Centralized data repository for trouble-free data access.
- Authenticated profile dependent access to data.
- User friendly interface requiring minimal learning and IT skills.
- Design for simplified scalability.
- Elimination of people dependent processes.
- Minimal data redundancy.

Some of the advantages to parents are:

- Frequent interaction with teachers.
- Reliable update on child's attendance, progress report and fee payment.
- Tracking of homework assigned by teachers to their child.
- Prior information about school events and holidays.
- Regular and prompt availability of school updates such as articles, discussions forums, image gallery and messaging system.

Classroom Management System

Advantages to teaching mechanism:

- Automated student attendance.
- Computerized management of marks and grades.

- Timetable creation in advance.
- Homework assignment to students and approval.
- Efficient and effective interaction with parents.
- Access to forum common to students and parents.
- Access to own and students attendance.
- Power on, power off, Reboot and Login to classroom computers remotely.
- Broadcast messages to groups or all network users in seconds.

Some key benefits are:

- Enhanced interaction with teachers, parents and peers.
- Online submission of homework.
- Access to their attendance, timetable, marks, grades and examination schedule.
- Liberty to publish articles and views, and participate in discussion forums.
- Freedom to browse through library books catalogue and identify the book(s) to be issued.
- Prior information about school events and holidays.

Thin Client System

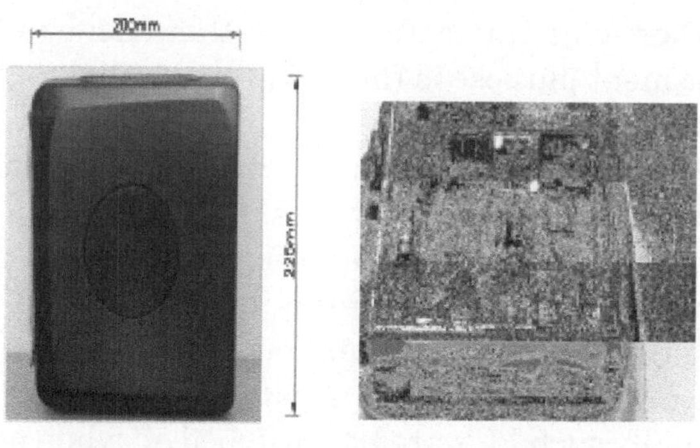

Plate 13.1 : Ideal thin client architecture

- Thin client is a general term for a device that relies on a server to operate.
- Thin client has display device, keyboard with mouse and basic processing power in order to interact with the server.
- An ideal thin client device contains no hard drives and CD or DVD-ROM

Advantages of the Technology

By using thin client technology rather than standalone PCs, it is possible to deliver a wide range of computer based educational and examination materials while restricting other resources that are usually accessible to the students if conventional PC system is to be used. With conventional PC based technology, it is difficult to prevent access to the Internet, chat services, mobile devices such as USB drive, documents previously stored by other students etc., which could allow simple cutting and pasting of answers into the assessment or exam sheets by students with thin client technology in place. It is simple for an administrator to disable USB port on thin client terminals for the duration of the assessment or examination time, thus further limiting the ability for student's accessing disallowed information to assist them in the assessment or examination.

Another major attraction of the thin client technology for assessment purpose is that it is very resilient, given the fact that they have no software or moving parts. Therefore there are unlikely to be an issue when the assessment are not been delivered due to faulty desktop devices. This causes unnecessary pressure on the affected student and the additional works involved to the invigilator. The issue of ensuring that PC's have the appropriate software available also affects PC's which are located in teaching spaces. Traditionally such PC's are left switched off when not in use which means that any automated software updates tend to fail or, worse, try to start when a teacher turns the PC on for a class. This can lead to anti-virus software not being updated, operating system vulnerability not being patched etc. the start up time of a PC system also causes difficulties, when a lecturer arrives in a classroom, there will be about 8-10 minutes start up time for the PC and to get the necessary software up and running; if any updated needed to be done this could delay the start of the class. Using thin client technology there is no need for the software updates and no need to worry about viruses. The user will always get the appropriate version of all the software via central server. The new upload of teaching material will be ready for teaching immediately as the student or teacher starts the class. Figure 13.2, shows the flow between teachers-students-parents-school in the school and class room management system.

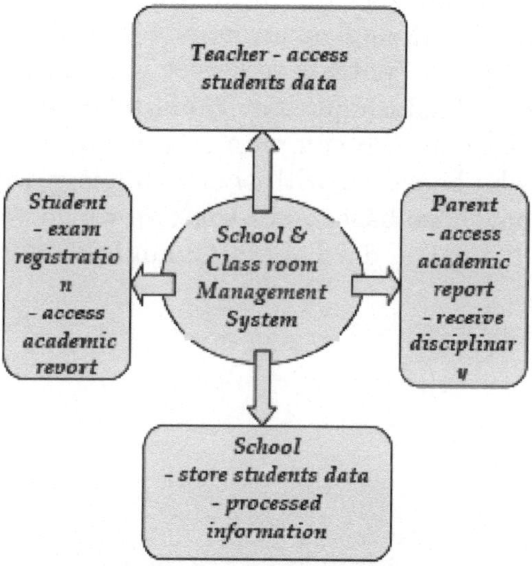

Fig. 13.2 : Data Flow between teachers-students-parent-school in the school and classroom management system

Conclusion

The school and classroom management system with thin client technology have not been fully integrated in the learning process in Malaysia. In last decade, the complexity of existing desktop machines, the capital investment needed for wide area network (WAN) access and lack of educational resources and multimedia content have prevented the potential of thin client based solution become reality.

Recently the convergence of community, business and government organizations in favor of client technology, have started to produce changes in education system. With the use of thin client technology, the teaching system will now can look forward into a new age of centrally manageable teaching technology, with equal access to information will be given to all students regardless of their background and geographical location. Rural students will be given full access to information and knowledge with tremendous reduction in communication time and infrastructure cost, knowledge can be shared with anybody from any part of the world for free. Coupling the centralized server with thin clients and the power of cloud computing, Tamil schools in Malaysia, soon will become the community information hub. The students who benefited with this technology will one day become knowledge based skill workers which will directly uplift the living standard of Malaysian Indian.

14

Embedding Co-features in 'OCR-Friendly' Fonts Will Go a Longway in Machine Reading of Texts

—N D Loga Sundaram

Preamble

The Regal superiority of digital world, crowned by its hyper speed-error-free signal transmission i.e. its unparallel dynamics in information handling. Because IT being made as retrofits to faculties handled by humans it gained popularity very quickly. Today they are ubiquitous products in the hands of informed community. Every one of us knows well that innovations in IT field are born worldwide, every minute, both in hardware and in software. By each of its million facets, they get deep-rooted mm by mm, in minute-wise human activity around the globe, recognizing that 'Continuous Improvement ' is one of the core theme for remaining in forefront in any business.

Playing Field

The overwhelming, inundating expansion of human activity in the digital virtual universe, i.e. in the interface between the human (with their archives), to the current digital machines are limited to, Vision and Sonics. Applications connected with vision and Sonics are already in use, over decades, one after another - Vision to digits and back, Sonics to digits and back, cross platform between Sonics and Vision thro digits.

Archives—CORE Instrument in Human Advancement

As pointed out elsewhere the whole spectrum of human advancement is sourced by the creation of huge voluminous Banks of Knowledge in visual/written format, which bypasses time and distance in human civilization. It is the vessel that accumulates and vends knowledge so that it can be continuously reviewed updated and suitably edited (evolution) to their customized needs on date. Archived written language (vision) is prone less to corruption and distortion than a spoken (Sonics) one and hence they survived perfectly such a long way since Stone Age until this digital era.

Primary In-put Medium to Human Knowledge

Modern civilized humans get their knowledge mostly through sight and sound, both in real world as well from archives, thro 'language' that is called Education'. The other faculties as taste, smell and feeling play lesser part quantitatively which still remains primitive and mostly limited to tangibles in front as non-virtual. The apparent necessity of quicker machine reading From times immemorial humans devised machines for many of their day-to-day activities by inherent laziness and to thrive with comfort in competitive world out of their disturbing ambience. This is true in digital world also, which plays an arterial roll on date in 'human resource'. By nature I.T. is one of the platform erected for high altitude launch of mechanization and automation.

In the present world of communication explosion and consumerism we see people everywhere like to, rather forced to, have anything done quickly and easily, seldom even by fancy mania. The digital gadgets ranging from tiny hand held devices crowded with numerous features to mammoth net search engine servers, are the gadgets white collared people have interface these days, before middling with their bowl of soup. Next to TV and consumer durables, cunning high-tech assisted marketing techniques paved way for deep penetration of desktop PCs with all of its army of useful peripherals and the gadget of the day the cellular Mobile. Hence the universe of digital gadgets is in reign today and its influence extends well beyond informed community.

Digital World and Its Contents

Aptness and forerunner ship in handling of contents whether in a simple and humble home paperlessoffice or goliath popular commercial portal; it can be achieved by size of handled quantity as well as by timely presentation. Hence a self-employed free-lancer or a web master, he/she has to handle their contents, as ease and efficient as possible. In most cases, when the source is not from ready-in-the-shelf digital form, they get them digitized through their peripherals. In most of the cases, they are compiled from contents of several other authors, in print media, which warrants first degree of conversion.

Anyone who wares the shoe of a web master or a mere single document initiator they have initial digitization hardships and hiccups by virtue of time and strain it takes to key-in the contents thro' human eye-fingers route. Therefore they always opt for an easier machine input process if available replacing the laborious ubiquitous keyboard route which causes fatigue, back pain and eye irritation from not so ergonomically designed work place.

Contents in Text Format

The contents available in texts format instead of an image format is preferred for memory size and more particularly when it has to be subjected to an analytical process as search compare and manipulate with mathematical or logical operators. Compiling is one of the core processes in any creation and hence pick a particular content or theme from the group is the necessity. Therefore text formats are first and foremost choice.

'Always Stands in Top'

Hence the case of machine reading from print media stands on top of wish list of authors. All the attempts focused to this theme, will be appreciated and hence they command huge market. By virtue of this commercial proposition, several OCR products were brought out already and serve well for about a decade.

Again a Review of the Need and Worth of Machine Digitization

Replacement of human activity in archiving information thro' digital machine paves way for:

1. Unbiased;
2. Quicker;
3. Faultless; and
4. Closely managed.

handling of information which leads to omnifarious economics. It shall even be the necessity in future high speed lanes in e-Management.

MICR is the Forerunner for OCR

Machine reading of printed characters are not new while it is about 30 years old, which is well before the advent of popular use of digital data with computers. It was introduced as magnetic character recognition in bank cheque nos known as MICR cheques. It was devised to avoid human failures and helps in speedy unbiased disposal by using a special kind of ink and a process to suit the machine reading along with safety. Initially it was limited to serial number of cheques (numerals) Now, design of same numerals of those safety cheques got modified, with simple distinct features in its normal printed glyphs. On date, one can see combination of thinner and thicker strokes or micro sized squares placed at a particular zone with disparity in each numeral's grapheme for providing easily traceable differentiating features between each of the characters in the set.

Barcode Reading

Then the digital era of barcode characters with 59 white and black bars was introduces and it is still a popular true workhorse at every marketing/vender outlet stores. Bar-coded price/product tags embed numerous particulars, which have bearings, both for seller as well as purchaser. As the bar code is devised purely for machine reading process, it is not suitable for normal/average human cognizance.

2D Checkerboard Type Tags

Now another innovation one can witness is a kind of tag (or nameplate) replacing bar-coded tag. It is a printed square box puzzle checkerboard matrix, which has rows of black and white optically, coded fields. By its 2D nature it contains more data than a barcode and evidently needs different reading writing devices to suit the system in design.

RFID

High volumes of digital activity also bring newer problems and we know about the necessity of safety of contents handled is an indispensable factor in any commercial/legal propositions. Mechanization in identification or authorization using a radio frequency signals and embedded 3D micro devised chips on to products are in use today for remote sensing at a distance which already started gaining popularity.

Currencies

We know that the safety features are inlaid in Currencies of most of the nations of the world have features for non-human cognizance serves automated or machine recognition.

Embeded Features in OCR Friendly Fonts

By applying the same basics in MICR, i.e. introducing an inlaid easily traceable secondary features to font characters/ glyphs, we can bring about automation/machine reading of contents along with visibility to human eye in print/display media. They shall be embedded with distinct features within the fields of a font character, which can be both in positive or negative videos or combination of both.

Even any of the other durable and safe means, in print friendly high-tech means such as magnetic electrostatic chemical and radioactive are not ruled out. Of course in those case the term 'OCR' itself may have to be substituted. Since OCR product with these new secondary features shall be designed with sensing mechanism focused to the particular zone of distinction in the field of a graphemes without wasting resources on confusing, inert and noise zones / feature, it is easier to design while the output shall be quicker and errorless.

Another advantage in introducing secondary features into graphemes in print media is that it will relieve many problems in design of OCR product for variations in colour, glyph size, style etc. while giving a font and print designer a free hand to their varieties as secondary features can even be made independent of normal optical visibility.

Forthcoming Contents

Being a newer introduction, it is for forthcoming contents in print media and not for existing contents in printed archives.

Early Deployment

To provide full fledged scope of freedom to font authors for their individuality and to cater their own specific vending zones no suggestions initiated at this stage other than a request to every one in digital planet to look into the scope for innovation and economics. This can cut short the take-off time.

Standardisation

For popularization of any product, standardization and universality is a natural prerequisite leading to general economics and convenience. This should be true for OCR products too. Therefore the developers of OCR-FRIENDLY fonts embedded with unique attributes can come to a common platform for standardizing their process and products so that plurality of vendor specific products has to be avoided since customer specific interests will always prevail upon in long term business.

I P Rights

This basic innovative theme of having a secondary feature in each of font grapheme cannot have intellectual property rights because it is merely a generalized idea re-presented. This lacks newness/state-of-art creative intelligence. But the design rights over a fonts' looks shapes and styles along with process/design of producing a secondary easily traceable visible or other feature remains with the author. Creation of distinct attributes between characters of a set/group when achieved through an innovative state-of-art process in the components of printing and reading like font printing ink or else and in the nature of medium over the print is made, the IP rights can still be enforced.

Tamil and Universality

Though the embedding co-features for OCR-FRIENDLY-NESS by virtue of universality, it shall be applicable to fonts/glyphs/graphemes of every language of the world, but when introduced in our Tamil as a pioneering work we can attract admiration from digital global villages. There will side effects and problems to be faced by Unicode Consortium in their monster Universal Character Set though their character-encoding scheme are not connected with shapes and looks and other features of fonts and graphemes.

Conclusion

I hope by virtue of its rationale printed graphemes embedded with secondary co-features will soon shine with its usefulness in the digital sky and contents with this innovation employed will be flooded with richness of every language, including Tamil, as an avalanche. The apparent fallout in having maiden digital Tamil contents initially from OCR friendly prints they can easily be converted/used in any other output mode as Sonics or Vision. If we find in the roadmap of having speech to text and text to speech applications until the initial sonic input route is less efficient and more cumbersome, the OCR route can be useful.

15

Creation of Annotated Tamil Handwritten Word Corpus for OHR

—Nethravathi B
—Archana C P
—Shashikiran K
—A G Ramakrishnan

ABSTRACT

Annotated datasets form a critical aspect in the development of robust technology for handwriting recognition and can be used for comparing results of different techniques used by various research groups. This chapter describes the efforts at MILE lab, IISc, to create a database for the design and development of Tamil Online Handwritten Recognition. 100,000 words have been collected from 500 writers in Tamil, so that as much variations in writing style is captured. The data collected incorporated all the symbols (base characters, Indo-Arabic numerals, punctuations and other symbols). An annotation tool has been developed which helps the study of various styles of writing, stroke directions and presence of delayed strokes. Quality tags like class A, B, C etc has been assigned to the words accordingly. The annotated data is stored in a standard XML format defined by OHWR Consortium.

Introduction

Databases are of great importance in any field of research, and handwriting recognition is no exception. A good database of handwritten data can be used to train and evaluate the performance of the recognition engine. Databases for scripts like Roman and Chinese already exist, whereas no such databases exist for Indic scripts. The database collected at MILE lab, IISc contains a comprehensive collection of words in Tamil, collected from many native Tamil people. Predefined word lists have been used to collect data, where the word list covers all the characters in the language. Here the focus is to develop a comprehensive database to support the development of a robust recognition engine. These databases facilitate comparison of different engines and also allow researchers to focus on recognition methodologies. A large database helps in removing bias of the engine towards particular styles of writing.

Tablet PC and G-Note have been used to collect data. The writer writes with an electronic pen on the electrostatic pressure sensitive writing surface of a Tablet PC or G-Note. The device captures the movement of pen tip on its screen in terms of *x*, *y* co-ordinates, sampled at equal intervals of time. It also captures the PEN_DOWN and PEN_UP information. The recognition is challenging because of varying styles of writing the same character. This chapter describes how the database of 100,000 words has been collected from different schools and colleges, which involved major field work. The collected data is annotated at the word, stroke group and akshara level using an annotation tool developed by MILE lab. An akshara in Indian languages is a cluster of graphemes that need to be considered together to obtain the correct Unicode representation. Aksharas can be consonants (C), vowels (V) or a combination of them such as CV, CCV and so forth. The output of annotation is stored in the standard XML format which was proposed by the OHWR consortium.

OHWR Consortium-funded by TDIL

A consortium made project was funded by Technology Development for Indian Languages (TDIL), Department of Information Technology, Government of India in January 2007 for research on online handwriting recognition. The project aims at developing Online Handwriting Recognition (OHWR) engines for Tamil, Kannada, Malyalam, Telugu, Bangla and Devanagari scripts. We at MILE Lab, IISc, are developing Tamil and Kannada engines. The academic partners of this project are IIT Madras, ISI Kolkata, and IIIT Hyderabad. The private and public industry partners are Learnfun Systems Chennai, CK Technologies Chennai and CDAC Pune.

Characteristics of Tamil Handwriting

Tamil compound characters (aksharas) are formed by graphically combining the symbols corresponding to consonants and vowel modifiers using well defined rules. Segmentation of words in these languages is more feasible than it is for English cursive writing as the characters are written separately without much overlap between them. In Tamil script, the majority of vowel modifiers are written as separate symbols and hence they are recognized separately.

Selection of Complete Constituent Symbols

Tamil: Tamil script comprises 313 characters. Of these, 12 are pure vowels and 23 pure consonants. Thus there are totally 12*23 = 276 consonant-vowel combinations. Apart from these, there are two additional symbols. The set of pure vowels in Tamil and its corresponding transliteration in English is depicted in Fig. 15.1.

அ	ஆ	இ	ஈ	உ	ஊ	எ	ஏ	ஐ	ஒ	ஓ	ஔ
a	A	i	I	u	U	e	E	ai	o	O	au

Fig. 15.1 : Set of Vowels in Tamil

We have established that only 155 symbols are required to represent all the 313 characters. The details are given below, 1) The vowel modifier for /A/ is depicted by a separate symbol and is written to the right of the consonant. Treating this vowel modifier as a separate class reduces the number of classes. A consonant /T/ combined with the vowel modifiers /a/ and /A/ are shown in two different rows of Fig. 15.2.

ட

டா

Fig. 15.2 : Consonants /Ta/ and /TA/

(2) Vowel modifiers of /i/, /I/ and /u/,/U/ create new symbols when combined with the consonants. These new symbols are treated as different classes, thereby adding to the total number of classes. An example of this is shown in Fig. 15.3.

டி டீ டு டூ

Fig. 15.3 : Consonants /Ti/, /TI/, /Tu/ and /TU/

(3) The vowel modifiers of /e/, /E/, /ai/ are separate symbols written to the left of the consonant. These symbols are also treated as separate classes, further reducing the number of classes. Fig. 15.4 shows an example of a consonant in combination with these vowel modifiers.

டெ டே டை

Fig. 15.4 : Consonants /Te/, /TE/ and /Tai/

(4) The vowel modifiers of /o/, /O/ have two separate symbols which are written on either side of the consonant. The consonant combined with vowel /o/ will have the modifier of /e/ to its left and the modifier of /A/ to its right. Similarly a consonant combined with vowel /O/ will have the modifier of /E/ to its left and the modifier of /A/ to the right. Since these symbols are already handled separately, the number of classes reduces further. Example of a consonant combined with these vowel modifiers is shown in Fig. 15.5.

டொ டோ

Fig. 15.5 : Consonants /To/ and /TO/

(5) The vowel modifier /au/ also has two symbols with one written on either side of the consonant. The symbol to the left of the consonant is the same as the modifier of /e/ and the symbol to the right is the same as the consonant /La/. These two symbols are already handled separately, similar to case 4, which also causes a reduction in the number of classes. A consonant combined with vowel modifier of /au/ is shown in Fig. 15.6.

டௌ

Fig. 15.6 : Consonant /Tau/

Along with the characters, special symbols like full stop and question mark are also incorporated in the symbol list. It is to be noted that in modern Tamil script, Tamil numerals are rarely used. Hence these symbols are not included in our dataset. Hindu-Arabic numerals have been included, and treated as special symbols in our work. The words have been carefully chosen so as to represent all possible symbols used in modern Tamil script.

Data Collection for Tamil OHR

Criteria for selection of acquisition devices

The devices used for data collection are the Tablet PC and G-Note. G-Note is more suitable for field work as it is sturdy, affordable and easy to carry. It is also easy for the user to write on a G-Note as the feel is the same as writing on normal paper or pad. The data collected in G-Note is stored as .TOP files. Tablet PC is suitable for individual use. It is heavy and difficult to carry. Also since it is expensive, it cannot be used for field work. The TabletPC data is stored in .txt format.

These devices are shown in Fig. 15.7. Predefined word lists have been used to collect data. A Tamil sample handwritten pages is shown in the Fig. 15.8.

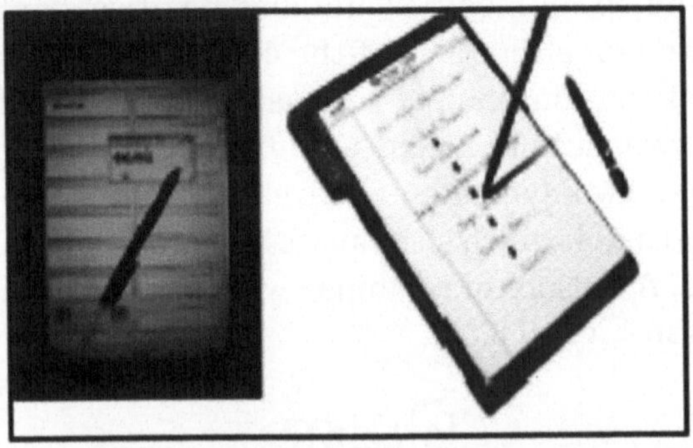

Fig. 15.7 : Tablet PC and G-Note 7000

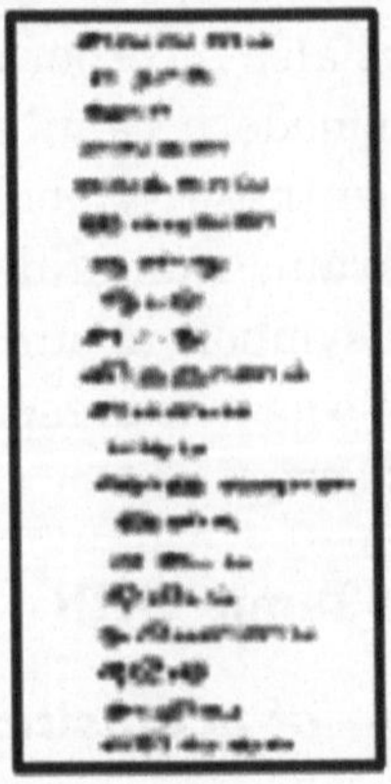

Fig. 15.8 : Sample handwritten Tamil Page

Selection of Writers

The criteria for selecting writers for data collection was that the person should be a native writer of the language and one who is currently writing regularly. Students and teachers were primarily chosen for data collection as they write regularly.

XML Standard for Annotation

The output of annotation is stored in a standard XML format which has been defined by the OHWR consortium. This standard XML includes all the details about the data, such as the writer details, the device information, the number of pages and words. The words are truthed at the word level annotation.

The aksharas and stroke groups are truthed at the character level annotation. All this information is stored in the XML. The XML also contains information about the quality assigned to each word, akshara, stroke group and stroke. This facilitates separation of Class A/good data from the Class R/reject data.

Annotation Details

Once the data is collected, the first process is to do the word level annotation. The collected set has multiple words on each page; hence determined word boundaries are to be used to obtain the strokes of a word. In word level annotation, each word is labeled, using a tool developed by IIIT Hyderabad. The output is stored in a standard XML format defined by the OHWR consortium. Next is the character level annotation, where the output of word level annotation is given as input. In character level annotation, words are separated into strokes, stroke groups and aksharas and they are labeled. Quality tags are also assigned to them based on the direction of writing, stroke order and validity of strokes. The output at this level is also stored in the standard XML format. This annotation at character level is performed using a tool developed at MILE Lab, IISc.

Quality Labels for Strokes, Stroke Groups and Aksharas

The strokes, stroke groups and aksharas are assigned various quality labels based on the nature of writing. The labels are defined as follows:

Class A: Denotes words written correctly with the expected number of strokes and in the expected direction. They are automatically segmented correctly by the segmentation module. Based on the statistics of writings from a huge number of native writers, there are multiple sets of stroke sequences valid for many stroke groups.

Class B: Denotes words which require manual segmentation and stroke groups with 10% or less overlap.

Class C: Denotes words where two or more normally separate strokes are written as a single stroke or vice-versa. It also includes strokes with overlap greater than 10% and delayed strokes.

Class D: Denotes words with extraneous strokes or overwriting and strokes written in the opposite direction. However, the resulting stroke groups must have the potential to be properly recognized using offline features.

Class R: This is the reject class, containing wrong words and/or strokes for which the likelihood of recognition is very low.

Conclusion

This chapter describes how the database has been created for Tamil Online handwriting recognition. The process of creating a reduced symbol list, which includes all the basic symbols of the character set has been described. The focus is on the process of collecting data, the devices used the criteria for selection of writers and why the reduction in number of symbols is required. This paper also tells how the data can be annotated for further use by researchers.

Acknowledgment

This entire data collection effort was funded by Technology Development for Indian Languages (TDIL), Department of Information Technology (DIT), Government of India. We thank Mr. Suresh, Mr. Rituraj, Ms. Chandrakala, Ms.

Archana, Ms. Saranya and Ms. Sountheriya for their efforts which made this task successful. We thank Prof. Deivasundram (University of Madras), AVM Matriculation Higher Secondary School, Govt. Boys Higher Secondary School, Sulur, Presidency College Triplicane, Virugambakkam, Chennai and IIT Madras for contributing to the data set. We also thank Dr. Anoop Namboodiri for giving us the word level annotation tool.

REFERENCES

1. K. H. Aparna, V. Subramanian, M. Kasirajan, G. V. Prakash, and V. S. Chakravarthy. *Online Handwriting Recognition for Tamil.* Proc. 9th International Workshop on Frontiers in Handwriting Recognition (IWFHR-9), 2004.
2. C. P. Archana, K. Shashikiran, and A. G. Ramakrishnan. *A Stroke Group to Word Annotation Tool for South Indian Languages.* submitted to ICFHR 2010, Kolkata, Nov 2010.
3. S. Behle, S. Chakravarthy, and A. G. Ramakrishnan. XML *Standard for Indic Online Handwritten Database.* Proc. International Workshop on Multilingual OCR, Barcelona, Spain, 2009.
4. A. S. Bhaskarabhatla and S. Madhvanath. *Experiences in Collection of Handwriting Data for Online Handwriting Recognition in Indic Scripts.* 4th International Conference on Language Resources and Evaluation, Lisbon, Portugal, 26-28 May 2004.

16

Difficulties in Developing OCR for Tamil Documents and an Integrated OCR Solution

—R. DhivyaBharathi
—A. BalaMurugan

ABSTRACT

In this chapter , the major difficulties arising in the development of OCR for Tamil language is presented with solutions. We have proposed a new approach of using a Neural Network integrated with an Encoded Character String Dictionary. Multiclass Hierarchical Support Vector Machines (MHSVM), Hidden Markov Model (HMM) and Radial Bass Function Neural Network (RBFNN) are used for accurate character recognition.

As MHSVM has shown excellent character recognizing results due to a strong mathematical foundation, it is chosen for the recognition process. HMM is chosen for recognizing online written letters. RBFNN is integrated with an Encoded Character String Dictionary and trained using the output of MHSVM and HMM for accurate character recognition. The three algorithms used here facilitate the recognition of Online, Offline and Printed Tamil characters which pave the way of developing an Integrated

OCR. The main advantage of developing an Integrated OCR is to decrease the memory requirement and to increase the processing time. The proposed model is expected to be 90 per cent-95 per cent accurate.

Keywords: *Optical Character Recognition (OCR), Hidden Markov Models (HMM), Multi Hierarchical Support Vector Machines (MHSVM), Radial Basis Function Neural Network (RBF-NN), Encoded Character String Dictionary.*

Introduction

The common problem in all type of algorithms used in OCR is the set of letters in Tamil which look very much the same, except for some minor differences (Example: *la* and *va*). And we face more problems with the slanting letters. Straightening these slanting letters introduces more noise due to the digital nature of the pixels. If we keep them in their original shape, splitting them into letters have to be handled carefully. These problems can be handled by looking at the previous letter or group of letters to decide the next letter using a dictionary of words. MHSVM provides excellent Offline and Printed character recognition. MHSVM requires little prior knowledge which saves a lot of time in training the neural network and minimizes risk. HMM is chosen for recognizing online written letters. Pen-up strokes are modeled using a left-to-right HMM and inter-symbol strokes are modeled explicitly in two states. This shows low performance in case of high lexicon size which can be eliminated using a statistical method. The statistical tool can be provided by the MHSVM explained earlier. HMM also avoids the segmentation problem, which is extremely difficult and error prone.

Proposed OCR Algorithm

The accuracy or efficiency of OCR purely depends on the

algorithm we deploy. The efficiency decreases when an algorithm fails to identify a character or if the algorithm detects an unrelated character. We have proposed a method where we can fuse two pattern recognition algorithms and evaluate the efficiency of OCR. Before fusing, the scanned document is preprocessed.

The steps in preprocessing involves:

(1) Histogram equalization and Gabor Filtering

(2) Binarisation

(3) ROI extraction

(4) Region Probe Algorithm

Preprocessing Steps

This section describes the preprocessing steps of the scanned document in detail.

Histogram Equalization and Gabor Filtering

The scanned document is first applied to Histogram equalization and Gabor Filtering. Histogram equalization usually increases the local contrast of many images, especially when the usable data of the image is represented by close contrast values. Through this adjustment, the intensities can be better distributed on the histogram. Then the Gabor filter is applied to the scanned document obtained by the previous step by spatially convolving the image with the filter. A Gaussian function multiplied by a harmonic function defines the impulse response of the linear filter, the Gabor filter. Because of the multiplication-convolution property (Convolution theorem), the Fourier transform of a Gabor filter's impulse response is the convolution of the Fourier transform of the harmonic function and the Fourier transform of the Gaussian function.

Where, $x' = x$ cose $+ y$ sine and $y' =$ "x sine $+ y$ cose

In this equation, *g* represents the wavelength of the cosine factor, *e* represents the orientation of the normal to the parallel stripes of a Gabor function, h is the phase offset, and i is the spatial aspect ratio, and specifies the ellipticity of the support of the Gabor function.

Binarisation

The binarisation process involves analyzing the grey-level value of each pixel in the enhanced image, and, if the value is greater than the global threshold, then the pixel value is set to a binary value one; otherwise, it is set to zero.

ROI Extraction

We perform morphological opening on the grayscale or binary image with the structuring element. We also performed morphological closing on the grayscale or binary image resulting in closed image. The structuring element is a single structuring element object, as opposed to an array of objects for both open and close. Then as the result this approach throws away those leftmost, rightmost, uppermost and bottommost blocks out of the bound so as to get the tightly bounded region just containing the bound and inner area.

Region Probe Algorithm

After all the above process, the image is passed to the segmentation phase, where the image is decomposed into individual characters. For this we have used region probe algorithm.

Algorithm Fusion

Then we have fused two algorithms meaning that both the algorithms are taken into consideration.

While fusing the two algorithms the following points are taken into consideration

(1) If one algorithm fails to identify a character, another algorithm may support in identifying the character.

(2) If one algorithm gives wrong character another may give a correct one.

(3) The possibility for same wrong identification by both the algorithms is less.

(4) If one algorithm gives wrong result the decision of choosing the correct result is done by neural network which is discussed later in the chapter.

We have chosen SVM, HMM for the fusion and discussed in the rest of the section.

Hidden Markov Model (HMM)

Hidden Markov Models are suitable for handwriting recognition for a number of reasons. The importance of HMMs in the area of speech recognition has been observed several ago. In the meantime, HMMs have also been successfully applied to image pattern recognition problems such as shape classification and face recognition. HMMs qualify as suitable tool for cursive script recognition for a number a reasons. First, they are stochastic models that can cope with noise and pattern variations occurring is human handwriting. Next, the number of tokens representing an unknown input word may be of variable length.

Moreover, using an HMM-based approach, the segmentation problem, which is extremely difficult and error prone, can be avoided. This mean that the features extracted from an input word need not necessarily correspond with letters. Instead, they may be derived from part of one letter, or from several letters. Thus the operations carried out by an HMM are in some sense holistic, combining local feature interpretation with contextual knowledge. Finally, there are standard algorithms known from the literature for both training and recognition using HMMs. These algorithms are fast and can be implemented with reasonable effort. Kundu and Bahl built an HMM for the English language. However, they require the input word being perfectly segmented into single characters.

The Hidden Markov Model is a straightforward generalization of ordinary probability distributions to the case of randomly generated sequences of discrete or continuous-valued events. A discrete density HMM produces strings *O=O1 ...OT* of symbols form a finite alphabet {*V1,....,Vk*} while the continuous density version creates sequences of real-valued feature vectors $x \in IR^d$.The generation of the observable output *t O* of the model is controlled by a doubly stochastic process. At each time instant *t* = 1,...,*T* the model is in one out of N possible states{*S1,...,SN*}. The state qt taken by the model at time t is a random variable which depends only on the identity of its immediate predecessor state. According to this assumption the state distribution is completely determined by the parameters.

$$\pi = p(q_1 = s_i) \text{ and } a_{i,j} = p(q_t = s_j \mid q_{t-1} = s_i)$$

in other words, the vector *j* = (*j1,... jN*)*T* of initial probabilities together with the (*NxN*) – matrix *A* = [*ai,,j*] of transition probabilities form a first-order Markov chain.

The actual state sequence taken by the model serves as a probabilistic trigger for the production of the output sequence. The *qt* themselves, however, remain hidden to an observer of the random process. According to a second model assumption, the probability distribution of an output symbol *Ot* (or an output vector, respectively) depends solely on the identity of the present state qt; thus, the distribution parameters. $b_{j,k} = b_j(v_k) = p(O_t = V_k \mid q_t = s_j)$ of a discrete density HMM constitute a (*N* × *K*) probability matrix B = [bj,k]. Consequently, the behavior of an HMM with discrete output is entirely specified by the cardinality *N* of the state space, the alphabet size , and a parameter array *g* = (*j* , *A, B*) of non-negative probabilities, obeying the (1+ 2*N*) normalization condition $\sum_i \pi_i = \sum_j a_{ij} = \sum_k b_{j,k} = 1$ Any of the state-dependent probability density functions (PDF) $b_j(x) = p(O_t = x \mid q_t = s_j)$ of an HMM with continuous output can be reasonably well approximated by a convex combination.

Support Vector Machines (MHSVM)

The utilization of support vector machine (SVM) classifiers has gained immense popularity in the last years. SVMs have achieved excellent recognition results in various pattern recognition applications. Also in offline optical character recognition (OCR) they have been shown to be comparable or even superior to the standard techniques like Bayesian classifiers or multilayer perceptrons. SVMs are discriminative classifiers based on Vapnik's structural risk minimization principle. They can implement flexible decision boundaries in high dimensional feature spaces. The implicit regularization of the classifier's complexity avoids over fitting and mostly this leads to good generalizations. Some further properties are commonly seen as reasons for the success of SVMs in real-world problems: the optimality of the training result is guaranteed, fast training algorithms exist and little a-prior knowledge is required, i.e. only a labeled training set. Here, we provide a brief introduction to support vector classification. For more details and geometrical interpretations please refer to the standard literature, e.g. by Burges or Cristianini and Shawe-Taylor.

Radial Bass Function Neural Network (RBF-NN)

To improve the accuracy, we have trained RBFNN with the output of both the algorithms. Different samples of Tamil Characters are taken and given as input to both HMM and SVM. If HMM or SVM gives a false character, the neural network is trained with the weightage of both the algorithms and the actual character. This process is done for all the possible false recognition of the two algorithms. During OCR

When both the algorithms not giving same character, trained RBFNN is used to retrieve the actual character. This way we can increase the accuracy of OCR. Radial Basis Functions emerged as a variant of artificial neural network in late 80's.RBF's are embedded in a two layer neural network, where each hidden unit implements a radial activated function.

Due to their non-linear approximation properties, RBF networks are able to model complex mappings, which perception by means of multiple intermediary layers. Radial basis networks can require more neurons than standard feed forward back propagation networks, but often they can be designed in a fraction of the time it takes to train standard feed forward networks. They work best when many training vectors are available. RBF networks have been successfully applied to a large diversity of applications including interpolation, image restoration, shape-from-shading, 3-D object modeling, data fusion, etc.

Encoded Character String Dictionary

Dictionaries obviously look like texts and share many features with other types of texts. However, users typically do not read a dictionary linearly, but access entries on the basis of a key (the headword) in order to retrieve various fields of information associated with that key (pronunciation, grammatical information, etymology, definitions, etc.). Electronic dictionaries now commonly available on CD ROM. In addition, although the display on the screen still looks more or less like a text, the internal representation is rarely that of a linear text. Here, a list of tamil words can be stored which will be used to find the occurrence of next letter of a word. This will enable the Neural Network algorithm to guess the word with more efficiency in case of confusing letters like la and va. These encoded dictionaries can be integrated with the neural network for efficiency in recognizing the characters.

Conclusion

In this chapter we have proposed a new method of Tamil OCR where we have fused three algorithms to get the maximum possible efficiency by integrating it with a encoded character string dictionary. Our work primarily deals with choosing a better algorithm, and fusing them finally to attain better accuracy. We have chosen HMM, SVM to be fused and finally used Neural network to predict the correct character when there arises a situation where two algorithms yield two different characters. Our future work is to increase the efficiency more by increasing the effectiveness of neural network.

REFERENCES

1. G. Nagy. *Twenty Years of Document Image Analysis in Pattern Analysis and Machine Intelligence*. IEEE Tran. PAMI, pp. 38–82, 2000.
2. Mantas, J., 1986. *An Overview of Character Recognition Methodologies*, Pattern recognition, 19 (6):
3. Govindan, V.K. and A.P. Shivaprasad, 1990. *Character Recognition—A Review*, Pattern Recognition, 23 (7): 671- 683.
4. Hewavitharana, S, and H.C. Fernando, 2002. *A Two Stage Classification Approach to Tamil Handwriting Recognition*, pp: 118-124, Tamil Internet 2002, California, USA.
5. Chinnuswamy, P., and S.G. Krishnamoorthy, 1980. *Recognition of Hand-printed Tamil Characters*, Pattern Recognition, 12: 141-152.
6. R.M. Suresh, S. Arumugam and K.P. Aravanan, "*Recognition of Handwritten Tamil Characters using Fuzzy Classificatory Approach*", Proc. The Tamil Internet 2000 Conference, Singapore, July 2000.
7. Siromoney *et al.*, 1978. *Computer Recognition of Printed Tamil Character*, Pattern Recognition 10: 243-247.
8. H. Bunke, M. Roth, and E. G. Schukat-Talamazzini. *Offline Cursive Handwriting Recognition using Hidden Markov Models*. Pattern Recognition, 28(9):1399–1413, 1995.
9. C. Burges. *A Tutorial on Support Vector Machines for Pattern Recognition*. Data Mining and Knowledge Discovery, 2(2):121–167, 1998.
10. N. Cristianini and J. Shawe-Taylor. *Support Vector Machines*. Cambridge University Press, 2000.

11. D. DeCoste and B. Scholkopf. *Training Invariant Support Vector Machines.* Machine Learning, 46(1/3):161, 2002.

12. G. C. Cawley. *MATLAB Support Vector Machine Toolbox (v0.50t).* University of East Anglia, School of Information Systems, Norwich, Norfolk, U.K. NR4 7TJ, 2000.URL http://theoval.sys.uea.ac.uk/~gcc/svm/toolbox.

13. Adrian G. Bors, "*Introduction of the Radial Basis Function (RBF) Networks*", Department of Computer Science, University of York, UK.

14. Haykin, S. (1994) *Neural Networks: A Comprehensive Foundation.* Upper Saddle River

15. Nancy Ide and Jean Veronis, "*Encoding Dictionaries*", Department of Computer Science, Vassar College, Poughkeepsie, New York 12601 (U.S.A.).

17

Recognition of Ancient Tamil Characters in Stone Inscription

—S. Rajakumar
—Dr. V. Subbiah Bharathi
—J. Navarajan

ABSTRACT

In our project, we simulate a technique for recognizing ancient Tamil characters in stone inscription of various centuries. Many medical mysteries and valuable historical secrets are hidden in stone inscription which only few people can understand. Though there are number of character recognition, there is no efficient system for Tamil language which has a large character set and huge amount of variation. In particular, there is no system that addresses either the morphological characteristics of stone inscriptions or accounts for ancient characters. We propose a 3-stage approach to increase the recognition efficiency of characters. The image of the sculpture is captured and converted to required dimensions. Segmentation of the character is done using Chan-vese algorithm which uses active contours for separating the characters from background. Chan-vese algorithm has resistance to the morphological characteristics of stone inscriptions as it uses active contours.

The noise in the image is removed using the area property.

Zoning of characters is done by which each character is divided into six regions each viz., three horizontal and three vertical regions. Feature extraction is carried out by extracting the geometric features of the character contour. These features are based on the basic line types that form the character skeleton. 54 features (nine for each region) representing the number and normalized length of line segments of is extracted. The feature vectors so generated are applied to neural network (which is trained in advance with the features extracted from the characters of training database) for pattern recognition. Post processing of the pattern obtained is done to identify the exact character.

Objective

The main objective of this thesis is to convert ancient Tamil characters of various centuries to modern character by training the computer. This thesis explains how the characters are extracted and recognized using neural networks.

Problem Definition

Though there are a number of Character Recognition systems available, Character recognition in Stone Inscription is still a challenging task due to the following factors:

- Texture of inscriptions
- Noise present in image
- Complex characters
- Matching characters of different centuries
- Large character set
- Size of letters etc.

Existing Systems

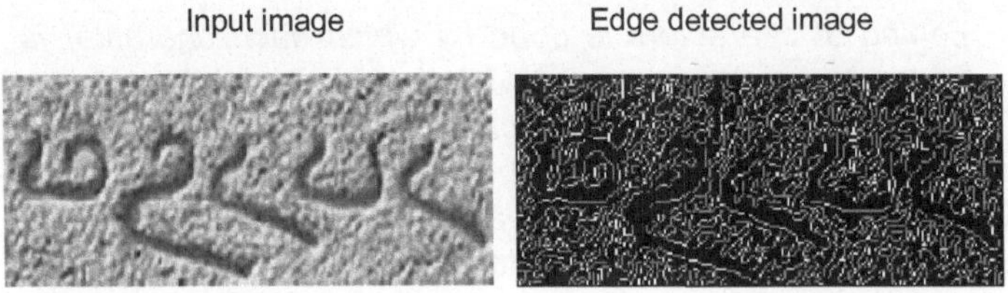

Edge detection is performed by computing gradients in an image. The contour of points with maximum gradient forms the edges in the image. Various operators used for these systems are Sobel operator, Roberts operators, Prewitt operators, Canny operator etc. These systems cannot be applied to stone inscriptions as the surface of the stones has ruggedness.

As shown in the above figure edge detection systems cannot be used in stone inscriptions due to its texture. Also the morphological characteristics of the stone inscriptions must be addressed during segmentation. In Thresholding, the mean values of the pixel values are calculated. Then, the histogram of the image is obtained. The mean value of the pixels is applied over the histogram to obtain the threshold value. Once the threshold value is obtained, all pixels having intensity greater than threshold are converted to the value of 255 and rest of the pixels is converted to 0. By performing the above operation, Binary image of the image is obtained having the value of 255 for characters and 0 for background of the image.

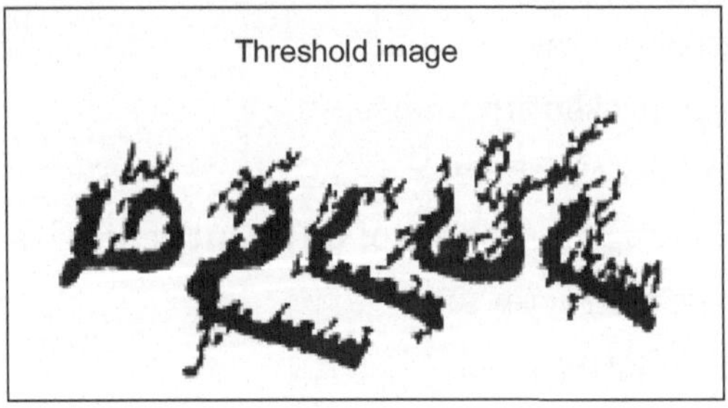

As shown in the above figure, when thresholding is applied the neighbours of the character is also taken as character due to the degradation function of the image. When the degradation function becomes significantly higher, the character cannot be segmented succesfully.

Proposed System

In our project, we propose a morphological segmentation that utilises the features of adaptive thresholding combined with dilation of centroids that eliminate the disadvantages of classic thresholding methods. The various steps involved in it are

- Specifying the ROI
- Morphological segmentation
  - Conversion to Gray image
  - Adaptive thresholding
  - Applying Median fiter
  - Use of Centroids

Input image Edge detected image

- Universe of Discourse
- Auto-correlation
- Neural networks

Specifying the ROI

Filtering a region of interest (ROI) is the process of applying a filter to a region in an image, where a binary mask defines the region. For example, you can apply an intensity adjustment filter to certain regions of an image.The multiROI function is used to obtain the region of interest from the image. The number of region of interest must be specified prior to running the program. Once it is specified, a figure window opens as shown in the image. The required region is selected by the polygon outline. The mask representing the region of interest is formed as shown in figure. This mask is used to extract the required character from the image.

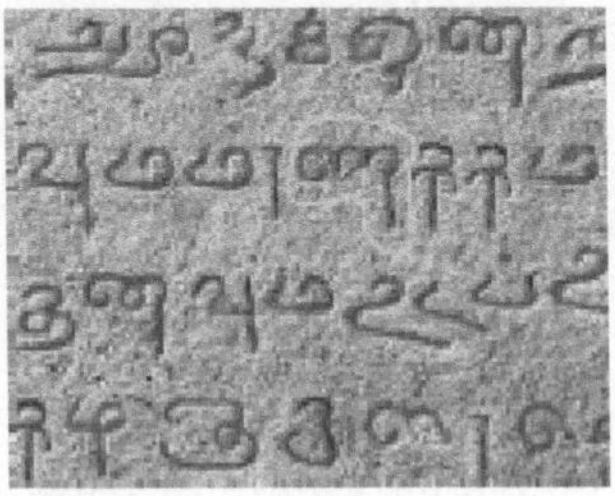

ROI Region

ROI Mask

Morphological segmentation: A grayscale image (also called gray-scale, gray scale, or gray-level) is a data matrix whose values represent intensities within some range. MATLAB stores a grayscale image as a individual matrix, with each element of the matrix corresponding to one image pixel. In RGB format, each pixel has three values one each for Red, Green and Blue colours. The mean value of the image for each colour are different and hence thresholding cannot be applied directly for RGB image. Hence it is converted into gray image before applying thresholding.The Gray value of the pixel can be calculated as

$$I = .3(R) + .59(G) + .11(B)$$

Where,

- I = Gray image intensity value
- R = Red component of RGB image
- B = Blue component of RGB image
- R = Red component of RGB image

Once the gray image is obtained, adaptive thresholding is done to convert it into a binary image. The histogram of the image is calculated for the image and the threshold value is calculated. All pixels having value greater than the threshold are converted into 0 and other pixels are converted into 1 as shown in figure. Median filtering is similar to using an averaging filter, in that each output pixel is set to an average of the pixel values in the neighborhood of the corresponding input pixel. However, with median filtering, the value of an output pixel is determined by the median of the neighborhood pixels, rather than the mean. The median is much less sensitive than the mean to extreme values (called outliers). Median1 filtering is therefore better able to remove these outliers without reducing the sharpness of the image. The medfilt2 function implements median filtering. A median filter is more effective than convolution when the goal is to simultaneously reduce noise and preserve edges.The noise which occupies large pixel values cannot be removed using median filter.

The area property of the bounded region is used to remove these noises. The bwlabel function is used for implementing the above step. The command, $L = bw$ label (BW, n), is used which returns a matrix L, of the same size as BW, containing labels for the connected objects in BW. n can have a value of either 4 or 8, where 4 specifies 4-connected objects and 8 specifies 8-connected objects; if the argument is omitted, it defaults to 8.The elements of L are integer values greater than or equal to 0. The pixels labeled 0 are the background. The pixels labeled 1 make up one object; the pixels labeled 2 make up a second object, and so on. The regionprops command is then applied over the matrix, L to obtain the area of each bounded region. The threshold of area is selected as 500 and bounded regions having area lesser than this are eliminated. The resulting image contains only the binarised characters.The region of interest mask obtained from the multiROI function is overlapped with the noise removed image to extract the specified character from the image. Once the required character is segmented universe of discourse function is applied over it to obtain the boundary of the character. Due to this function, the variation in the size of letters is removed as all characters will be transformed into the same size.

Universe of discourse function finds the lowest number of the row that contains a non-zero element (a), the highest value of the row that contains non-zero element (b), the lowest number of the column that contains a non-zero element (c), the highest value of the column that contains non-zero element (b). These values are used to extract the required character. The required character can be now described as bounding box extending from a to b in x-direction and c to d in y-direction. The character obtained is complemented and converted to the dimension of 256 X 256 before comparing with the database to make it compatible with the images in the database.

The character after being resized is cross-correlated with every image in the database. In image processing, cross-correlation is a measure of similarity of two images as a function of a time-lag applied to one of them. This is also known as a sliding dot product or inner-product. The correlation is done in 2 dimensions and is obtained as

$$R(i,d) = \frac{E[(Xi - \mu i)(Xd - \mu d)]}{\sigma i * \sigma d}$$

Where

- '*i*' is the input character
- '*d*' is the image from database
- '*E*' represents expectation value
- '*X*' represents mean
- '*n*' represents intensity of individual pixel
- ' ' represents the standard deviation

The above equation is applied over every pixel in each image in database. The correlated values obtained are given as input to the neural network. The neural network selects the image that has maximum correlation in the database as the recognised character.

Output Image

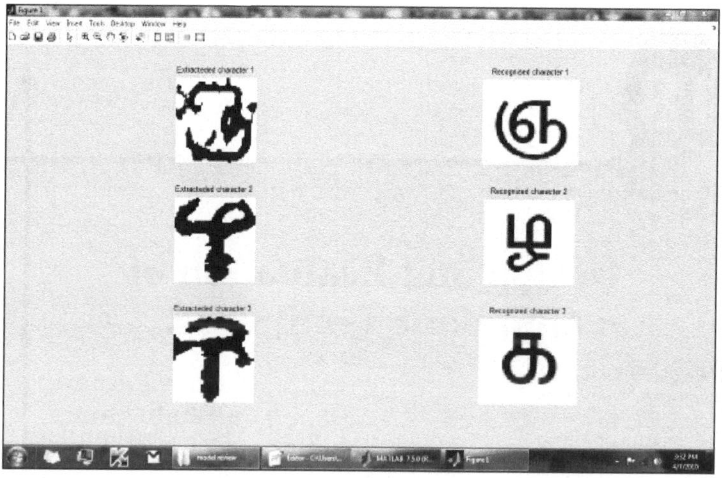

REFERENCES

1. *An Adaptive Technique for Handwritten Tamil Character* Recognition-IEEE 2007, Sarveswaran.K and Ratnaweera.D.A.A.
2. *Enhancing the Performance of Handwritten Tamil Character recognition by slant removal and introducing special features*—Journal of soft computing-2008.N.Shanthi and K.Duraiswamy.
3. *Recognition of Hand Printed Tamil Characters*, Pattern Recognition -1980, Chinaswamy and S.G.Krishnamoorthy.

18

Design and Evaluation of Omnifont Tamil OCR

—Tushar Patnaik
—Shalu Gupta
—Santanu Choudhury

IISc Bangalore has developed a recognition engine for Tamil printed text, which has been tested on 1000 document images of pages scanned from books printed between 1950 and 2000. IIIT Hyderabad has developed a XML based annotated database for storing the 5000 images of scanned pages and the corresponding typed text in Unicode. CDAC, Noida has developed an efficient evaluation tool, which compares the OCR output text to the reference typed text (ground truth) and flashes the substitution, deletion and insertion errors in different colours on the screen, so that the design team can quickly identify the issues with the OCR and make corrective steps for improving the performance. IIT Delhi has proposed and developed a novel scheme for segmenting only the text regions from document images containing pictures. The OCRs uses Karhunen-Louve transform (KLT) as features and a support vector machine (SVM) classifier with RBF kernel in a discriminative directed acyclic graph (DDAG) configuration. They assume an uncompressed input image of the document page, scanned at a minimum of 300 dpi with 256 gray levels (not binary or two-level). Tamil OCR currently gives over 94% recognition accuracy at the Unicode level, evaluated on over 1000 printed pages, some of them also containing old Tamil letters.

The features of the OCRs are

Omnifont: Any normal font used by books is handled. We don't say it is font-independent, because ornamental or stylized fonts cannot be handled.

Merged Characters: To a certain extent, the OCR is capable of identifying and segmenting the merger between two adjacent characters in a old, printed book.

Noise Tolerance: Certain types of breaks in the character are handled successfully.

Old Tamil or Kannada Script: The pre-1970 (prior to script revision due to E V Ramasamy Naicker) Tamil CV combinations such as NA, RA, nA, Nai, lai, Lai and nai are all recognized, along with the revised representations of the same. Similarly, old Kannada (halegannada) characters of La and zha and their vowel combinations are all handled seamlessly.

Unicode Output: The output is given in UTF-8.

Testing: Both OCRs have been tested by CDAC, Pune using an annotated corpus of over 1,000 document images of pages scanned from books printed between 1950 and 2002.

Consistency: The OCRs produce consistent and graded performance with font, size and quality variations.

Future Enhancement: The current average performance of 94 per cent for Tamil and 84 per cent for Kannada at the character level is without the use of any language model for postprocessing. Thus, there is a good potential to improve the performance of both OCRs further.

Medical Intelligence and Language Engineering Laboratory has teamed up with Bookshare.org, an

International non-profit organization, to provide Tamil and Kannada digital books (copyright free or permitted by authors) online to print-disabled people (visually challenged, old people with vision disabilities and people with other disabilities that make it impossible for holding a book and turn pages of it). A Text-to-speech engine in the respective language will also be provided to the registered user, who can then directly listen to the printed content on their desktop or laptop. We look forward to partners, who can give us copyright free books (hard or soft copies) or direct us to sources of the same. They are also welcome to directly partner with bookshare.org or Worth Trust at Chennai or Enable India at Bangalore.

Figure 18.1 shows a screen shot showing the performance of the system, as well as the convenience and use of the GUI. Figure 18.2 shows the confusion matrix shown by the evaluation tool, which helps in identifying common confusion and improve the OCR accordingly. Figure 18.3 shows the evaluation tool, comparing the XML annotated Tamil text

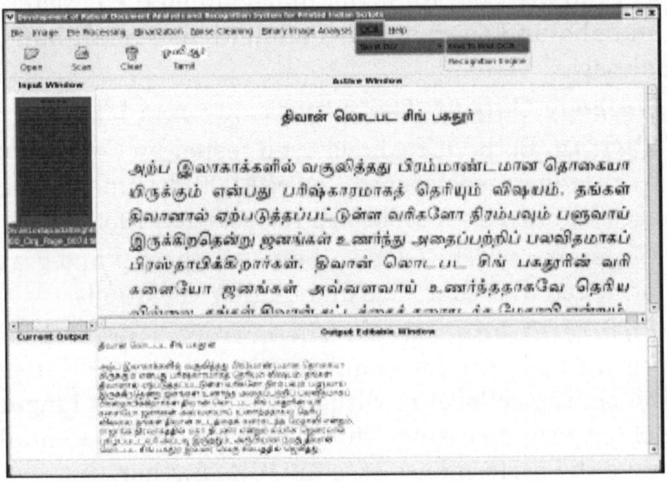

Fig. 18.1 : A screen shot from the OCR, showing the input image and the output text

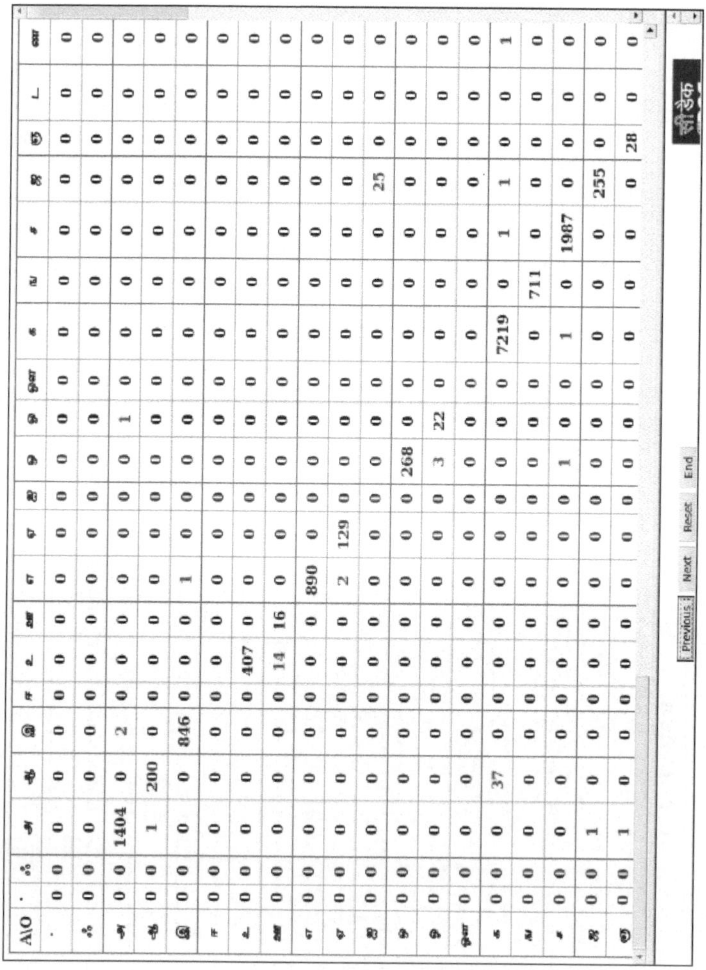

Fig. 18.2 : Display of Confusion matrix for a page recognition

for the page and the OCR's output in Unicode. Use of such convenient tools accelerated the development of the OCR accuracy, and it is currently giving a performance of over 95 per cent for good quality printed pages.

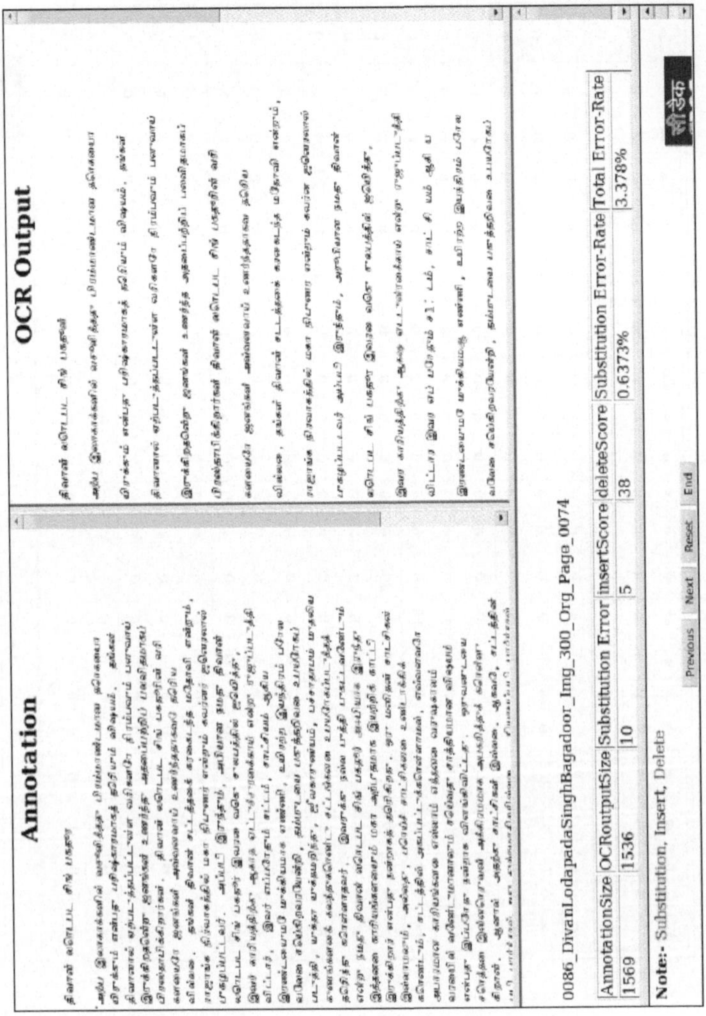

Fig. 18.3 : Evaluation Tool showing substitution, insertion and deletion erros

19

A Novel Hybrid SVM-Neural Approach to Recognize Handwritten Tamil Characters

—N. Shanthi
—K. Duraiswamy

ABSTRACT

In this chapter a Tamil handwritten character recognition algorithm based on hybrid SVM-Neural approach is presented. Initially SVM and Neural network is individually tested to know the performance of each classifier. The recognition accuracy of SVM is 90 per cent and the recognition accuracy of neural network is 81 per cent. So a hybrid approach is used to improve the recognition accuracy. Data samples are collected from different writers on A4 sized documents. They are scanned using a flat bed scanner at a resolution of 300dpi and stored as grey scale images. Various preprocessing operations are done on the input document image to enhance the quality. The characters are segmented and normalized to uniform size of 64 X 64. These uniform sized characters are projected onto a grid of fixed size 8 X 8. The pixel density is calculated for each grid and used as the feature vector. These features are given to well known support vector machines in the first stage. Few characters with low recognition accuracy are selected and are given to neural classifier. Since few classes are given to the neural network the recognition accuracy is improved. The new hybrid approach yields a recognition accuracy of 91.25 per cent.

Introduction

Machine simulation of human reading is one of the areas, which has been the subject of intensive research for the last three decades, yet it is still far from the final frontier[1,2]. Works on offline recognition of handwritten characters has been done well on Chinese, Arabic and few other scripts of the other nations[13,14,15]. However, there is less progress towards recognition of handwritten characters of Indic scripts. Recognition of handwritten Indian scripts is difficult because of the presence of vowel modifiers and compound characters. Most of the existing works are concerned about Devnagari and Bangla script characters, the two most popular languages in India. Few works are reported on the recognition of other languages like Telugu, Oriya, Kannada, Punjabi, Gujarathi[4] etc.

There are few attempts to recognize printed or handwritten Tamil characters[3,6,8,9,17,18]. This chapter proposes a recognition system for handwritten Tamil characters. The paper is organized as follows. The following section presents a brief description of Tamil language. The proposed hybrid SVM-Neural approach is presented in section 3. Finally, in section 4 conclusion and future works are given.

Tamil Language

Tamil, which is a south Indian language, is one of the oldest languages in the world. Sanskrit has influenced it to a certain degree. Its history can be traced back to the age of Tolkappiyam, the earliest extant Tamil grammar generally to 500 B.C. Tamil language is a member of the Dravidian / South Indian family of languages. Among the Dravidian language it is least influenced by 'Sanskrit' though there is a certain degree of influence. Most Tamil letters have circular shapes partially due to the fact that they were originally carved with needles on palm leaves, a technology that favored round shapes. The Tamil script is used to write the Tamil language in TamilNadu, SriLanka, Singapore and parts of Malaysia.

Tamil is the official language of the Indian state of TamilNadu, classical language in India, and has official status in India, Sri Lanka and Singapore. With more than 77 million speakers, Tamil is one of the more widely spoken languages in the world. The script for Tamil Language was conceived since time immemorial and the present form is after undergoing various changes at various periods of time. During its long cherished existence, it underwent various changes, corrections, modifications and has arrived at the present form based on its applicability and adoptability in the ever changing writing method and devices from time to time. The present form of the Tamil script is believed to have been evolved based on its "adoptability" for handwriting mechanisms.

Tamil Alphabets

Tamil alphabet consists of 12 vowels, 18 consonants, a special character (akh) and 216 combinational alphabets obtained by combining the vowels and consonants. Tamil language is relatively simpler compared to other Indian scripts. The rules for character composition are far fewer than in other Indian scripts. The only category of composition allowed is of Consonant-Vowel type, where a structure corresponding to a consonant and another corresponding to vowel are combined to form a C-V type character with a unique shape. Even though the total number of alphabets is 247, the graphical characters required to represent all of them are only 106. The C-V combination results in unique shape when அ, இ, ஈ, உ, ஊ are combined with consonants. When the remaining vowels are combined with consonants, ா then the combination results in horizontally isolatable structure. For example by adding க with அ we get க. similarly when all the consonants are added with அ, we get 18 unique characters. Then by placing the character after these characters we get one alphabet. Following க we get கா; following ங we get ஙா; following ச we get சா. In this manner there are eighteen alphabets with the character coming after different consonants. So the composite characters can be recognized as the sequence of െ, േ, ൗ characters. Due to this flexibility the total number of characters to be recognized is reduced to 106. If these 106 characters are recognized then all the 247 characters can be recognized. In addition to this the other unique characters to be recognized are ം[illegible], and [illegible].

Hybrid SVM-Neural approach

For relatively small class problems a single classifier system provides acceptable accuracies. But when the number of classes is more, the recognition accuracy is less. So hybrid approach can be used to recognize complex character recognition problem. Classification with multiple classifiers has been an active research area since early 1990s. Many combination methods have been proposed, and the applications to character recognition problems have advantage over individual classifiers. Generally, a character recognizer involves three tasks: preprocessing, feature extraction and classification.

Preprocessing

Various preprocessing operations are performed prior to recognition to enhance the quality of the input image. Preprocessing operations performed prior to recognition are:

1. Thresholding is to convert a gray scale image into binary by determining a value for gray-scale (or threshold) below which the pixel can be considered to belong to the writing and above which to the background; Here Otsu's method of histogram-based global thresholding algorithm is used[11].
2. Skew detection and correction is to detect the skew present in the image and to correct it. A document skew detection algorithm using wavelet transform and horizontal projection profile[19] is used in this work.

3. Line segmentation, the separation of individual lines of text; Horizontal histogram profile is used for segmenting the lines[10].
4. Slant correction, Removal of angle between the vertical direction and the direction of the strokes; a new method for slant estimation is used based on the combination of the projection profile technique and wavelet transform.
5. Character segmentation, the isolation of individual characters; Vertical histogram profile is used for segmenting the characters[10].
6. Skeletonization is the process of peeling off of a pattern as many pixels as possible without affecting the general shape of the pattern[12]; Here Hilditch's algorithm is used for skeletonization.
7. Character size Normalization, Size normalization is a transformation of an input image of arbitrary size into an output image of a fixed pre-specified size, while attempting to preserve structural detail[7]; Bilinear interpolation technique is used to convert the random sized image into normalized image of size 64X64.

Figure 19.1 shows the sample input image and Figure 19.2 shows the preprocessed image of the last line.

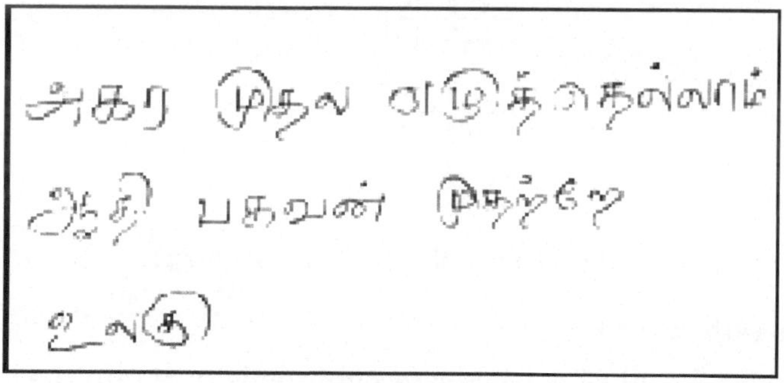

Fig. 19.1 : Sample input image

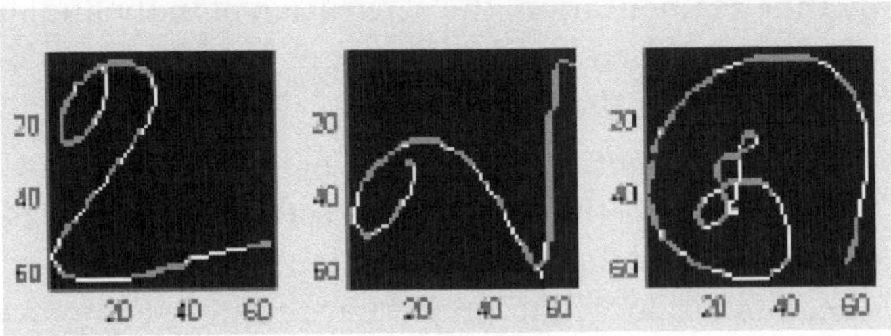

Fig. 19.2 : Preprocessed image

Feature extraction

Feature extraction is the problem of extracting the information from the preprocessed data, which is most relevant for classification purposes, in the sense of minimizing the within-class pattern variability, while enhancing the between-class pattern variability[20]. Selection of feature extraction method is the most important factor in achieving high recognition performance[5]. Here a simple feature of pixel density is used as feature. An 8 X 8 grid is superimposed on the character image, and for each of the 64 zones the average number of pixels is computed which results in 64 features. The pixel density varies from 0 to 64.

The Figure 19.3 shows the zoning of character image.

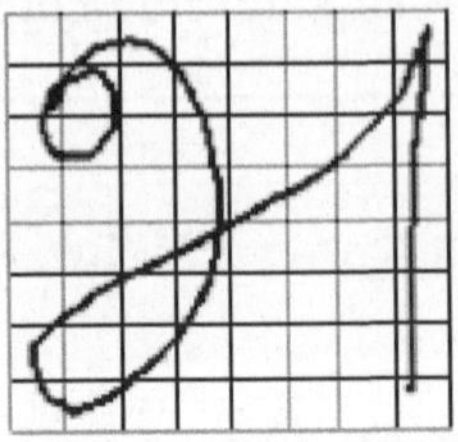

Fig. 19.3 : Zoning of character image

Classification

The final goal of character recognition is to obtain the class codes of character patterns. On segmenting character or words from document images, the task of recognition becomes assigning each character or word to a class out of a pre-defined class set. Different classifiers are used for recognition. Support vector machine and artificial neural network are used in this work for classification.

Support vector machines

The SVM is a new type of hyperplane classifier, developed based on the statistical learning theory of Vapnik[16], with the aim of maximizing a geometric margin of hyperplane, which is related to the error bound of generalization. The application of SVMs to character recognition has yielded state-of-the-art performance. Initially SVM alone is used for training and classification of the Tamil characters.

SVMs are mostly considered for binary classification. For multiclass classification, multiple binary SVMs, each separating two classes or two subsets of classes, are combined to give the multiclass decision. Here "one-against-one" approach in which k(k"1)/2 classifiers are constructed and each one trains data from two different classes. For training data from the ith and the jth classes, the following binary classification problem is solved:

$$\min_{w^{ij}, b^{ij}, \xi^{ij}} \quad \frac{1}{2}(w^{ij})^T w^{ij} + C(\sum_t (\xi^{ij})_t)$$

subject to

$$((w^{ij})^T \phi(x_t)) + b^{ij}) \geq 1 - \xi_t^{ij}, \text{ if } x_t \text{ in the } i^{th} \text{ class},$$

$$((w^{ij})^T \phi(x_t)) + b^{ij}) \geq -1 + \xi_t^{ij}, \text{ if } x_t \text{ in the } j^{th} \text{ class},$$

$$\xi_t^{ij} \geq 0.$$

Here max-wins voting strategy is used for classification. The recognition accuracy using SVM is 90 per cent.

Artificial neural networks

An artificial neural network is defined as a computing

structure consisting of a massively parallel interconnection of adaptive neural processors. The main advantage of artificial neural networks lies in the ability to be trained automatically from examples and good performance with noisy data. Artificial neural networks have been widely used in the field of character recognition produced promising results. Back propagation feed forward neural network (BPN) is used for training and testing the network. The recognition accuracy is only 81 per cent. Neural network took large time to train and the recognition accuracy is also low. So we have decided to use the benefits of both the classifiers.

Introduction to SVM-Neural Classifier

Even though the recognition accuracy of SVM is higher when compared to the other classifiers, still there is a scope for further improvement. The analysis of the Tamil character set reveals that a few characters are closely identical to each other in structure. So when all the characters are given to SVM then there is a difficulty in recognizing the identical characters. The characters identified and their percentage of recognition using SVM is shown in table 19.1. For example when the classification result of character ண is analyzed, the result shows that many a times the character ண is recognized as ஞ or ன. This is because of the reason that these characters look identical in structure. Hence in order to solve this difficulty a hybrid two stage classifier approach is proposed.

Table 19.1 : Characters with low recognition accuracy

S.No.	Characters with low recognition accuracy	Similar characters	Recognition accuracy %
1	ஏ	எ, ர	78.45
2	ஓ	ஒ	72.8
3	ஞ	ணு	77.7
4	பூ	பு	81.29
5	ண	ஞ, ன	74.85

The hybrid approach consists of 2 stages. SVM is chosen as the classifier in the first stage since it produced the highest recognition accuracy. When the performance of the SVM classifier is analyzed it illustrated that the 64 × 64 sized image with overlapping zones produced the best recognition accuracy. So those 225 features are calculated and given as input to the SVM classifier in the first stage. The output of SVM revealed that the recognition accuracy of the characters எ, ஓ, ஞ, பு and ள are low because they are identical to other characters in structure. The groups of such identical characters are (எ, ஏ, ர), (ஒ, ஓ), (ஞ, ஞு), (பு, பூ) and (ள, ன, ண).

In the second stage a separate classifier is designed for each group of identical characters. Both SVM and ANN are used in the second stage and the performances of both the classifiers are analyzed for all the groups. Table 19.2 shows the characters with low recognition accuracy, their identical characters and improved recognition accuracy using SVM-SVM approach. Table 19.3 shows the improved recognition accuracy of SVM-Neural approach. From the Tables it is evident that the performance of ANN is good in the second stage when compared to SVM. Hence in the proposed hybrid approach SVM and ANN are combined sequentially to improve the classification performance. This hybrid approach improves the overall recognition accuracy by 1.5 per cent.

Table 19.2 : Recognition Accuracy of SVM-SVM Approach

S.No.	Characters with low recognition accuracy	Identical characters	Recognition accuracy %	Improved recognition accuracy %
1	எ	ஏ, ர	78.45	85.08
2	ஓ	ஒ	72.83	80.93
3	ஞ	ஞு	77.71	85.71
4	பு	பூ	81.29	87.71
5	ள	ண, ன	74.86	80.00

Table 19.3 : Recognition Accuracy of SVM-Neural Approac

S.No.	Characters with low recognition accuracy	Identical characters	Recognition accuracy %	Improved recognition accuracy %
1	எ	ஏ, ர	78.45	90.61
2	ஓ	ஒ	72.83	84.39
3	ஞ	ஞு	77.71	89.71
4	பு	பூ	81.29	89.47
5	ள	ண, ன	74.86	81.14

This hybrid approach improves the overall recognition accuracy by 1.5 per cent from the original 90 per cent and improves the recognition accuracy of each identical character by 6 per cent to 12 per cent. SVM and ANN are combined effectively in the proposed hybrid approach to improve the overall recognition accuracy and the recognition accuracy of identical characters.

The architecture of the proposed hybrid SVM - Neural approach is shown in Fig. 19.4.

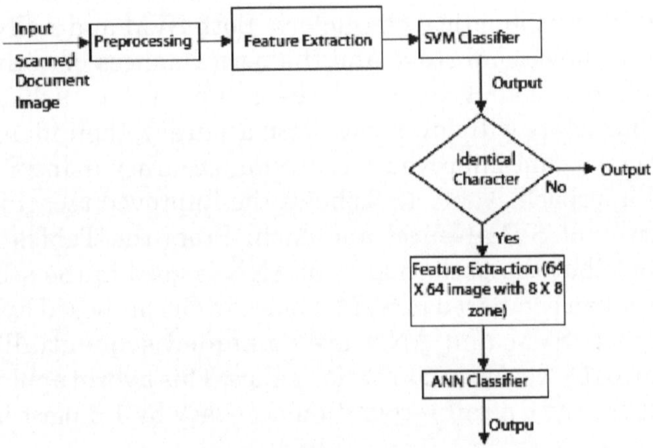

Fig. 19.4 : Architecture of the Proposed Hybrid SVM-Neural Approach

Conclusion

This study presents a novel hybrid system to recognize offline handwritten Tamil characters. The experimentation result shows that the simple SVM approach produces a cumulative recognition accuracy of 90 per cent and the recognition accuracy for different characters varies from 72 per cent to 99 per cent. When neural network is used for recognition, the recognition accuracy varies from 63 per cent to 98 per cent with an overall recognition accuracy of 81 per cent. But when SVM-neural approach is used the recognition accuracy is increased to 91.5%. This recognition accuracy is achieved with a simple feature of pixel densities in various zones of the images. The main recognition errors were due to abnormal writing and ambiguity among similar shaped characters. Future work can include more robust invariant features to achieve better discrimination power and neural classifier can be constructed for other characters.

REFERENCES

1. J.Mantas. *An Overview of Character Recognition Methodologies.* Pattern Recognition, 19(6):425-430, 1986.
2. V.K.Govindan and A.P. Shivaprasad. *Character Recognition—A Review.* Pattern Recognition, 23(7):671-683, 1990.
3. P.Chinnuswamy and S.G.Krishnamoorthy. *Recognition of Hand-printed Tamil Characters.* Pattern Recognition, 12(3):141-152, 1980.
4. U.Pal and B.B.Chaudhuri. *Indian Script Character Recognition: A Survey.* Pattern Recognition, 37(9):1887-1899, 2004.
5. Trier, Anil K. Jain and Torfinn Taxt. *Feature Extraction Methods for Character Recognition—A Survey.* Pattern Recognition, 29(4): 641-662, 1996.
6. G.Siromoney, R.Chandrasekaran and M.Chandrasekaran. Computer Recognition of Printed Tamil Characters. Pattern Recognition, 10(4):243-247, 1978.
7. Srihari *et al. On-line and Off-line Handwriting Recognition: A Comprehensive Survey.* IEEE PAMI, 22(1): 63-84, 2000.
8. R.M.Suresh *et al., Recognition of Hand-printed Tamil Characters Using Classification Approach.* ICAPRDT'99, 63-84, 1999.
9. S.Hewavitharana and H.C.Fernando, *A Two Stage Classification Approach to Tamil Handwriting Recognition*, Tamil Internet 2002, California, USA, 118-124, 2002.
10. N.Shanthi and Dr.K.Duraiswamy. *Preprocessing Algorithms for the Recognition of Tamil Handwritten Characters.* 77-82, Third International CALIBER 2005, Kochi.
11. N.Otsu. *A Threshold Selection Method from Grey Level Histogram,* IEEE Trans. System Man and Cyber. 9(1):62-66, 1979.

12. Lam, Lee, Suen. *Thinning Methodologies—A Comprehensive Survey*, IEEE PAMI, 14(9): 869-885, 1992.
13. S. N. Srihari, X. Yang and G. R. Ball. *Offline Chinese Handwriting Recognition: An Assessment of Current Technology*. Frontiers of Computer Science in China, 1(2):137-155, May 2007.
14. L.M.Lorigo, V.Govindaraju. *Offline Arabic Handwriting Recognition*: A Survey, IEEE PAMI, 28(5):712 – 724, 2006.
15. S. Jaeger, M. Nakagawa, C.L.Liu. *A Brief Survey on the State of the Art in On-Line Handwriting Recognition for Japanese and Western Script*, IEICE Conference on Pattern Recognition and Media Understanding, 1-8, March 2002.
16. Chih-Wei Hsu, Chih-Chung Chang, and Chih-Jen Lin. *A Practical Guide to Support Vector Classification*. 2003.
17. U.Bhattacharya, S.K.Ghosh, and S.Parui. *A Two Stage Recognition Scheme for Handwritten Tamil Characters*. 1: 511-515, ICDAR 2007.
18. N.Shanthi and Dr.K.Duraiswamy, *A novel SVM-based Handwritten Tamil Character Recognition System*. Pattern Analysis and Applications: Vol. 13, Issue 2 (2010), p. 173.
19. Shutao Li, Qinghua Shen, Jun Sun, "*Skew Detection Using Wavelet Decomposition and Projection Profile Analysis*", Pattern Recognition Letters 28, pp.555 - 562, 2007.
20. Trier, Anil K. Jain, Torfinn Taxt, "*Feature Extraction Methods for Character Recognition—A Survey*", Pattern Recognition, Vol. 29, No.4, pp. 641-662, 1996.

20

Effective Tamil Character Recognition in Tablet PCs Using Pattern Recognition

—Dr. T. Ravi
—Prof. R. Velayutham

ABSTRACT

Tamil Character Recognition is done for many applications using various novel methodologies. But the recognition of Tamil characters in Tablet PCs is a challenging one. Various methodologies like SVM, Preprocessing, interpolation etc were used in the past but were not satisfactory to friendly-user point of view. In this paper we introduce a new methodology pattern matching for Tamil Character Recognition. This method was tested to be a better approach for Gujarati scripts. As our Classical Language Tamil characters also has more curls and twists like Gujarati scripts, we utilized the same methodology for Tamil Character Recognition. This methodology uses a series of operations on the digitally written character. Scanning, Inversion, Grayscale conversion and trimming are done in the preprocessing section. Back propagation using neural networks in the middle tier and at last pattern matching algorithms areemployed. In this last phase instead of pattern matching done, we come forward with a modified pattern matching algorithm. We have termed this algorithm as

Thellodai Line Fitting Algorithm. As a result of this series of operations, the recognized output is obtained. For tablet PCs the output was simulated in Matlab's Neural Network and Image Acquisition toolbox. After analyzing the simulated results, the recognition rate of this methodology is found to be about 70-80 per cent on an average where as the other methodologies were tantalizing between 60s and 70s for character recognition of the Classical Language Tamil.

Key Words: *Pattern Classification, Thellodai Algorithm*

Introduction

This chapter deals with the new methodology implied for the effective pattern matching of Tamil character recognition in tablet PCs. Tablet PCs English characters are easily recognized by just scribing on the touch module. But for Tamil Characters, the mechanism is not available as of now in the case of Tablet PCs. English characters are easy and faster to recognize because, it has only 26 characters. There lies a difficulty for Tamil Character Recognition. It has 247 letters excluding the old scripting letters. So there is a need to classify the Tamil characters in a simple way and reduce the character set to a minimal extent. Gujarati scripts as in are given with a set of matching. They are checked for templates and pattern matching of the particular character. This is possible for Gujrati scripts because the number of characters used are less. But when this technique is implied Tamil, certain difficulties are experienced in the performance of execution. Tamil Characters are totally 247 in number, excluding the other language influential characters.

Similarly some methodologies are given for handwritten Tamil character recognition also. In section II, the difficulties in execution of the various methodologies are discussed. In section III, the newly proposed Thellodai line fitting algorithm is discussed in detail. In section IV, the proposed model is elucidated. In section V, the performance measures and the modules for real time implementation are discussed and finally section VI concludes the entire work with the possibilities to execute this project in real time.

Related Work

The base work is selected as, because Gujrati also has curvy writings similar to Tamil. So we are taking the technology used in as the backbone for our proposed model. The model stated in fails for Tamil because, Tamil characters are large in number and they take larger time when compared to the Gujrati scripts. Various methodologies are being proposed for Tamil Handwritten Character Recognition. The models stated in, has various good features for larger devices or enterprise level solutions. But these methodologies are found to be less effective when we take in the case for Tablet PCs.

Tablet PCs normally deal with the device driver synchronization, character compression and well classified set of characters. Tamil character set consists of 247 characters totally. In the previous models proposed in [3], [6] and [7], the classification is not efficient to the expected levels of Tablet PC synchronization. English characters find easier in the tablet PC because, it has only 26 singlet characters for classification. After thorough analysis on the Tablet PC architecture, the problem statement is framed as follows: "There lies a need for classifying all the 247 letters in Tamil to a maximal extent. The number of patterns used should be reduced to a minimal extent. A new algorithm based on line fitting for pattern recognition needs to be framed. This system should be developed in such a way that the device driver synchronization for Tablet PCs is to achieved."

Thellodai Algorithm

As mentioned in the problem statement at the end of the previous section, we have developed a new algorithm-based on line fitting. We term it as Thellodai Line Fitting algorithm.

Thellodai pronounced /θ llaudeı/. Thellodai means "Clear stream" in Tamil. As per this algorithm concerned, this has the well classified set of Tamil characters. All the 247 characters are classified efficiently and 35 patterns are framed. Many letters are recognized as a combination of two or more other patterns.

The Thellodai algorithm has a predefined trained set of 35 characters. These characters are termed as Frequently Used Patterns Uf, Rare Patterns Rp and Original Pattern Op.

Algorithm 1: Thellodai Line Fitting Algorithm

```
Function match()
{
 Var Uf, Rp, Op;
 Wait for input;
 Set the combination;
 Decide on the permutation;
 If permutation is Uf
  {
```

The sub patterns are matched;

```
  The sub patterns are matched;
  }
  If permutation is Rp
  {
   Rp sets are matched;
  }
  If permutation is Op
  {
   Move to next input;
  }
  If match is formed
  {
   Indent to next space and wait for input
  }
}
```

The above algorithm is framed specially for the Tamil character set. The patterns possible are reduced to a minimal set of just 35 patterns. These patterns are studied for the usage. According to this study, many of the characters are not used nowadays for casual usage. So we don't need to concentrate much on these characters. Thellodai algorithm is included as an additional feature in our proposed system and it will be good for rarely used characters also. The frequently used characters are indexed in an Ajax based system and it will show the possibilities of character identification.

Proposed Model

The proposed model is based on the architecture mentioned in the system is simulated in matlab 7.0 using the image acquisition toolbox and neural network toolbox. The image acquisition toolbox is used or simulating the patterns and neural network tool box for simulating the frequently used pattern set.

Fig. 20.1 : Expected output for the Tamil Character Recognition in Tablet PCs (Modelled)

Fig. 20.1 shows the expected output of the simulated set of data. For example, if we scribe '*ah*', it will give he possibility for '*aah*' also. The main aim is to study the efficiency of handwritten character ecognition for aharam, aaharam, eharam, eeharam, uharam, ooharam, aeharam, aeharam, oharam, oharam and ouharam set of characters. In Fig. 20.1, the character 'ah' is scribed by the user. The system dentifies as 'ah' and gives the possible extension for 'aah' also. The scribed character is displayed in lack and the permuted extension is displayed in grey.

The recognition sector deals with the following processes: Scanning, Inversion, Grayscale conversion nd trimming are done in the preprocessing section. Back propagation using neural networks in the iddle tier and at last pattern matching algorithms are employed. In this last phase instead of pattern atching done, we come forward with a modified pattern matching algorithm. We have termed this lgorithm as Thellodai Line Fitting Algorithm. As a result of this series of operations, the recognized utput is obtained.

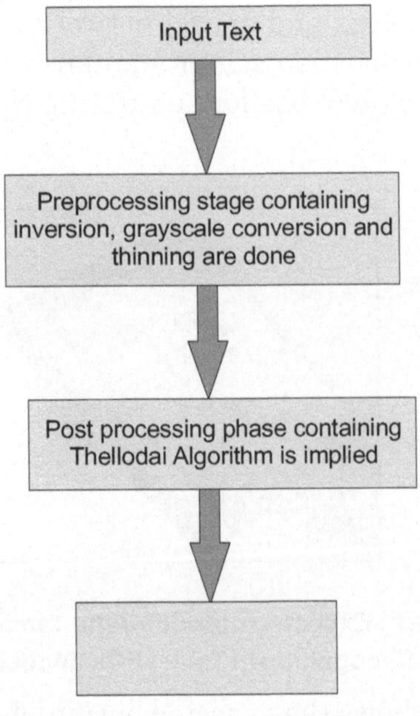

Preprocessing Phase

The preprocessing phase has the steps of Inversion, grayscale and thinning. During inversion, the haracter input is converted to the inverse color. Then during the grayscale phase, it gets converted to lack and white. During thinning the edges are fitted.

Supervised phase

During the supervised phase, the Neural network principles

come into act. The back propagation and rained intelligence modules will analyze the output of the preprocessing phase. Then by using the rained intelligence, the extensions are predicted. A popular and simple NN approach to the problem is ased on feed forward neural networks with back propagation learning. In the training step, we each raining sample is represented by two components: possible input and the desired network's output iven that input. After the training step is done, we can give an arbitrary input to the network and the etwork will form an output, from which we can resolve a pattern type presented to the network. As per he requirement of the Neural Network algorithm the information content that is area within the borders eeds to be digitized. This is achieved by dividing this area into a 12 x 12 grid. This 12 x 12 grid is canned, and every time 1 is detected that particular block is flagged. This procedure is referred to as digitizing.

Fig. 20.2 : Undigitized output for 'Ka'

The undigitized output is obtained in this phase. This output is now fed as input to the post processing phase.

0	0	0	0	0	0	0	0	0	0	0	0
0	0	1	1	1	1	1	1	1	1	1	0
0	0	1	0	0	0	0	1	0	0	0	0
0	0	1	0	0	0	0	1	0	0	0	0
0	0	1	0	0	0	0	1	0	0	0	0
0	0	1	1	1	1	1	1	1	1	0	0
0	0	1	0	0	0	0	1	0	1	0	0
0	0	1	0	0	0	1	1	0	1	0	0
0	0	1	1	0	1	1	0	1	1	0	0
0	0	0	1	1	1	0	1	1	0	0	0

Fig. 20.3 : Digitized output as a result of the post processing phase

Postprocessing phase

Post processing phase is the final phase for this proposed methodology. This phase implies the Thellodai algorithm for the efficient pattern matching of the digitized tamil characters.

0	0	0	0	0	0	0	1	0	0	0	0
0	0	1	1	1	1	1	1	1	1	1	0
0	0	1	0	0	0	0	1	0	0	0	0
0	0	1	0	0	0	0	1	0	0	0	0
0	0	1	0	0	0	0	1	0	0	0	0
0	0	1	1	1	1	1	1	1	1	0	0
0	0	1	0	0	0	0	1	0	1	0	0
0	0	1	0	0	0	1	1	0	1	0	0
0	0	1	1	0	1	1	0	1	1	0	0
0	0	0	1	1	1	0	1	1	0	0	0

Fig. 20.4 : Output obtained as a result of Thellodai algorithm in the post processing phase

The purple colored cell in Fig. 20.4 indicates that the extension is possible for this character for 'key' and 'keey' characters. When the user scribes on the purple extensions, it will automatically guide the user to incorporate the extension for the particular character to be finalized.

Performance Measures

The performance of the proposed methodology are found for the various subsets aharam, aaharam, eharam, eeharam, uharam, ouharam, aeharam, aaeharam, aiharam, oharam, ooharam and ouuharam. The combination of 35 singlets is combined with each other and the characters are found for efficiency of matching. It is found that, the subsets of aharam, aaharam, aeharam, aaeharam, aiharam, oharam, ooharam and ouharam are in no need for any difficulty in recognizing the character. But eharam, eeharam, uharam, ouharam finds little difficulty. This is just for the reason for some characters

Table 20.1 : Recognition rates of various subsets of Tamil character series

Character Subset	Recognition rate in%
Aharam	80
Aaharam	77
Uyir	79
Mei	80
Eharam	72
Eeharam	70
Uharam	71
Ouuharam	69
Aeharam	76
Aaeharam	78
Aiharam	80
Oharam	75
Owharam	74
Ouharam	75

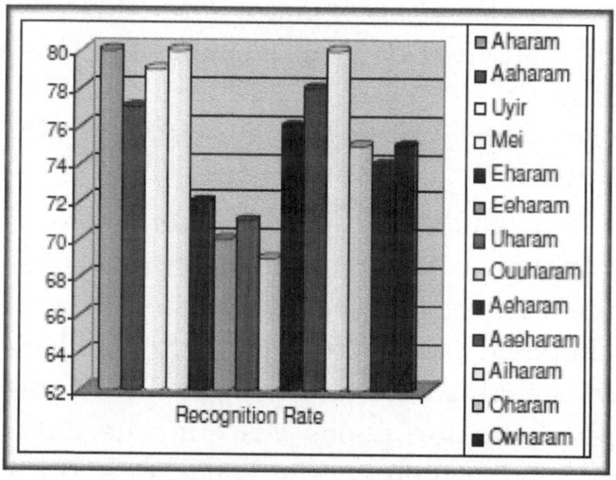

Fig. 20.5 : Graph showing the performance and recognition rates of various subsets of Tamil character set

like 'Do' are in need of totally different shape transformation when compared with the other characters.

As shown in Fig. 20.5, it is evident that the efficiency of the character recognition is found to be nearing 80 per cent for most of the character subsets. Only 4 out of the 14 subsets, the efficiency is in the early 70s. The recognition rates for eharam, eeharam, uharam, ouuharam are found to be nearing the early 70s because there are chances for asymmetric matching. When comparing with the recently existing systems, it is clear that our proposed model will be better in its every aspect. The fidelity of the letters will be more. Handwritten performance of the user will increase.

There are many advantages for this system. When comparing to the transliteration system, the user is in no need to have English phonetic proficiency to type in Tamil. The proper pronunciations and spellings are possible. There is an issue of confusion with the lla and zha characters. This problem can be eliminated by using the proposed approach. Tablet PCs as of now are not designed for Tamil Characters. This is because of the lack of proper hardware modifications. The modifications need to be done in such a way that Tamil characters can also be recognized. After this issue is fixed, real time implementation is possible for this proposed methodology.

Conclusion

From the above elucidated proposed methodology, it is clear that this technology is successful at the level of simulation. The efficiency for most of the cases comes above 75 per cent and the Thellodai Line Fitting algorithm holds better than many of the existing pattern matching algorithms. The real time implementation needs the Unicode data of Tamil characters to be included in the Tablet PCs. If it is done so, then the real time implementation can be done. Tamil Tablet PCs are no longer to wait.

REFERENCES

1. Prasad JR, Kulkarni UV, Prasad RS, *Offline Handwritten Character Recognition of Gujarati Script Using Pattern Matching*. IEEE ASID 2009.
2. http://www.touchscreens.com
3. J. Sutha, N. Ramaraj, *Neural Network Based Offline Tamil Handwritten Character Recognition System*. IEEE Intl Conf on Computational Intelligence and Multimedia Applications 2007.
4. Ramanathan *et al*, *Tamil Font Recognition Using Gabor Filters and Support Vector Machines*, IEEE Intl Conf on Computing, Control and Telecommunication Technologies 2009.
5. KH Aparna *et al, Online Handwriting Recognition for Tamil*. Proc IEEE IWFHR-9 2004.
6. RM Suresh, L Ganesan, *Recognition of Printed and Handwritten Tamil Characters Using Fuzzy Approach*. Proc IEEE ICCIMA 05.
7. U Bhattacharya *et al, A Two Stage Recognition Scheme for Handwritten Tamil Characters*. Proc IEEE ICDAR 2007.
8. Sarveswaran K, Ratnaweera, *An Adaptive Technique for Tamil Handwritten Character Recognition*. Proc IEEE Intl Conf on Intelligent and Advanced Systems 2007.
9. Suresh Sundaram, AG Ramakrishnan, *A Novel Hierarchical Classification Scheme for Online Tamil Character Recognition*. Proc IEEE ICDAR 2007.
10. Seethalakshmi *et al, Optical Character Recognition for Printed Tamil text using Unicode*. Journal of Zhejiang University SCIENCE, 2005.
11. J. Venkatesh, C. Suresh Kumar, *Handwritten Tamil Character Recognition Using SVM*. Intl Journal of Computer and Network Security (IJCNS) Dec 2009.
12. Hiroki Mori *et al, Japanese Document Recognition Based on Interpolated N-gram Model of Character*. Proc IEEE ICDAR 1995.

21

Design of Intelligent Robotic Arm Writing Tamil for Physically Challenged

'A Boon for Physical Ailment'

—Seima Saki S
—Sabita Devi D
—Manoj S
—Mr. R. Vimalathithan

ABSTRACT

Physically impaired people find hard to subsist in this challenging world. Here forth is advancement in technology to provide comfort to handicapped and visually disabled to convey their thoughts through pen and paper. Inventions made so far didn't prove a great amount of benefit to them. The working model proposed here is much novel and proves to be a well-worn technology. The central notion is to design a robotic arm that writes upon dictation. We use speech analysis techniques to convert it into text. Writing is brought by finding the mathematical equation of each alphabet, character or a number and converting into values that drives the arm. We use 3 degrees of freedom design for X,Y and Z axis motion. The values of the equations are stored in the memory of the micro controller and are sent to motors corresponding to the incoming text. Hence not only one but many styles of writing can be brought up by a single system by feeding their corresponding equation values. This not only assists disabled persons, but also supports people who need a proxy for their hand writing. This technique is much practical and shows best results.

Introduction

Researchers spend their valuable time in inventing novel methods to impede the disabilities of physically impaired. Previously developed devices were not that effective to make the needy feel relieved from all his necessities. Some tasks like signing the documents and writing in his own hand writing seemed to be impossible. Can a robot take up these jobs of a human...? The technology invented here is to couple human voice with the mechanical arm. Speech is analyzed by software and converted to digital format. The hand writing is mathematically formulated as discussed below. Further, the system allows selecting upon different styles among the ones present in their memory. The rest of the chapter is organized as follows: Section II presents a brief overview of fundamental building blocks, Section III gives the overview of Hardware description, Section IV presents the construction details and Mathematical formula of text are discussed in Section V. Finally, Conclusion and Future work are presented in section VI.

Fundamental Building Blocks

Our aim is to make the arm trace the letters in accordance with the speech. Arm movement can be brought up with pulleys and stepper motor. For this, each alphabet, number or a special character is to be represented by a unique values, so called as 'fonts', and fed into a memory. And motor carries out the activity in relation to those values. And we need a microcontroller to take up memory and control activities. We require a speech analyzer to convert human language into text and text is processed further into digital data. Microcontrollers work with digital inputs. So the speech has to be converted into digital string. To position and orient the robotic arm, manipulators of 6-DOF or 3-DOF can be employed. The DOF of the manipulator or the arm are distributed into sub assemblies of each axis. Given below is the outline of technical blocks of the robotic humanoid hand.

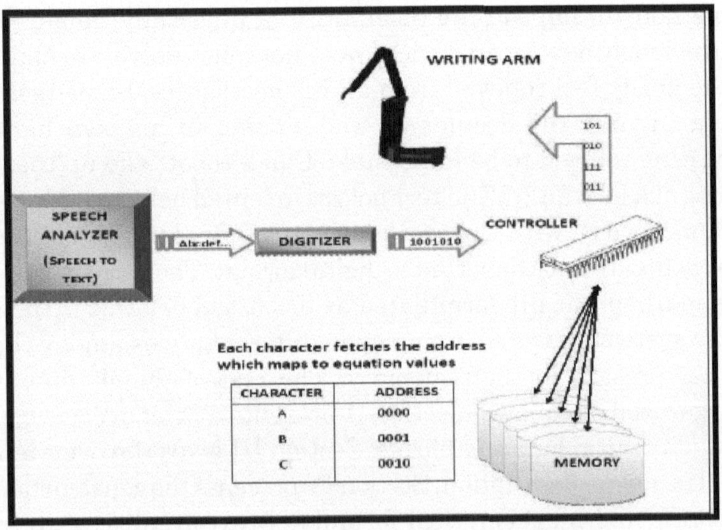

Fig. 21.1 : Basic Building Blocks—Overview

Hardware Descriptions

Micro Controller Unit

We use the basic 8051 family micro controller Atmel 89C51. It has 4KB on-chip program space, 128bytes RAM, 2 timers,4 I/O ports, 1 serial port and 6 interrupt sources. 8051 is a 8-bit processor meaning that the CPU can work on only 8 bits at a time. Data larger than 8 bits has to be broken into 8-bit pieces to be processed by the CPU. Micro controller unit used here performs the task of matching the incoming text with already stored binary equivalents of the letters and alphabets. MCU makes decision of which data has to be written to the port where motors are interfaced. We require 3 motors for 3 Degrees of Freedom.

Stepper motor interface

Stepper motor is widely used device that translates electrical pulses into mechanical movement. In applications such as hard disk, dot matrix printers, and robotics the stepper motor is used for position control. The most common stepper motors have four stator windings that are paired with a centertapped. This type of stepper motor is commonly referred to as a four phase or unipolar stepper motor. The center tap allows a change of current direction in each of two coils when a winding is grounded, thereby resulting in a polarity change of the stator. The stepper motor shaft moves in a fixed repeatable increment, which allows one to move it to a precise position. This repeatable fixed movement is possible as a result of basic magnetic theory where poles of same polarity repel and opposite poles attract. The step angle determines number of rotations per minute and the delay given for each step determines the speed of rotation. Due to incremental steps, accuracy is high.

Pulley Mechanism for Navigation

Movement of the arm can be brought about by using a manipulator that is fixed to a pulley belt. Pulley is operated by a stepper motor. The setup of stepper motor controlling the pulley with its shaft is shown in the figure. For x,y and z axis movement we use three pulleys with motors in it. Motion of one arm affects the other there by bringing up a relative translation over the entire 3 dimensional space.

Fig. 21.2 : Stepper Controlled Pulley System

Construction

Module 1- Mechanical Perception

3 DOF design

To enhance robot hand dexterity, the robot should be designed to have a redundant number of degrees of freedom. In order to avoid ill poised nature and to minimize its inability to act as a human hand, we go for a 3 Degrees of freedom design. The over view of the design is shown in the figure. X,Y and Z are the Cartesian co-ordinates, $q1$,$q2$ and $q3$ denotes vector of joint angles. $L1$,$L2$ and $L3$ is the distance between two vector of joint angles. Movements in Z axis is used to lift the whole set up and place it in its origin for the start of a new page or a new line and movement in X and Y axis is for writing on the plane.

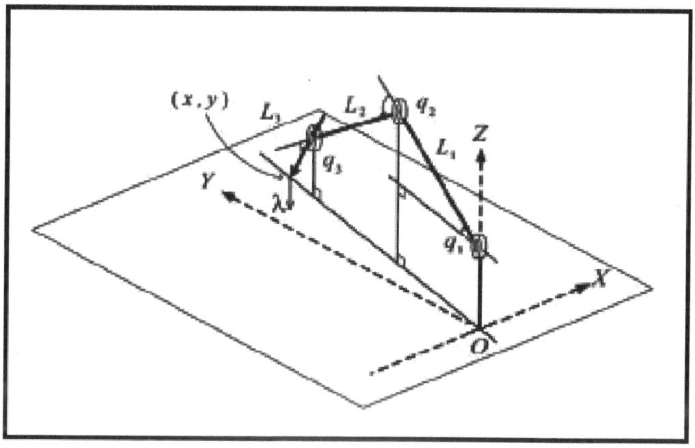

Fig. 21.3 : DOF Design

Mechanical setup

The entire built set up is shown in the figure. Pulley is supported by metal rods. As mentioned above we use three pulleys. Each of the pulley is driven by stepper motor, which gets signals from the micro controller for its movement. The strength of the pen on the paper is adjusted by varying the Z axis dimension. Also the speed of the stepper motor determines the accuracy of writing.

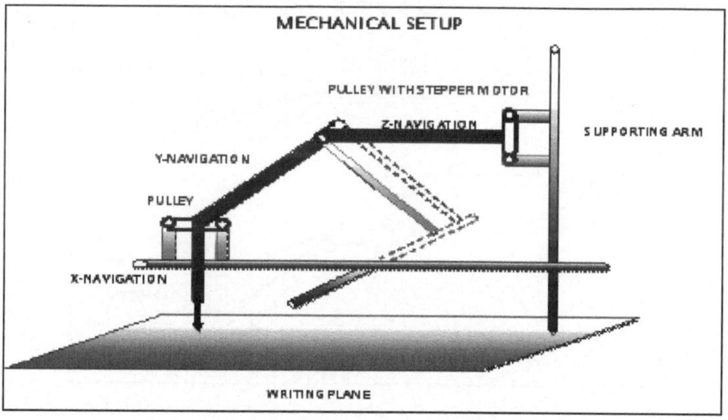

Fig. 21.4 : Mechanical Setup

Module 2—Programming Conception

Speech to text

The speech is converted to text using the third party software as mentioned above. The text data is converted to binary form and sent serially to MCU. Hence each word maps to certain set of binary values, i.e. set of letters in binary form. The pronunciations of words vary from person to person. Hence it is hard to differentiate between words having similar pronunciation. Bear can be interpreted as bare or *vice versa*. These types of verbal mistakes are much common with this type of systems and can be minimized by training the system continuously with most common words. If the software used is able to compare the words with the context of the sentence and then check for verbal errors, then it would be much efficient. As a key point, the text is converted to digital context and serially sent to the controller.

Text Identification

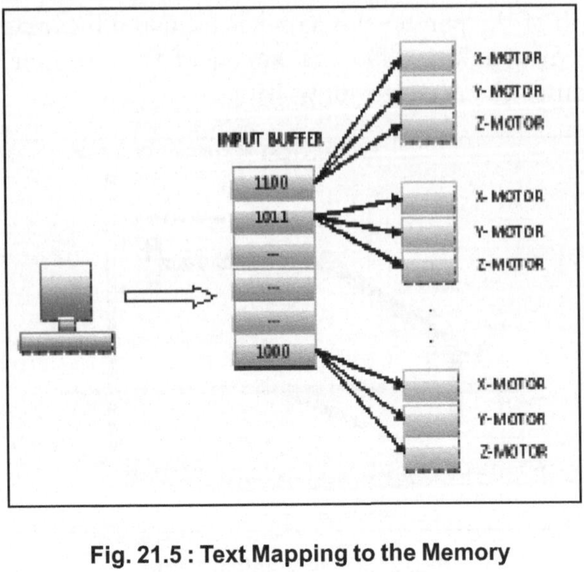

Fig. 21.5 : Text Mapping to the Memory

The values of each alphabet, character or number is already stored in heap of memory of the controller. This heap of values maps to set of locations which contains the values that are to be sent to the pen in order to bring about the letter. These values are nothing but the mathematical formulation of letters, i.e. the equations formed by those letters when endorsed in a 2 dimensional *XY* plane.

Mathematical Formulation of Text

The entire text is imagined as combination of lines and curves in *XY* plane. Let the size of character be in the ratio of 1:2 (width: height) for English and 1:1 for Tamil. Hence each character is expressed in equations of x and y. For the word to be written, values of the entire axis have to be given simultaneously. For slanting lines, slope has to be specified and for curves its corresponding curvature values has to be specified. With this type of method, any character can be represented and be stored as specific fonts in the MCU memory. This allows multiple hand writings to be written by a single system.

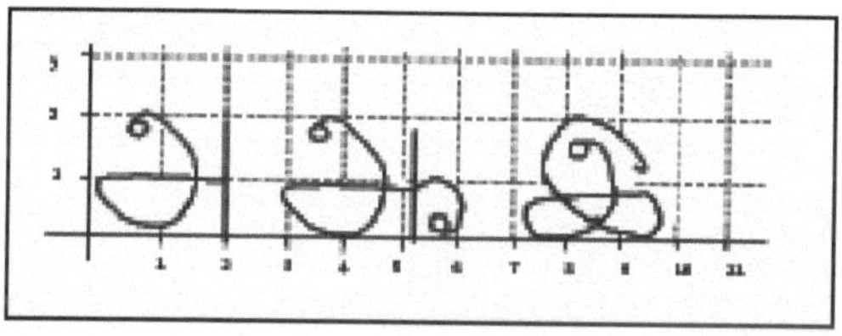

Fig. 21.6 : Graphical Outlook of a Sample Letter

Conclusion

The algorithm for formulation of the text was derived. Speech analysis was found tricky with many errors. But it was minimized when the system was trained with the common words. Mechanical arrangement was designed and the errors were significant while retrace. Yet it proved to be efficient. If this technology is released as a real-time product it would really be a boon for physical ailment.

REFERENCES

1. R K Mittal, I J Nagrath: "*Robotic and Control*", Tata McGraw-Hill Publications.
2. Frederick: "*Stastical Methods for Speech Recognition*" (Chapter 1) -1997 MIT.
3. 8051 *Microcontroller and Embedded Systems*, Muhammed Ali Mazidi, Janice Gillispie Mazidi, McKinley
4. IEEE Transaction on "*Robottics and Automation*", March 2003, Vol. 10, Issue 1.
5. Third International Conference on "Information Technology and Applications" 2005.Vol. 2, Issue 4 to 7 pp. 21 to 24
6. IEEE Transaction on "*Speech and Audio Processing*", July 2004 Vol. 12, Issue 4.
7. Ravi P. Ramachandran, Richard Mammone: "*Modern Methods of Speech Processing*", Kluwer Academic Publications 1995. p. 236.
8. Third International Conference on "*Information Technology and Applications*", July, 2005. Vol. 2, Issue 4.

22

LaaLaLaa
A Tamil Lyric Analysis and Generation Framework

—Sowmiya Dharmalingam
—Madhan Karky

ABSTRACT

Over 1000 Tamil lyrics are being written every year. Tamil films, advertisements, private pop albums are the main contributors of Tamil lyrics. This chapter presents LaaLaLaa, a framework for Tamil lyric analysis and generation. For the analysis part, a set of 2000 Tamil lyrics collected over a period of 50 years penned over different themes is mined for various statistics and morphological patterns. The analysed statistical data is then used for the generation of the lyrics. This chapter explains the different components in the framework such as lyric generator, rhyme finder, lyric miner, template selector, morphological generator and WordNets for lyric generation. We introduce three scoring mechanisms for the properties of flow, rhyme and meaning of a lyric. These scoring methods are used to compare the quality of the generated lyric. Discussing the results, the chapter concludes with open problems and future directions.

Introduction

Tamil is a vibrant language with a rich grammar, vocabulary, an inherent poetic flavour and music is synonymous with its culture. Tamil Lyrics have evolved in a dramatic fashion from the many historical poems of the Sangam literature including Ettuthogai and Pathuppaattu, narrative poem Silappatikaram, compositions of the Tamil Saiva saints such as Appar, Thirugnana Sambanthar ,Manikkavaasagar and compositions of Tamil hymns known as Thiruppugazh to the medieval period philosophies dominated by songs to the present day's rap culture. There are about 1000 lyrics being written every year as private albums, jingles and as original soundtracks of mainstream movies. In this chapter, we propose LaaLaLaa, framework that can analyse lyrics for various statistics on words, their morphological patterns and generate lyrics in Tamil concordant to the input music and selected theme. Computational creativity is particularly very challenging, as it requires understanding and modelling knowledge, which almost cannot be formalized. Generating meaningful lyrics to a given tune and in a given domain can be treated as an optimisation problem that aims at maximizing the various features of lyrics such as meaning, rhyme and flow.

This chapter is organised into four sections. The second section discusses a few contributions to lyric generation and how LaaLaLaa differs from the rest of the lyric generation systems. The third section presents the LaaLaLaa lyric analysis and generation framework and in detail discusses the various components of the system. The section also presents suggestions for three scoring mechanisms to ongoing research and future work.

Background

Several poetry generation systems have been developed in the past which broadly fall into the following categories—template based, generate and test approaches, evolutionary approaches and case-based reasoning approaches[6]. The Tra-la-Lyrics system[7] generates Portugese lyrics given a MIDI by calculating syllabic division and syllabic stress identification of words and the strength of each beat. It however doesn't handle the semantic aspect and produces completely random words and also doesn't use metric patterns that can serve as an exact template for the words.

The Automatic Generation of Tamil Lyrics for Melodies[12] identifies the required syllable pattern for the lyric and passes this to a sentence generation module which generates meaningful phrases that match the pattern. A corpus of poems and stories is used as a source of phrases. This system is constrained by the size of the phrases/patterns and generates phrases that are independent of the previous phrases which lead to lyrics that are meaningful in parts, but meaningless on the whole. Secondly the system presented in[12] generates rhyme based on maximum substring match and fails to make use of edhugai, moanai and iyaibu, the three rhyming patterns that are specific to Tamil language.

Other remarkable works in this domain include poetry generation in COLIBRI[3] and An expert system for the composition of formal Spanish poetry[5] which translate a user specified prose message into formal Spanish poetry, Hisar Manurung's McGonnagall[10] where the poem generation process is formulated as a state space search problem where a state in the search space is a possible text with all its underlying representation, and a move can occur at any level of representation, from semantics to phonetics. The POEVOLVE system which implements the architecture proposed by Levy[9] creates texts that satisfy the form specifications of limericks. The WASP[4] system splits a given block of text into shorter fragments to identify reference patterns and uses the words in the text to produce verses that match these patterns. In his thesis, Manurung[11], defines a poem to be a text that meets three properties: meaningfulness, grammaticality and poeticness. Our system currently handles the grammaticality and meaningfulness aspects to a certain degree while work is going on to enhance these factors, to meet the poeticness factor (LaaLaLaa framework proposed in this paper uses edhugai monai and iyaibu properties to achieve this) and handle other limitations of existing systems.

LaaLaLaa Framework

The LaaLaLaa framework presented in figure 22.1, can be divided into four major subsystems. Music-To- Template, Lyric Analysis, Lyric Generation and Lyric Scoring are the four subsystems that constitute the LaaLaLaa framework. The following sections describe the subsystems in detail.

Music to Template

MIDI(Musical Instrument Digital Interface) is a format for representing music in digital devices. A MIDI file is the input to the system. The MIDI file is processed by a MIDI-to-ABC[1] converter. The ABC notes[8] are processed by ABC-To-

தானானானன்னானானானா | thaanaanaanannaanaanaanaa

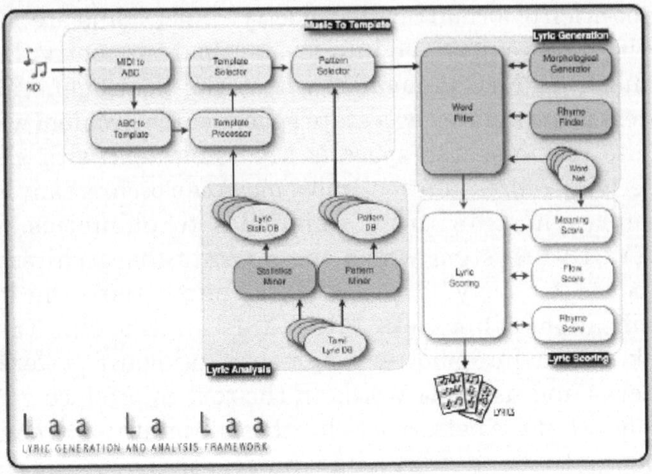

Fig.22.1 : LaaLaLaa Lyric Generation and Analysis Framework

Template converter which transforms the ABC notes to Tamil Textual Place Holders, we call them Templates. A template can be formed using combinations of a short vowel (tha | na), a long vowel (thaa | naa) and a consonant (n). An example line template is provided below.

A template such as the one provided in the example can be split into numerous combinations of smaller chunks. The objective of splitting the line template into smaller chunks is to treat the chunks as placeholders for fitting words. We solve the problem of minimising the number of templates based on results from the analysis subsystem. A Lyric Stats DB provides information on average word lengths and average number of words per sentence for a template of given length. This statistic is used to split the given template into smaller chunks of placeholders for words. The line template example provided above may be split into one of the following options based on statistics available in Lyric Stats DB for line of length 9.

தானானா நன்னானா நா நா | thaanaanaa nannaanaa naa naa
தானா நானன் நானா நானா | thaanaa naanan naanaa naanaaa

Template Selector selects templates that can be matched with the previous line to maximise rhyme score, which will be explained in the Lyric Scoring. The selected template will then be tagged for patterns. Pattern of a line will the part-of-speech tags associated with each word of the line. This POS tag for each word of the template is obtained from Pattern DB, populated as a result of Pattern Mining in the Lyric Analysis system. Pattern DB & Stats DB are explained in next section. The following tagged template is example of a selected pattern. It is also to be noted that a single template may match multiple patterns and a pattern is selected at random. This pattern tagged template forms the input to the Lyric Generation subsystem.

தானா<adjective+clitic> நானன்<noun+locative> நானானானா<verb+1st person + singular + future>

Lyric Analysis

Lyric Analysis is an offline system where a Tamil lyric corpus is analysed for various statistics and patterns. Lyrics collected from various sources are formatted by tagging them with appropriate headers and section tags (pallavi, anupallavi, saranam,..) The formatted lyrics are fed as input to a statistics miner and a pattern miner. A statistics miner analyses lyrics for statistics corresponding to length of sentences and words, length of co-occurring words.

Table 22.1 : Lyric Statistics

n = Length (s)	AvgWPS(n)	AvgWLN(n)
5	2	3
10	3	3
15	4	4
20	5	4
25	6	4
30	7	4
35	8	4
40	8	6
45	8	6

Table 22.1 provides some statistics obtained from our implementation of lyric miner over 2000 Tamil lyrics collected from multiple sources. The Length(s) denotes the character count for a given sentence. AvgWPS (n) denotes the average words per sentence for sentences with length n. AvgWLN (n) denotes the average character count of words for sentences with length n. It is to be noted that the average is computed over the lyric corpus. The template processor uses this information to efficiently split templates for word fitting.

Table 22.2 : Sample Output Pattern Miner

wps	pattern	pattern
2	4	< Noun > < Pronoun + Sandhi + Clitic >
3	10	< Interrogative Noun + Clitic > < Pronoun > < Interrogative Noun + Clitic >
4	3	< Infinitive > < Verb + Past Tense + Verbal Participle > < Time > < Noun >

A sample output from our pattern miner is provided in Table 22.2. wps denote the words per sentence and | pattern | denotes the number of times a particular pattern occurs. The pattern gives information on what pos and morphological suffixes are used[2]. Pattern Selector module uses these results to tag templates for lyric generation.

Lyric Generation

The Lyric Generation Subsystem uses domain specific WordNets, Morphological Generator and a Rhyme Finder. The domain specific WordNet consists of words and their associations specific to a certain domain such as nature, love, history, geography, religion, zoology and more. Given a root word and appropriate tags, it can generate nouns and verbs. The information obtained from the Pattern Tagger is used to generate words according to the tagged pattern. The Rhyme Finder is used by the Lyric.

நா <verb> ளா <verb> ளாளா <noun+clitic>
நா <verb> ளா <verb> ளாளா <noun+clitic>

Generator to choose words that match one or more of the three Rhyme properties (edhukai, moanai, iyaibu). The edhugai property states that the second letter of two parallel words match. Two words are considered to be parallel if they occur in the same position of two different sentences. The moanai and iyaibu properties state the same for first letter and last letter to match respectively. Let the above example be considered as two template patterns for parallel sentences sent to Lyric Generator.

The above given lyrics are two options generated by the lyric generator. The words poovae and theevae are not obtained from the WordNet as the WordNet comprises of root words only. The morphological generator uses the noun+clitic pattern for naanaa word template and chooses noun roots from Word Net to generate morphological suffixes that meter-match the template.

வா வா தீவே | vaa vaa theevae
போ போ போவே | poa poa poovae

வா வா தீவே | vaa vaa theevae
போ போ பூவே | poa poa poovae

Two words are considered to Meter match if the two words have same character length and every character of a word meter matches with the corresponding character of the other word. The meter matching of two words is again obtained from ancient Tamil grammar definition of maathirai aLavu (meter length). Rhyme finder minimises the search space for generating the second line by restricting the list of word to match edhugai monai or iyaibu properties. Choosing same length roots with same clitic or matching the first second or last characters of words enables choosing rhyming words.

Lyric Scoring

We propose a lyric scoring subsystem that takes an entire lyric as input and gives three different scores for the lyric namely flow score(f), rhyme score(r) and Meaning Score(m).

Flow of a lyric can be modeled as a property influenced by the phonetic properties of words in the lyrics. Tamil alphabets are sensibly classified into short vowels, long vowels, soft consonants, hard consonants and mid consonants. We use this classification along with doublings in words to determine the score of a word, a sentence and thus a lyric. Rhyme score (r) analyses various rhyming patterns and rhyming properties mentioned in the previous section determine a score for a lyric. Meaning score (m) is the challenge. We do not have any formal method to analyse if a given sentence is meaningful. If meaning can be a property that can be achieved through associations of words in a sentence and connection between sentences, then domain WordNets can be used to determine a meaning score for a lyric.

Conclusion and Future Work

The objective of this chapter is to present the LaaLaLaa framework for lyric analysis and generation. Very few parts of the LaaLaLaa framework have been implemented. The word generator has been implemented in parts and a very small WordNet corresponding to nature is used for testing. A basic statistics and pattern miner modules have been implemented. Developing multi domain WordNets and implementing the meaning score will be a challenging task. Improving the speed of generation by building a special index based on meter length of words will be part of our future work.

Acknowledgements

We would like to thank Dr. T. V. Geetha and Dr. Ranjani Parthasarathi for providing valuable inputs to this chapter. We also would like to acknowledge the contributions of Gayathri Lakshman, Prathyusha Senthil Kumar towards initial implementations of the LaaLaLaa framework.

REFERENCES

1. Allwright, J., *The abcMIDI Project 2002*, http://abc.sourceforge.net/abcMIDI/.
2. Anandan, R. Parthasarathi, and Geetha, *Morphological Analyser for Tamil*. ICON 2002, 2002.
3. Diaz-Agudo, B., P. Gervas, and P.A. Gonzalez-Calero. *Poetry Generation in COLIBRI*. in ECCBR 2002. 2002.
4. Gervas., P. Wasp: *Evaluation of Different Strategies for the Automatic Generation of Spanish Verse*. in Proceedings of the AISB00 Symposium on Creative & Cultural Aspects and Applications of AI & Cognitive Science. 2000. Birmingham, UK: Wiggins, G. (Ed.).
5. Gervas., P., *An Expert System for the Composition of Formal Spanish Poetry*. Journal of Knowledge-Based Systems, 2001. 14.
6. Gervas., P. *Exploring Quantitative Evaluations of the Creativity of Automatic Poets*. in 15th European Conference on Artificial Intelligence. 2002.
7. Goncalo, H.R., et al. *TraLaLyrics: An Approach to Generate Text-based on Rhythm*. in Fourth International Joint Workshop on Computational Creativity, IJWCC'07. 2007. London.
8. Gonzato., G., *The abc Plus Project*. 2003, http://abcplus.sourceforge.net.
9. Levy, R.P. *A Computational Model of Poetic Creativity with Neural Network as Measure of Adaptive Fitness*. in ICCBR- 01 Workshop on Creative Systems. 2001.
10. Manurung, H.M., *An Evolutionary Approach to Poetry Generation*. 2004, University of Edinburg.
11. Manurung, H.M., G. Ritchie, and H. Thompson. *A Flexible Integrated Architecture for Generating Poetic Texts*. In Fourth Symposium on Natural Language Processing. 2000. Chiang Mai.
12. Ramakrishnan, A., S. Kuppan, and S.L. Devi. *Automatic Generation of Tamil Lyrics for Melodies*. In NAACL HLT Workshop on Computational Approaches to Linguistic Creativity. 2009. Colorado.

23

Language Independent Emotion Recognition System for Web Articles Using NLP Techniques

—D. Mahendran
—S. Gunasundari
—Prof. B. Rajalakshmi

ABSTRACT

In recent years, suicide of college students has been a universal phenomenon in the world. And the phenomenon has become more and more severe because of the complex and drastic competitions. With the popularization of internet and the development of information processing technologies, a lot of people have established their own blog websites to write down their experiences and express their feelings at times. It will be very helpful if the computer can recognize the emotions expressed in blog pages automatically. And then it will be convenient for teachers or psychological consultants to monitor the affective information of college students and take measures for the depression prevention when necessary.

Owing to the advances in Affective Computing and Natural Language Processing, researches have begun to pay more attention to the emotion recognition in NLP all over the world. This leads to construct an Emotion Recognition System. It is based on the lexical contents of words and structural characteristics of blog articles. The emotion recognition system is composed of five modules: data collection, data processing, morphological analyzing, emotion tagging, and emotion computing. This algorithm independently works for web articles in any language. We checked articles in English and Tamil and the response of the system is good.

Keywords: *Suicide, Depression, Natural language processing, Emotion classification, Emotion recognition*

Introduction

In recent years, suicide of college students has been a universal phenomenon all over the world. Furthermore, the number of college students who suicide themselves has been increasing with amazing speed in a worldwide scope, around 100 million persons every year. In the year of 2003, World Health Organization (WHO) appointed September 10th as "World Suicide Prevention Day (WSPD)" to give a caution to the society. And it has adopted many suicide prevention programs and projects to avoid unnecessary death. At the same time, the problem of mental health among college students has raised great attention from more and more psychologists, educators and people in all the other Professions University or college. However, some college students are afraid to talk about their private experiences with other people face to face, and refuse to consult psychological consultants when they meet troubles. In late decades, the popularization of internet and the development of information processing technologies have greatly changed the communication ways of mankind. More and more people have established their own blog websites over the internet where they write down their experiences, put forward their opinions, and express their feelings at times. While some people feel embarrassed to confide their troubles to others face to face, they may feel free to express their emotions in blogs without any pressures.

It can be anticipated that in the near future, almost everyone in the world especially every college student will possess his or her own blog website. At that time, it will be very helpful if the computer can recognize the emotions expressed in blog articles automatically. In this case, an Emotion Recognition System is needed. If the system detects that some college student has been in a blue mood for continuous days (for example, for continuous three days), it is recommended that the teacher should pay more attention lately and have a talk with him or her regularly so that the depression can be treated in time. That's why this research has been taken on. In this chapter, we outline a new approach to recognize the author's emotion from his or her blog articles. Based on the approach, an Emotion Recognition System has been constructed. The results of our experiments on blogs prove the feasibility of the means.

System Structure

The emotion recognition system is composed of six modules: data collection, data preprocessing, dictionary creation, morphological analysis, emotion tagging, and emotion computing shown in figure 23.1. In the following we will introduce the flow of how the system works step by step. Firstly, the blog articles are collected from various authors with their emotion category mentioned. The collected articles are preprocessed to remove unwanted data from the blog articles. Then the preprocessed articles are subjected to morphological analysis. Here in morphological analysis the articles are split into sentences then the sentences are split into words for comparing with the emotion dictionary to find the emotion category. In emotion tagging, emotion category for each words and sentences are assigned.

Finally, with the emotion category of each sentence, the Emotion Computing module will compute the weight value of emotion categories of all sentences in a blog article according to the blog structure rules, and output the emotion result for the whole article.

Data Collection

Our emotion recognition system will work effectively on group of sentences. That's the reason we go for blog articles where people express their emotions in blogs without any pressures. In our country the blogs are not that much famous. This is the issue we faced on collecting the data. The personal blogs are popular in US, China, Japan which is not that much popular in our country. What we did is, we created a proxy to access the US websites for English blogs. But in Tamil, we got only few web articles.

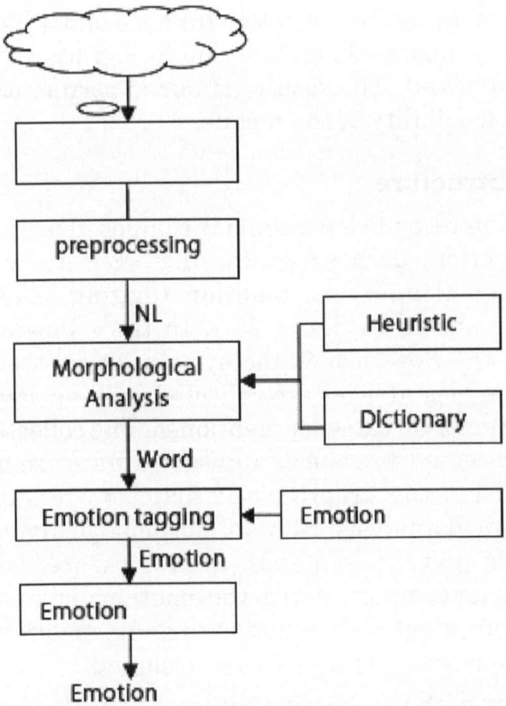

Fig. 23.1 : Framework for the emotion recognition system

Around 300 English blog articles were collected from the internet among various authors.

Data Preprocessing

The collected blog articles contain images, videos etc. Raw data cannot be used directly in our emotion recognition system. So, that the data has to be preprocessed. Here in data preprocessing the unwanted elements are removed from the articles like HTML tags, images, videos and other multimedia files are removed. HTML Parser is used for data preprocessing. The HTML Parser module analyzes the blog webpage that has been downloaded, and extracts each blog article in the webpage. Then it divides the blog article into paragraphs and sentences which are stored for further processing. Delimiters used for separating the sentences are (dot),? (question mark) and !(exclamatory mark). Other special characters like -, @,#,$ etc are removed from the articles. And for Tamil articles, the format is changed to Unicode for easier implementation.

Morphological Analysis

Morphology is the identification, analysis and description of the structure of words (words as units in the lexicon are the subject matter of lexicology). While words are generally accepted as being the smallest units of syntax, it is clear that in most languages, words can be related to other words by rules. Here in our system we have created the own morphological analyzer. It contains Heuristic rules, English and Tamil dictionaries (noun dictionary, verb dictionary, adverb dictionary). User interface of one of the dictionary is shown in figure 23.2. Binary search tree algorithm is a node based binary tree data structure which we have used in these dictionaries. Therefore the searching efficiency will be more. The heuristic rules are rules to extract the root words from the sentence. For example: The word 'happily' is an adverb.

Root word for 'happily' is 'happy'. Likewise 'anju' is a root word for Tamil word 'anjinen' for each natural language sentence, the Morphological analyzing module will analyze the lexical characteristics of the sentence and extract words from it based on the rule database according to analyzer rules. The words are used for further processing. Morphological analysis part has been made of automatic.

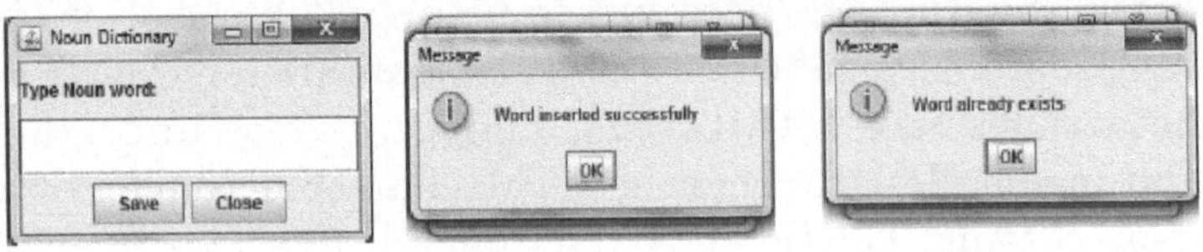

Fig. 23.2 : User interface of the Noun dictionary

Emotion Dictionary

Emotion dictionary is constructed which is to be used in emotion tagging module. In emotion dictionary, the data structure, Binary search tree algorithm is used to improve the searching efficiency. Emotion dictionary is made as semi-automatic. User interface of the emotion dictionary is shown in figure 23.3. Here two separate emotion dictionaries are used for English and Tamil languages. Numerous words have been inserted in the emotion dictionary with their appropriate category. It contains three fields, word, category and weightage. The weightage field stores the weight values for each word. Weight values of each word play a vital role in emotion recognition system. Emotion category is found out based on weight values.

In the past, emotion has been simply divided into two categories 'pleasure' and 'displeasure' which are too ambiguous to assess rich emotions of human. Ekman has defined 7 universal affective categories based on unique facial expressions which seem still less while applied into a practical system. In contemporary Chinese, 39 emotional categories are specified for vocabulary, nevertheless part of which is seldom used in daily communications.

In our Emotion Recognition System, we classified emotion based on the affective categories defined by Ekman plus some important categories found in blogs with high frequency of use. They are totally 26 categories: happy, sad, fearful, disgusted, angry, surprised, love, expectant, nervous, regretful, praiseful, shy, respectful, proud, impatient, doubtful, hateful, grievance, critical, depressed, exited, thankful, annoyed, scornful, haughty, envious. When there is no emotion expressed in a blog, we named the mental state as 'neutral'. Some examples of the emotional vocabularies for Tamil are listed in Table 23.1.

Table 23.1 : Emotion vocabularies for Tamil

Emotion category	Happy	Angry	Sad
vocabulary	Santhosham Subam Sugam	Sinam Veruppu Padhatram	Thukkam Thuyaram Varutham ....

Emotion Tagging

In morphological analysis the article is split into sentences and words. Those extracted words are passed to emotion tagging module. The words are compared with the emotion dictionary. If the corresponding word is present in the emotion dictionary then the weight values and emotion category is assigned to that word.

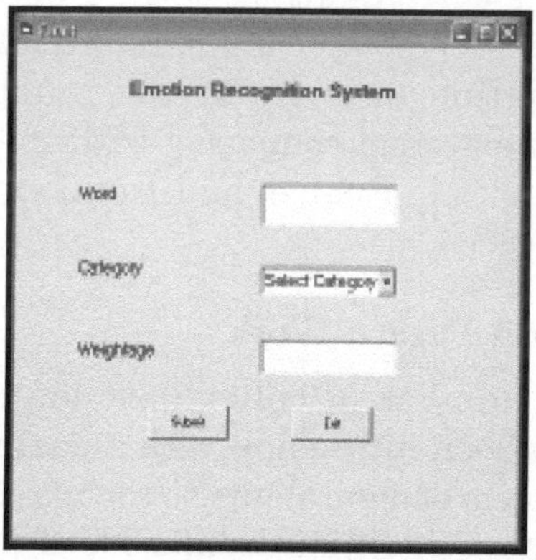

Fig. 23.3 : User interface of the emotion dictionary

Emotion Computing

Finally, with the emotion category of each sentence, the Emotion Computing module will compute the weight value of emotion categories of all sentences in a blog article according to the blog structure rules, and output the emotion result for the whole article. Let us suppose that there are j (j=1, 2, 3,....m) sentences in an article. For each sentence j, there is a emotion weight value Wj assigned. Ea is one of the 26 emotion categories (a=1,2,...26). Ea with maximum sum of all the corresponding Wj is the emotion of the whole article.

Experimental Results

Emotion recognition system is implemented in Java language. And we have attained the expected results. It is still an issue for the evaluation. By now there is not a good evaluation method generally accepted. Since different people may have different opinions even on the same text, it is common for them to give different evaluations of emotion manually. In our experiments, we carried close test based on the manual evaluation of emotions as a standard set which is judged by evaluators in advance.

Close Test

The close test is carried out on several blog articles. Our algorithm of emotion computing is realized in our system. And the evaluation is to count the number of correct prediction by the system compared with the standard set. We checked articles in English and Tamil and the response of the system is good.

Conclusion and Future Work

Recently, the number of college students who suicide themselves has been increasing with amazing speed in the world. The problem of mental health among college students has raised greater attention from a lot of people in many professions. With the popularization of internet and the development of information processing technologies, more and more people have established their own blog websites. It will be convenient for teachers or psychological consultants to monitor the affective information expressed in blog articles in order to prevent the depression of students. The advances in Affective Computing and Natural Language Processing enable the emotion recognition from blog articles automatically.

In this chapter, we have outlined the approach to develop an Emotion Recognition System. Firstly we decided the classification of emotions, and introduced the model of the System. Based on the lexical contents of words and structural characteristics of web articles, a method have been proposed for emotion computing. The experiments for testing have been carried out. The approach was proved to be feasible and pointed out the future's direction of the research. We find that some parts need to be improved in the future: The first task to improve the emotion dictionary by expanding the vocabularies and arranging them better, for it plays a very important role in the emotion sensing. Since different people have different styles in writing blog articles, in the future we will choose more web articles of different authors for the algorithm analysis and system test, which are supposed to achieve a better performance. Currently we are developing a system to find emotions from Hindi language blogs. We are in research of developing a language independent emotion recognition system for all languages. That is, identifying an emotion from all language blog articles by the help of Unicode.

REFERENCES

1. P. W. Picard, E. Vyzas, J. Healey, "*Toward Machine Emotional Intelligence*", IEEE Transactions on Pattern Analysis and Machine Intelligence, Vol. 23, No.10, pp. 1175-1191, October 2001.
2. P. Ekman, W. V. Friesen, P. Elsworth, "*Emotion in the Human Face*", Cambridge University Press, London, 1982.

3. X. Y. Xu, J. H. Tao, "*Emotion Dividing in Chinese Emotion System*", the 1st Chinese Conference on Affective Computing and Intelligent Interaction (ACII'03), pp. 199-205, Beijing, China, December, 2003.
4. K. Matsumoto, J. Minato, F. J. Ren, S. Kuroiwaÿ "*Estimating Human Emotions Using Wording and Sentence Patterns*", Proceedings of the 2005 IEEE International Conference on Information Acquisition, pp. 421-426, 2005.
5. D. Kulic, E. A Croft, "*Affective State Estimation for Human-robot Interaction*", IEEE Transactions on Robotics 23 (5), pp. 991-1000, Oct. 2007.
6. Xiaoxi Huang, Yun Yang, Changle Zhou, "*Emotional Metaphors for Emotion Recognition in Chinese Text*", Springer Berlin / Heidelberg Publication on Affective Speech Processing, pp. 319-325, November 15, 2005.
7. R. Cowie, E. Douglas-Cowie, N. Tsapatsoulis, G. Votsis, S. Kollias, W. Fellenz, J.G. Taylor, "*Emotion Recognition in Human-computer Interaction*", IEEE Transactions on Signal Processing Magazine, Vol. 18, No.1, pp. 32-80, January 2001.
8. Y. Zhang, Z. M. Li, F. J. Ren, S. Kuroiwa, "*Semi-automatic Emotion Recognition from Textual Input Based on the Constructed Emotion Thesaurus*", Proceeding of NLP-KE'05, pp. 571-576, November 2005.
9. Ye Wu, F. Ren, "*Emotion Recognition Based on Negative Words and Pattern Matching for Chinese Negative Sentences*", Proceeding of NLP-KE'08, pp. 1-5, October 2008.
10. H. Li, N. Pang, S. Guo, H. Wang, "*Research on Textual Emotion Recognition Incorporating Personality Factor*", Proceeding of ROBIO'07, pp. 2222-2227, December 2007.
11. http://www.tamilcafe.net/

24

An Integrated Intelligent Framework for Automatic Story Generation in Tamil

—G.V. Uma

ABSTRACT

Story is a description of a chain of events told or written in prose or verse. It is an interesting way to transfer knowledge from one person to other in the form of narrated sequence of events. The sequence of events is arranged in a chronological order to convey the message to other. An intelligent framework is developed using ontology to benefit the system in order to generate the story automatically and to reason the system generated-stories based on their conceptual consistency and validity. Ontology has the significant role in constructing semantic stories by the system. Ontology is a formal explicit shared conceptualization, which contains domain knowledge for the story construction. This research work developed a framework for automatic story generation in Tamil.

Introduction

Everyone in the world have their own interest to read the stories and like them very much. Stories are naturally has their own way of attraction from children to old age people. Children learn their moral and social obligations in the form of stories narrated to them by their guardians and peers[1]. The basic characteristics of human beings can be explained through stories to the youngsters to inspire them.

Hence, they play a vital role in everyone's life and their traits can be shaped well, based on the characters in the story. For example, Mahatma Gandhiji was influenced by the story "Harichandra" for speaking the truth in any kind of difficulties, and the 'shravana story' for obedience to his parents. People can gather a lot of information from the story based on their perceptions. The ASG system tries to make the computer and Artificial author' to construct new stories dynamically. The story is a natural verbal description of objects / human beings, their attributes, relationships, beliefs, behaviours, motivations and interaction. It is a message that tells the particulars of an act, and an occurrence or course of events are presented in the form of writing. It can also be described as follows:

- It is a description of the sequence of events
- It is a piece of fiction that narrates a chain of related events
- It focuses on only one incident, has a single plot, a single setting, a limited small number of characters, and covers a short period of time.

The automatic story generation system helps to generate a variety of new stories dynamically as per the reader's interest. The user has the choice to select any characters, locations, settings for generating a story. The theme may be conceived either automatically or by the user; similarly, existing stories can be revised to remake new ones. Any kind of story can be restructured and reasoned based on the author's requirement and specification. Ontology provides full support for story generation by preserving the concepts, attributes and the relations among them, which help for semantic reasoning. The language generator helps to generate suitable sentences with beautiful words for the construction of new stories.

This story generation framework enables the user, to act as reader as well as the author of the story. They can generate stories based on their wish and with necessary ingredients like characters, settings, location, food, etc. A simple story is started with initial situation and which has an active element to precede the story interestingly and finally comes to final situation. The generated stories are helpful for kids to know about the world knowledge. Story generation framework comprises of three levels of computation such as theme conception, story generation and semantic reasoning. Ontology plays a major role in each of these three phases. Ontology is a formal explicit specification of shared conceptualization[2]. It can be expressed as the basic terms and relations comprising the vocabulary of a topic area as well as the rules for combining terms and relations to define extensions to the vocabulary for a specific domain. The ontology is constructed based on the components of story domain. It involves characters, location settings like forest, palace, home and etc.

The ontology posses the events and the order of events/ functions /activities leads the story generation system. Even though constructed ontology is domain specific, it can be updated, modified, reengineered, reused for other purposes also. The main reasons[3] for using ontology for story generation system is

- To share common understanding of the structure of information among people or Software agents
- To enable reuse of domain knowledge
- To make domain assumptions explicit

- To separate domain knowledge from the operational knowledge
- To analyze domain knowledge

The structure of the chapter organized as follows: Section 2 discusses the related work and Section 3 provides the framework for automatic story generation. Section 4 devotes in the role of ontology in automatic story generation. Section 5 focuses on the role of ontology in story generation and reasoning. Section 6 discusses the conclusion and future works.

Related works

There are different types of story generators available for the purpose of automatic story generation and their evolution is described below. Propp[4] discussed the story generation as; a tale is a whole that may be composed of thirty-one moves. A move is a type of development proceeding from villainy or a lack, through intermediary functions to marriage, or to other functions employed as a denouement (ending). One tale may be composed of several moves that are related between them. One move may directly follow another, but they may also interweave; a development, which has begun pauses and a new move, is inserted. Bailey[5] described an approach towards automatic story generation based on the twin assumptions that it is possible for the generation of a story to be driven by modeling of the responses to the story of an imagined target reader, and that doing so allows the essence of what makes a story work (its 'storiness') to be encapsulated in a simple and general way.

Charles, F *et al*[6], presented results from a first version of a fully implemented storytelling prototype, which illustrates the generation of variants of a generic storyline. These variants result from the interaction of autonomous characters with one another, with environment resources or from user intervention.

Dimitrios N. Konstantinou *et al*[7] discussed the story generation model HOMER. It receives natural language input in the form of a sentence or an icon corresponding to a scene from a story and it generates a text-only narrative apart from a story line and it includes a plot, characters, settings, the user's stylistic preferences and also their point-of-view.

Riedl *et al*[8] had provided planning algorithm for story generation. The story planners are limited by the fact that they can only operate on the story world provided, which impacts the ability of the planner to find a solution story plan and the quality and structure of the story plan if one is found, but which lacks semantics.

George miller[9] provided a wonderful environment to have the collection of words and their synonyms and they are put together to form a lexical database. It helps to retrieve the meaning for any kind of word in any language. This framework helps to generate stories automatically and to overcome the semantic lacking of stories which can be resolved by reasoning the stories in a systematic and efficient way using the efficiencies of ontology.

Framework Automatic Story Generation

This framework for automatic story generation shown in Figure 24.1 and it helps to provide a systematic approach to generate and analyze stories both syntactically and systematically. This framework mainly divided into five phases such as Theme conception, Sentence generator, Parser, Syntactic checker and Semantic checker.

Theme Conception

There are two main approaches for conceiving theme such as:

- Static conception - is a predefined order of events to describe the flow of a story.
- Dynamic conception - refers to the order of events which are selected and organized during the phase of story generation.

Set of built-in themes are available in the theme repository; the user can select the necessary theme for the story based on the characters involved. Also, a new theme can be conceived using events from the repository.

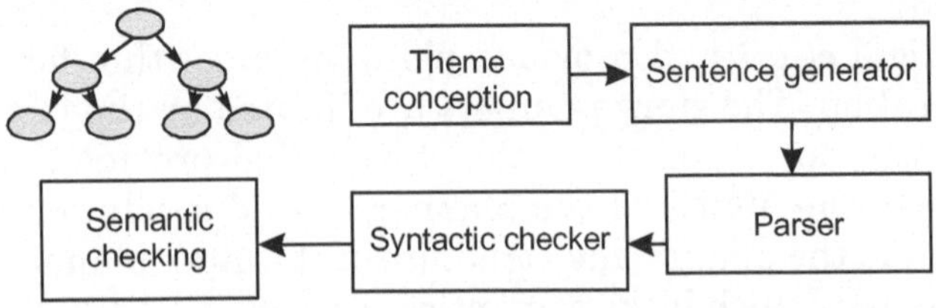

Fig. 24.1 : Framework for automatic story generation

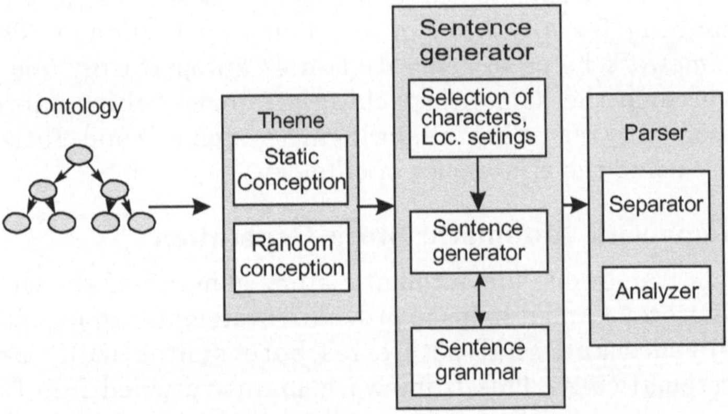

Fig. 24.2 : Detailed Framework for Sentence Generator

Figure 24.2 depicts the detailed framework for generating simple sentences. The inputs of the Sentence generator are sentence type, sentence grammar and necessary terminal values. Using the sentence type, the corresponding sentence grammars and their production rules are retrieved from ontology. The necessary terminal values are checked with given production rules. There is no standard sentence structure for Tamil. The following grammar rules were framed and based on the rule sentence structures is obtained[11,12].

1. NC —> adj N / N / ADJC N / NNC
2. VC —> adv V/ adv rpl / ADVC V / vpl / V
3. NNC —> S con
4. ADJC —> NC VC
5. ADVC —> (NC)* vpl
6. S —> (NC)* (VC)

Fig. 24.3 : Sample grammar for sentence generation

Figure 24.3 depicts the sample grammar for sentence generation in Tamil which is used for stories. By applying if then—rules, suffixes are updated with root words. Parser contains the two phases namely separator and analyzer. Separator helps to separate the story into story segments called sentences. The separation of sentences helps to check the sentences by its form of sentence structure and the meaning of the story. Analyzer used to identify the noun, verb, settings, location and etc from the story which helps in semantic validation.

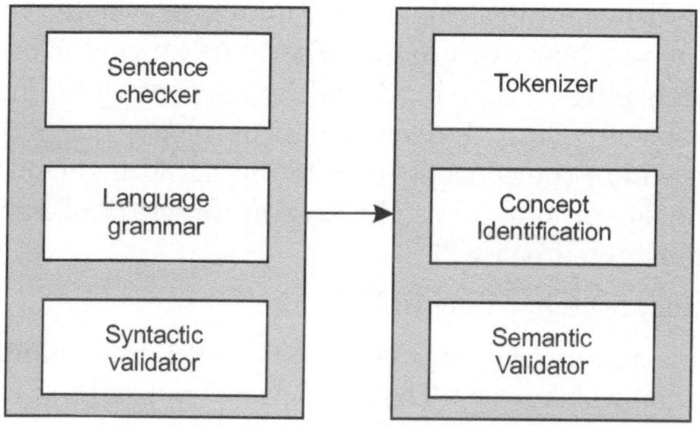

Fig. 24.4 : Detailed Framework for Semantic Reasoner

Figure 24.2 depicts the detailed description about the semantic reasoner which divides into two such as syntactic validation framework and semantic validation framework. Syntactic validation framework helps to check the sentence structure of the sentences based on the sentence grammar whereas semantic checker detects the meaning of sentences whether it is valid or invalid.

Role of Ontology in ASG

Nowadays ontologies have significant role in information processing. They are important for story generation, which holds the various concepts that are relevant to the story domain. Initially, the ontology is built with minimal knowledge, in later stages; ontology can be extended whenever new concepts are introduced. One of the primary purposes of constructing ontology is to provide a standard, unambiguous representation of a particular domain of knowledge.

OWL has the language expressive representative formalism and reasoning power. Because OWL was derived from DAML+OIL, it can take advantage of the existing reasoning algorithms in Description Logics (DL). The semantic of OWL allows us to define a ranking function that distinguishes multiple degrees of matching. There are three types of matches: exact match where the concept to be found is found, plug-in match where the concept to be found is more specific than the concept in ontology, and subsume match where the concept to be found is more general than the concept in ontology. The scoring function of matching degree is given below[10]:

Exact Match > Plug in Match > Subsume Match

This matching degree helps to identify the semanticness of the generated story. The basic properties of the Lion is

Living being → animals → wild → Lion (king, legs, anger, roar, kill

→ Domestic → Rat (small, legs, frightens)

→ Bird → crow (black, legs, fly)

If the generated sentence states that '

action cannot be performed by animal. So the basic properties of Lion are preserved. It helps to improve the quality of the story. Consider another sentence, 'எலி சிங்கத்தை கொன்றது.' in this sentence, the domestic animal 'mouse' killed the wild animal 'Lion'. In reality, it is not possible and then the system detects it, based on the strength of the animals which are categorized in ontology.

The semantic reasoner detects and corrects the sentence as, So, எலியை சிஙகம கொனறது. the basic properties of Lion and rat are preserved. The sample story generated by the system is given in the Figure 24.5.

சிங்கம் காட்டில் தூங்கியது.
சிங்கத்தை எலி எழுப்பியது.
சிங்கம் கோபம் கொண்டது.
எலியை சிங்கம் கொன்றது.

Fig. 24.5 : Sample story generated by the system

Results

The above framework has been implemented in Java and uses the Java JDBC to connect to MySQL server and retrieve the relevant values. GUI is developed using Java Swing. The necessary basic concepts and their attributes are retrieved for semantic checking. The framework has been built and tested for various stories. The system parses the sentence to the framework for the reasoning purpose. Charles[6] proposed a set of factors that are considered to check the quality of the story. These factors are utilized to check the quality of stories by reasoning. Based on the above factors, the generated stories are given to a group of people to give their opinions about the generated stories with following scaling factors and with above said features. Excellent - 5; V.Good - 4; Good -3; Fair -2; needs improvement-1;

Table 24.1 : Factors for Assessment of Story

Sl.No.	Factor	Describes
1.	Overall	How is the story as an archetypal fairy tale?
2.	Style	Did the author use an appropriate writing style?
3.	Grammaticality	How would you rate the syntactic quality?
4.	Flow	Did the sentences flow from one to the next?
5.	Diction	How appropriate were the author's word choices?
6.	Readability	How hard was it to read the prose?
7	Logicality	Did the story seem out of order?
8.	Believability	Did the story's characters behave as you would expect?

Table 24.2 : Results of Story Assessment

Sl.No.	Parameters	Before reasoning (max=5)	After reasoning (max=5)	Improve-ment
1.	Overall	4.3	4.7	1.09
2.	Style	4.0	4.5	1.13
3.	Grammaticality	4.1	4.8	1.17
4.	Flow	4.2	4.5	1.07
5.	Diction	2.8	3.4	1.21
6.	Readibility	3.7	4.0	1.08
7.	Logicality	3.6	4.1	1.14
8.	Believability	4.4	4.7	1.07
	Average	3.885	4.33	1.12

The Table 24.1 shows the assessment value of story. The Table 24.2 depicts the calculated values for the stories before reasoning and after reasoning. After reasoning, the quality of the story is improved on an average of 22.4 percentage better than the before reasoning. The believability factor and overall content have very good feedback among other factors. The other factors like style of the story, grammar content in the story, flow of the story are the good factors in the next level and also the other good factors in the next level are diction, readability, and legibility. Figure 6 depicts results of story assessment of stories.

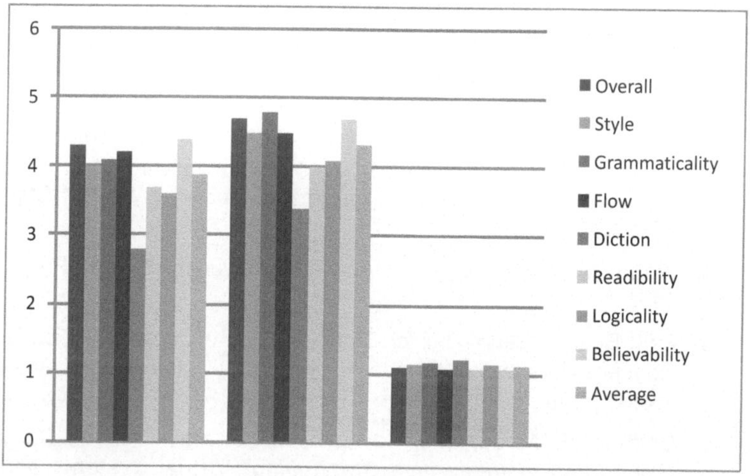

Fig. 24.6 : Results of Story Assessment

Conclusion

Thus the framework helps to generate a simple short story in Tamil with simple sentences and semantic reasoning. It also proves that the framework is efficient, by comparing the results of the generated stories with before and after reasoning. In future, the project work can be extended to generate medium size stories, novels and picture based stories. Also, ontology can be extended with more number of concepts, attributes and their relation. Similarly, Reasoning can be extended to complex type sentences too.

REFERENCES

1. Bilasco, I.M., Gensel, J., Villanova-Oliver, M.: *STAMP: A Model for Generating Adaptable Multimedia Presentations*. Int. J. Multimedia Tools and Applications, Vol 25 (3) (2005) 361-375.
2. Thomas R. Gruber Toward Principles for the Design of Ontologies Used for Knowledge Sharing. Originally in N. Guarino and R. Poli, (Eds.), International Workshop on Formal Ontology, Padova, Italy. Revised August 1993. Published in International Journal of Human-Computer Studies, Volume 43 , Issue 5-6 Nov./Dec. 1995, pp. 907-928, Special Issue on the Role of Formal Ontology in the Information Technology
3. Natalya F. Noy and Deborah L. McGuinness. "*Ontology Development 101: A Guide to Creating Your First Ontology*". Stanford Knowledge Systems Laboratory Technical Report KSL-01-05 and Stanford Medical Informatics Technical Report SMI-2001-0880, March 2001
4. Propp. V "*Morphology of the Folktale*", University of Texas Press, 1968.
5. Paul Bailey, "*Searching for Storiness: Story Generation from a Reader's Perspective*" Symposium on Narrative Intelligence, AAAI Press, 1999.
6. Charles, F.; Mead, S.J.; Cavazza, M. "*Character-driven Story Generation in Interactive Storytelling*" Virtual Systems and Multimedia. Proceedings. Seventh International Conference on Virtual Systems and Multimedia. 25-27 pp no: 609-615, Oct. 2001
7. Dimitrios N. Konstantinou , Paul Mc Kevitt , "*HOMER: An Intelligent Multi-modal Story Generation System*" Research plan. Faculty of Informatics, University of Ulster, Magee, Londonderry, 2002.
8. Riedl, M. and Young, RM, "*Open-world Planning for Story Generation*" Proceedings of the 19th International Joint Conference on Artificial Intelligence. California USA 2004.
9. George Miller , "*WordNet. An Electronic Lexical Database*". Edited by Christiane Fellbaum, with a preface by . Cambridge, MA: MIT Press; 1998. p 422

10. Ong Siew Kin, Tang Enya Kong, "*Conceptual Modelling and Reasoning using Ontology* "National Computer Science Postgraduate Colloquium 2005 (NaCSPC'05).

11. Saravanan, K., Ranjani Parthasarathi, Geetha.T.V., "*Syantactic Parser for Tamil*", Tamil internet, 2003.

12. T. Mala , T.V. Geetha, '*An Intelligent System for Picture-based Tamil Sentences*' International forum for information technology in Tamil and Insititute of Indology and Tamil Studies, Germany, 2009.

25

Evaluation of Tamil Descriptive Passages Using Concept Maps

—Mahalakshmi G.S
—Sendhilkumar S
—Shankar B

ABSTRACT

e-Learning has changed the way of education. With the wide-spread applications of e-Learning technologies to education at all levels, we need to focus on learner-centric knowledge management in order to complement the conventional learning system. This chapter examines the pioneering application of concept mapping as a follow-up study strategy for learning from text. With the great advancement in language processing tools in Tamil, we have proposed a novel mechanism which will evaluate Tamil descriptive answer passages based on the pre-stated prose. The idea is achieved by generating concept maps equally from prose and descriptive answer passages, and thereby evaluating the contents via generation of concept maps.

Introduction

With the widespread applications of information technology to education at all levels, we need to focus on learner-centric knowledge management in order to complement the conventional learning system. To enhance self-learning and assessment especially in learning subjects that require high knowledge retention, application of concept maps to promote education has been a proven success worldwide.

Academic Significance

The first difficulty someone who attempts to comprehend a text faces is to understand what it is all about. That is, to grasp the global sense of the communication, understand its elements and the relationships among them. In this context, the student may understand some of the concepts involved in the definition. These concepts are linked by words forming whole sentences that seem to make sense. However, trying to understand the overall conceptual structure is more difficult. It is probably easier for many students to grasp a whole sense of the concept frame of reference when faced with a graph like the structure. This is due to the powerful visual effect that a graph has in order to facilitate understanding of a concept or a conceptual structure.

Contribution to Knowledge

Concept Maps help to improve understanding of a given subject and facilitate building student's own knowledge, as long as the student has the opportunity to use, criticize, analyze, question or improve expert's maps or Concept Maps generated by his own peers.

The implementation of concept maps in the classroom allows both the teacher and the student discovering and describing meaningful relations among the concepts object matter of the study, making it possible to create connections between them and the context in which activities are developed. The concept map helps the learners to have a better overview of the course and what aspect he/she should pay attention. Concept maps constructed are very useful for teachers as an evidence of the way as each one of the parties involved in the process assumes his/her own learning. From their follow-up and analysis, experiences can be designed to help their students overcome weaknesses or to reinforce strengths acquired in learning process.

This motivated us to apply technological advancement and research in contributing better methodologies for education with a special focus on students whose medium of instruction is any regional language (for our study: Tamil) other than English. Although concept maps have been proven to be a successful resource for grade improvement in abroad, their use is little explored in Indian education. The detailed literature analysis conducted for the same revealed the fact that almost no work reported the development and use of concept maps to promote education in regional language—Tamil. In this context this chapter concentrates on development of concept maps that eliminates the need for memorization and helps the students with active participation, to learn the subjects in their respective regional languages. With the objective of applying ICT in Regional Language Education, in this chapter we express the methodology of developing concept maps for various subjects at the higher secondary/pre-collegiate level.

Related Work

As it is known, an essential aspect in the learning process (either electronic or traditional) is the possibilities to evaluate the students. It is very important both for professor and student to test the understanding degree of the course. One of the best possibilities is to ask questions from the studied course. It is tested this way the degree of understanding of each studied material and the integration of new knowledge with the previous ones (that should already be known). These facts will have as a result an in-depth understanding of the learning materials. Here we discuss the study and research done in connection with the proposed topic, by various experts outside India.

Question Generation for Learning Evaluation

Taking into consideration the high number of learning material existing in electronic format, the importance of the testing and evaluation systems has increased. The authors [McGough *et. al.*, 2008] present an interesting solution to the problem of presenting students with dynamically generated browser-based exams with significant engineering mathematics content. Here, the main idea is to generate the questions automatically based on question templates which are created by training on many medical articles. Liana et al [Liana Stanescu *et. al.*, 2008] tried to design and implement a software instrument (Test Creator) that permits generation of questions based on electronic materials that students have. The solution implies teachers to have a series of tags and templates that they have to manage. These tags can be used to generate questions automatically.

Concept Maps Applied for Question Generation

Concept maps are a result of Novak and Gowin's (1984) research into human learning and knowledge construction. One of the powerful uses of concept maps is not only as a learning tool but also as an evaluation tool, thus encouraging students to use meaningful-mode learning patterns. Concept mapping may be used as a tool for understanding, collaborating, validating, and integrating curriculum content that is designed to develop specific competencies. Concept mapping, a tool originally developed to facilitate student learning by organizing key and supporting concepts into visual frameworks, can also facilitate communication among faculty and administrators about curricular structures, complex cognitive frameworks, and competency-based learning outcomes.

However, the only issue is that the learner must choose to learn meaningfully. The one condition over which the teacher or mentor has only indirect control is the motivation of students to choose to learn by attempting to incorporate new meanings into their prior knowledge, rather than simply memorizing concept definitions or propositional statements or computational procedures. The indirect control over this choice is primarily in instructional strategies used and the evaluation strategies used. Instructional strategies that emphasize relating new knowledge to the learner's existing knowledge foster meaningful learning. Evaluation strategies that encourage learners to relate ideas they possess with new ideas also encourage meaningful learning.

Concept Maps in e-Learning

Recent researches have demonstrated the importance of concept map and its versatile applications especially in e-Learning. Concept maps creation for emerging new domains such as e-Learning is even more challenging due to its ongoing development nature. Concept maps can provide a useful reference for researchers, who are new to the e-Leaning field, to study related issues, for teachers to design adaptive learning materials, and for learners to understand the whole picture of e-Learning domain knowledge.

Concept Map Mining

There is yet another approach [Villalon and Calvo, 2009] for automatic concept extraction, using grammatical parsers and Latent Semantic Analysis. Essays, as any other text, represent both the knowledge and the writing skills of its author; hence, an Automatic Concept Map from Essay (ACME) should reflect both. Therefore, the words for the concepts and relations must be extracted literally from the document, and the hierarchy of concepts must reflect the importance of the concepts relative to what was written in the particular document. However, the performance is related to the way concepts are chosen by humans. We believe that understanding this phenomenon and using it for the automatic selection of concepts could lead to big improvements.

Evaluation Mechanism

The proposed answer evaluation system creates concept-maps from the prose and the answer passages, that involves the extraction of concept-words from the passages by parsing the input text [Saravanan *et al*, 2004], creating a dependency model among the concept-words within the passage, visualization of concept-maps that has two levels viz., words level and the sentence pattern level that helps us to analyze what are the key concepts needed in a passage, Comparison of the concept-maps created and finally evaluation of the answer passages. The evaluation of the passage does not handle the content comparison part alone but also analyzes the finer aspects like the structuring of the passage, repetitions, duplications, and also the additional aspects used by the students like causation, summarization, expansion at instance, etc. These finer aspects have been inspired from 'nannool', a Tamil prose that presents the needed and irrelevant aspects of a prose.

For drawing light on the evaluation mechanisms followed, we choose a specific prose and answer and evaluate them. The total number of words in the prose above which was considered for the evaluation is 15. The comparison procedure followed is presented below.

Missing Concepts

Comparing the prose and answer we find that the third sentence in prose is completely missing in answer. These three words will subtract 3 from 15. The last sentence in answer is not present in prose that's an irrelevant concept and we don't add any marks for it.

Marks=15-4 = 11

(11/15)*100 = 73.33% (word_match)

Duplicates

In answer the first two sentences are one and the same. We detect this with the help of the relation table. There are 59 relations generated and only 28 matches. So this module score is (28/59) * 100 = 47.45% (pattern).

Repetition

Sentence one is repeated again, so we deduct one mark. Therefore one mark should be deducted from the total score.

Value Addition

The evaluation method, value addition is computed based on causation and summarization, expansion at instance, argument by example. Here, the answer passage has summarization. Therefore one mark is to the total marks.

Score

From the values calculated above, the final score can be determined. Here, the given answer passage was evaluated to obtain the score 60.39% ((73.33 + 47.45)/2 + 1 – 1). Below the answer evaluation system results for the same prose and answer is provided.

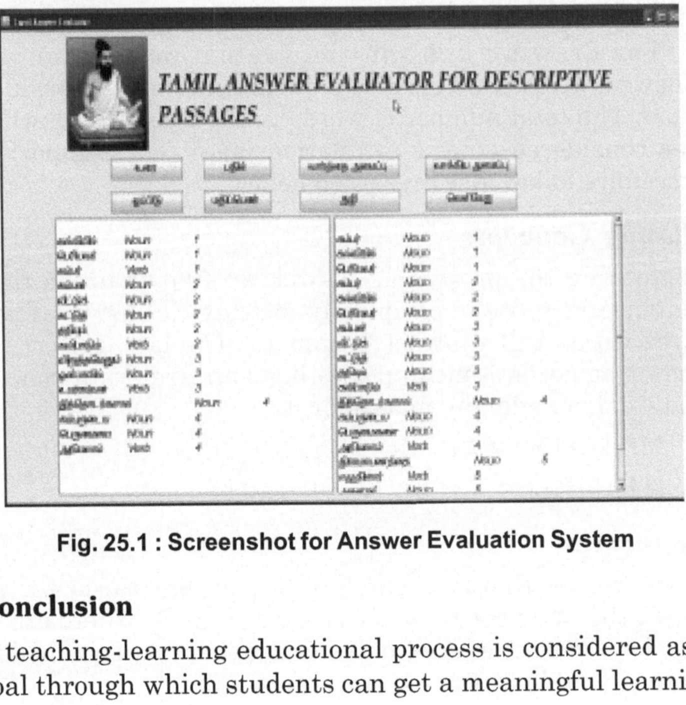

Fig. 25.1 : Screenshot for Answer Evaluation System

Conclusion

If teaching-learning educational process is considered as a goal through which students can get a meaningful learning of stated concepts, which extend and articulate their network of relations and can apply them in different contexts, it is necessary that teachers include tools to speed up act performance of agents involved in the construction of the new knowledge. In our case, applying a concept map tool in the classroom will allow students being themselves more motivated to carry out proposed activities and to participate in the construction of their own knowledge. The methodology of developing concept maps discussed in the paper shall be (*i*) Extended to impart concept map based learning in other regional languages; (*ii*) Applied to generate associated concept animations for enriching automated content development; (*iii*) Applied to automated answer evaluation thereby taking part in self-assessment activity of pre-collegiate examinations; (*iv*) Used to dynamically generate questions and further continue the answer evaluation process in an e-learning setting; and (*v*) Applied for automatic document summarization

REFERENCES

1. Jorge Villalon, and Rafael A. Calvo, "*Concept Extraction from Sstudent Essays, Towards Concept Map Mining*", Ninth IEEE International Conference on Advanced Learning Technologies, 2009. pp.221-225
2. Liana Stanescu, Cosmin Stoica Spahiu, Anca Ion, Andrei Spahiu, "*Question Generation for Learning Evaluation*", Proceedings of the International Multiconference on Computer Science and Information Technology, pp. 509-513, 2008 IEEE
3. McGough J., Mortensen J., Johnson J., Fadali S., "A Web-based Testing System with Dynamic Question Generation". LNCS 1611-3349, 2008, pp. 242-251.
4. Novak J. and Gowin, *Learning How to Learn*. New York and Cambridge, UK: Cambridge University Press, 1984.
5. R. Saravanan, Ranjani Parthasarathi and Geetha T.V., '*Vaanavil—Parser for Tamil*', Resource Center for Indian Languages – Tamil, Dept. of Computer Science and Engineering, Anna University Chennai, India, 2004.

26

A Machine Translation System for Converting Tamil Text-to-Sign Language

—D. Narashiman
—Dr. T. Mala

ABSTRACT

This scheme enhances a remarkable approach to decipher the given Tamil text into sign language. The system suggested here is cross modal. It gives a wider interaction of textual input and generates corresponding sign language output in one or a number of sign variants. The application receives Tamil text sentences as input and provides output in 3D animated sequence that can be visualized.

Keywords: *Sign language, 3D animation, machine translation.*

Introduction

Sign language is a universal language and signs are common features in all the countries around the world. This system has been developed for the deaf community to enhance their communicative ability. This system was developed in such a way that it accepts text as input through keyboard(tactile mode) and generates animated sign symbols as output (visual mode).The benefits of this system include: (*a*) maneuvered for many personal and real time confessions; (*b*) essential and vital tool for educative purpose to people who are interested in knowing the sign language; (*c*) The 3D animated output, endows the user to visualize the signs effectively for number of purpose such as news broadcasting and picture animation. This chapter talks about the interactive system which translates Tamil text to sign language by compiling of sign language video[5], mapping of tokens and sign symbols[10,11] and creating animated output[3,12]. The sections are arranged as follows: Section two presents the literature survey on sign language. Section three describe the system architecture in general and also explain various phase in generating sign language in detail. Section four gives the method for evaluation of the translation output. Last section deals with conclusion and future enhancement of the system.

Literature Survey

Sign language is represented by non gesture, gesture coding. Non-gesture features include hand movements alone whereas gesture features include hand, face, shoulders, head and facial expression combined with hand sequences. Since sign variants are comparatively fewer than Tamil words the system should be able to generate sign for that corresponding word instantly. Sign language is lexically backward, it has become inventible for a sign generator to exhibit some degree of creativity in assigning concept-to-sign correspondence. When converting the Tamil text into sign language the creative method like finger spelling is used. The sign language mainly deals with non-gesture and gesture features of the signer. In practice however it is highly impossible to separate the context from the given text. Instead we prefer the semantic or conceptual representation of the source text. Various works were carried out earlier to solve this problem. Former approaches for converting text sign language are:

Example-based Method

Morrisey and way investigate corpus-based methods for example-based sign language translation from English to sign language of the Netherlands. With the small corpus and no available lexicon, the system is robust for sentences already encountered in the training set but has problems with unseen combinations of corpus chunks as well as corpus parts that it is unable to align[7].

Theoretical Methods

This method deals with the theoretical issues arising during machine translation of written text to sign language for example a notation for sign which use the 3D space around the signer to form complex expression[3,4].

Rule-based Method

Safar and Marshall propose a decomposition of the translation process in two steps: initially they translate from written text into a semantic representation of the signs. Afterwards graphically oriented representation is done. Both the steps use rule-based techniques for a specific domain in British sign language[6].

Interlingua Method

An interlingua try to capture the generic fact-stating capacity of language using two different strategies: the first attempts to construct a universal grammar that generalize over the semantics nuances of many language, while the second is knowledge intensive allows for the incorporation of heterogeneous common sense into translation process[8].

Statistical Machine Translation Method

This method is used to automatically transfer the meaning of the source language sentences into a target sentence by applying the phrase-based statistical machine translation based on morpho-syntactical analysis[1,2].

System Architecture

The system architecture design is given in figure 26.1. The system mainly focuses on the construction of the direct knowledge repository and incremental knowledge repository. The finger spelling knowledge repository (F.S K.R), spatial knowledge repository and rule based knowledge repository comprise the incremental knowledge repository. System uses the knowledge repositories to translate given text to sign language. The pre-processor unit fed with parallel corpus. It converts the given input Tamil text and Sign videos into a suitable form for statistical analysis. The input text is divided into tokens using the white space as delimiter. The sign videos are also segmented. These tokens and corresponding signs are stored in a direct knowledge repository. The tokens for which signs are not available directly are generated and stored in incremental knowledge repository.

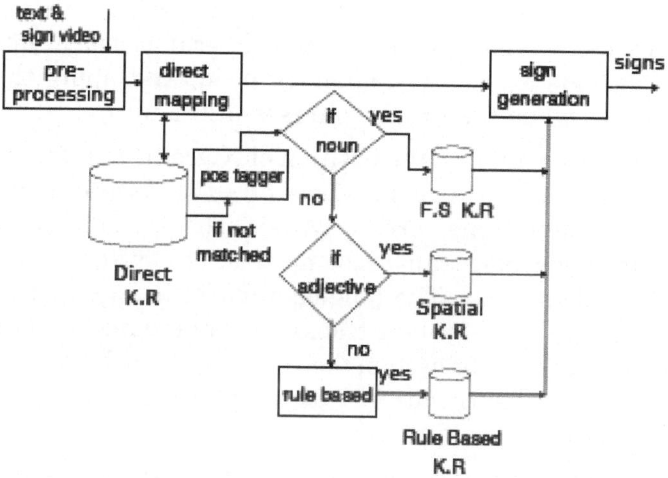

Fig. 26.1 : System Architecture

A. Creation of Direct Knowledge Repository

The creation of direct knowledge repository is shown in figure 26.2.

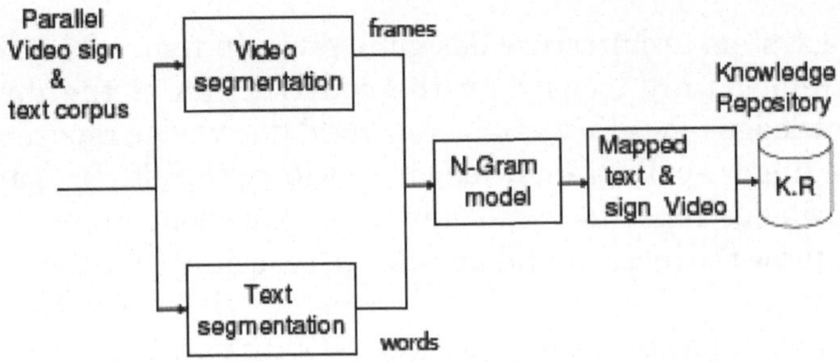

Fig. 26.2 : Creation of Direct knowledge Repository

Pre-processing is to convert the given input Tamil text and Sign videos into a suitable form. The text is processed by removing unimportant stop words, special characters and splits into words. Then the preprocessed words are stored in a table along with probability of occurrence using N-Gram methods. This is training the system. While training, statistical systems track common N-grams, learn which translations are most frequently used, and apply those meanings when finding the phrases in the future.

They also analyze the position of N-grams in relation to one another within sentences, as well as words grammatical forms, to determine correct syntax. The system uses the training to develop translation models. The system is fed by the parallel corpus. The language model is applied to the sign images. The system tracks bi-grams and builds the language model. The system then develops translation model from the parallel corpus and uses its training to translate new sentences.

The Direct Knowledge repository contains the index image in which segmented videos are indexed and stored in a database, alignment matrix is constructed in order to obtain the matching of word-to-sign coherence, and Language Model Probability. The language model is applied to the target language (sign language) for reordering and arrangement of the signs. N-Gram calculations are applied and probability of the sign occurring is calculated and stored in the table. Where probability of the output sign depends on the given text and probability of that sign generated for the given text.

A. Creation of Incremental Knowledge Repository

The word which does not inherit appropriate sign by using direct knowledge repository is exhibited using incremental knowledge repository. The incremental knowledge repository is created by finger spelling, spatial and rule based method as shown in the figure 26.3. The purpose of this to generate sign for the words not present in the direct knowledge base. The proper noun words, descriptive word and ambiguous words come under this category.

The parts of speech tagger is used to group the words according to proper noun, adjective, ambiguous and action words. Depending upon the classification the sign are generated from respective incremental knowledge repository. The word whose sign are not generated by direct knowledge repository are generated by incremental knowledge repository. The preprocessed word is tagged using the pos tagger which gives the information about the word whether proper noun, action and descriptive words according to the classification the process is carried out.

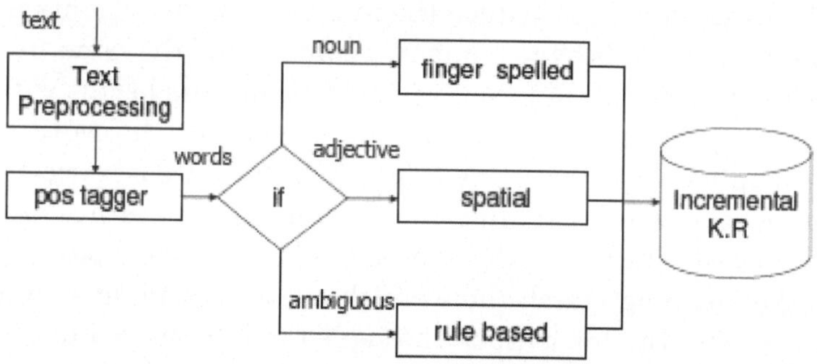

Fig. 26.3 : Creation of Incremental knowledge Repository

The proper noun words are represented using this knowledge repository. The process is shown in figure 26.4. This repository contains sign for individual alphabet. The word is tagged by POS tagger if the word is proper noun it is again rechecked using the word net dictionary if synonyms is available it is signed using direct knowledge repository otherwise the word is separated into individual characters and signed respectively. Eg: பெயர்சொல்- ê□õè£ñ□. The name is separated into signal characters and they are signed.

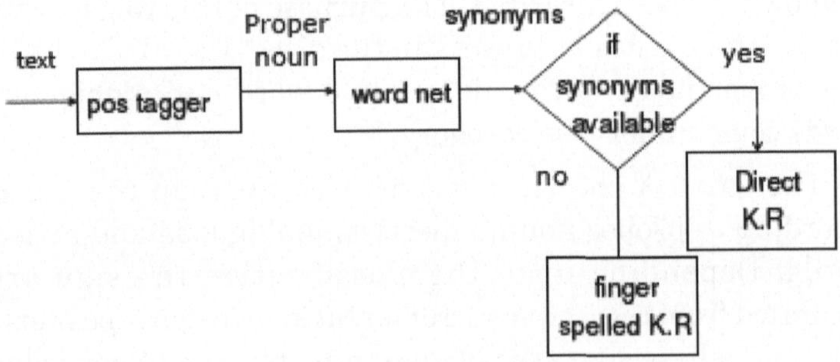

Fig. 26.4 : Finger Spelling method

Spatial method is used to represent the descriptive words. The method is shown in figure 26.5. Usually these words describe the place, nature, behavior etc. The main purpose of this module is to reduce the number of sign variants as the certain words have common meanings and the same sign is represented for different words. This process begins with the tagging of the word and check whether the word is descriptive (adjectives), the meaning for the word is retrieved using the word net dictionary then the meanings are compared with the words in the spatial knowledge repository if the meaning match the word then corresponding sign is generated. By this method the signs for different words are generated easily with minimum number of signs video in the database.

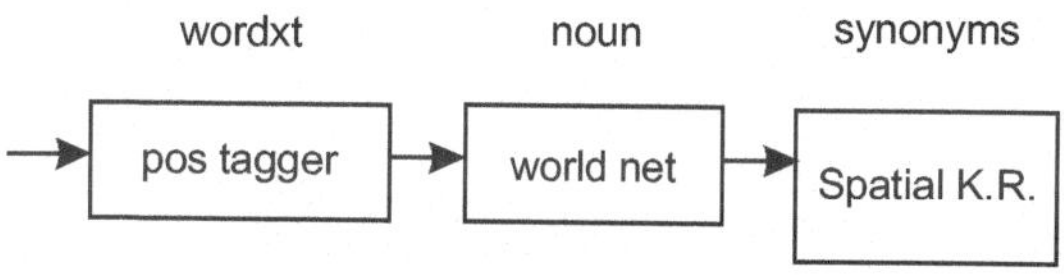

Fig. 26.5 : Spatial method

Rule based method is used represent the ambiguous word. The task of disambiguation is to determine which of the senses of an ambiguous word is invoked in a particular use of the word. A word is assumed to have a finite number of discrete senses often given by a dictionary and task of the forecast is to make a forced choice between these senses for the meaning of each usage of an ambiguous word based on the context of use. This procedure is termed as context based disambiguation. The word is tagged if the tag is ambiguous then the pervious word tag is considered depending on previous word the sign is generated. The alternative method is using n-gram model. An n-gram is a type of phrase within a document that has a set of n number of words. N-grams are the basic linguistic unit with which a statistical machine translation system works. The n-gram gives the maximum probability of word occurring together. This is used to check the word occurrence in the context and along with the other words in sequence. This also used to determine the word that are unable to decode correctly, by checking the context and word occurrence. From this the sign for ambiguous word are generated The rule based method is shown in the figure 26.6.

Finally signs are arranged in the logical sequences and the final output is generated. The final output is in the form of 3D animation. If sign for corresponding word not found in the direct knowledge repository then the word is tagged using pos tagger. According to the tag, if the word is proper noun then the signs are generated using finger spelling knowledge repository, if the word is an adjective then spatial knowledge repository is used and if the word are ambiguous the rule based knowledge repository is used.

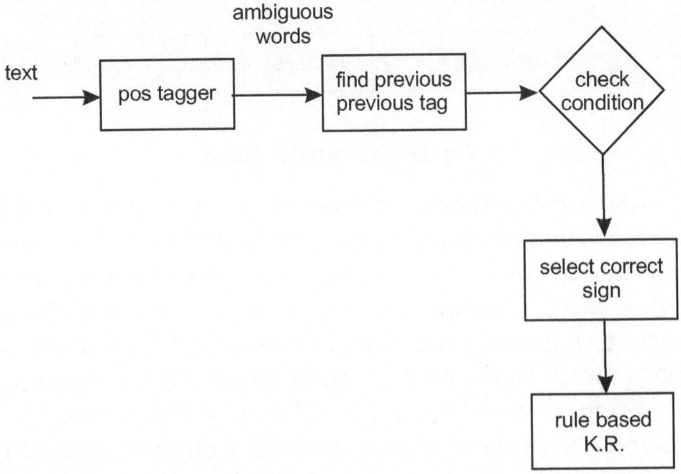

Fig. 26.6 : Rule based method

Evaluation Criteria

The output of the system is final as it should generate the correct sign for the given text. The generated output should be clear, understandable and correct. The hand and facial movements should clear and various actions are understandable. The correct matching of sign and the word should be done. The output of the system is validated using the confusion matrix. The confusion matrix is plotted by taking into consideration the actual generated sign and how it understood. The first quadrant represent the correct sign and understood correctly, second quadrant represent the correct sign but understood incorrectly, third quadrant represent incorrect sign generated but understood correctly and the last quadrant represent the incorrect sign generated and understood incorrectly.

The confusion matrix shown in the figure 26.7 about 50 words are given as input and output signs are checked, The value in the first quadrant 30 are the signs generated are correct and understood correctly. The value in the second quadrant is obtained when there is difference in retrieval of sign number from the database. The value in the third quadrant is obtained as there is difference in generating spatial sign. The fourth quadrant value is obtained when there is difference in retrieval of sign for the given word as the word is an ambiguous word.

actual \ understood	true	false
true	TP 30	FN 5
false	FP	TN

Fig. 26.7 : Confusion matrix

Conclusion

The system described here is very useful for the deaf community. The process starts by breaking the sentence into tokens, mapping the tokens with the sign symbols, generating the perfect symbol in accordance with the conditions and rearranging of symbols to generate the correct meaning of the sentence. The output is a real visualization of sign language and enables interactive application. The main challenge of the system is mapping the sign , generating the new sign if not available in the database and rearranging the symbols according to the meaning of the text checking the grammar of the sentence, adding to the database for future reference. As it is not the only way to generated sign symbols it can be always impoverished to the native speakers. The animation output is selected as it will be pleasing for the viewers. This is mainly designed as a non-human interpreter for sign language. Future development in this system is to increase the sign symbols for the words that are commonly used in day to day life and also generalizing the symbols irrespective of native speakers, to customize the output image according to their interest. The system can be extended to any language by using a language translator with little modification and it also an be extended to translate speech to text and then to sign language.

REFERENCES

1. Daniel Stein, Jan Bungeroth, and Herman Ney, "*Morpho-syntax based Statistical Methods for Automatic Sign Language Translation*," In Proceedings of European Association for Machine Translation , 2006, Vol. 10,pp.169-177.
2. S.Kanthak, D.Vilar, E.matusov, and H.Ney, "*Novel Rendering Approaches in Phrase-based Statistical Machine Translation*," in proceedings of Association of Computer Linguistics Workshop, 2005, pp.167-174.
3. Maria Papadogiorgaki, Nikos Grammalidis, Dimitrios Tzovara s, and Michael G.Strintzis," *Textto- sign Language Synthesis Tool*," In Proceedings of European Signal Processing Conference, 2005, pp.130-134.
4. Matt Huenerfauth,"*Spatial and Planning Models of ASL Classifier for Machine Translation*," In Proceedings of Theoretical and Methodological Issues in Machine Translation,2004,pp.65-77.
5. Mohamed Mohandes,"Automatic Translation of Arabic Text to Arabic Sign Language", Artificial Intelligence and Machine Learning, 2006, vol.6(4), pp.15-19.
6. E.Safar and I.Marshall, "*The Architecture of an English Text -to-Sign Languages Translation System*," In Proceedings of Recent Advance in Natural Language Processing,2001,pp.223-228.
7. Sara Morrissey and Andy Way," An Example-based Approach to Translating Sign Language," In Proceedings of Example-based Machine Translation, 2005, Vol.11, pp.106-116.
8. Tony Veale, Brona Collins, and Alan Conway, "*The Challenge of Cross–modal Translation Proceedings of Association of Machine Translation*, 2000, Vol.13 (1), pp.81-106.
9. R.Zens, O.Bender, S.Hasan, S.Khadivi, E.Matusov, J.Xu, Y.Zhang, and H.Ney," *The RWTH Phrase-based Statistical Machine* Translation System," In Proceedings of International Workshop on Spoken Language Translation, Oct 2005.

10. R.Zens, F.J.Och, and H.Ney, "*Phrase-based Statistical Machine Translation," In Proceedings of German Conference in Artificial Intelligence*, 2002, Vol. 2479, pp.18-32.

11. Yuging Guo, Josef van Genabith, and Haifeng Wang, "*Dependency -based Ngram Models for General Purpose Sentences Realisation*," in Proceedings of International Conference on Computational Linguistics '08,2008,pp.297-304.

12. D.Narashiman and T.Mala , "*An Interective System for Converting Text-to-Sign Language*," in Proceeding of International Conference on Information Systems and Software Engineering,2009, PP.164-167.

27

Tamil Hyper Grammar

—0Uma Maheshwar Rao G
—Christopher M
—Parameswari K

ABSTRACT

Grammatical descriptions of human languages are the results of efforts in modelling of the design features and the internal organization of the structures and the mechanisms. Therefore, Linguistics is about language modelling, designing and studying their theoretical and practical implications. However the activity of grammatical descriptions itself is molded by the specific needs of aims and the goals such as Teaching and Learning a language, investigating the issues related to the evolutionary biology with regard to discovering the universals of human language and development, philosophical and functional aspects of language and Linguistic Computing. Here, we would like to discuss certain issues towards building a Hyper grammar for a given language.

Concept

A Hyper grammar is a non-linearly organized dynamic grammar based on the hypertext format. It is intended to simulate certain functions of a native speaker. It can be used both as learning and teaching tool besides as a reference grammar.

It is comprised of a number of non-linearly arranged texts each with a comprehensive note on various grammatical facts of Tamil, with hyper-links. It can be accessed and retrieved for various purposes involving language, to experience the effect of a native speaker and hearer of the language. Functionally it serves better than any of the existing printed grammars, which are simply flat and linear. In a way the existing printed grammars are non-communicative i.e. passive, hence, they are monologues and do not participate or reciprocate to pass judgments about the linguistic facts of the respective languages. A grammar in order to reciprocate should have some of the computationally implemented tools like a morphological generator, analyzer, chunker, parser, lexical accessor etc. The Hyper grammar is intended to be a reciprocative grammar, as it involves some of the properties like the native speaker's ability to make judgements on the grammaticality of the linguistic facts. This single feature makes it distinct from the printed grammars. Hyper grammars are extremely useful from the point of learning, teaching and as reference material. The design features are borrowed from the hypertext format but conceived as a computationally cognitive model. The contents are being developed from both the published and unpublished sources carefully selected and rewritten in the hypertext format.

The Contents

The content of Tamil Hyper grammar has two main components, viz. 1. the description of grammar in hypertext format and 2. the applicational aspect of the Tamil Language as a language manager.

The Tamil Grammar

The grammar part includes a number of comprehensive

descriptive notes on certain linguistic facts of the Tamil Language. It is conceived in terms of a Computational Grammar. It deals with the Orthography, the design features of Tamil script, the orthographic syllable, the information on the frequency distribution of written syllables etc.

As part of the Tamil morphology, we have information on Tamil categories viz. nouns, adjectives, verbs, adverbs, numerals, pronouns etc. In each of these, there is information regarding the setting up of paradigm types and a list of paradigmatic forms under each category. One can access information regarding the most frequent hundred words, five thousand words and ten thousand words in terms of their frequencies, and communicative contribution to the coverage in Tamil Texts. As regards to the frequency of Tamil characters and syllables as they occur in the 3 million-word corpus, one can find the relevant information. One of the most important and crucial is the lexical component. A number of bilingual dictionaries like Tamil-Hindi, Tamil-Kannada, Tamil-Tamil, Tamil-Oriya, Tamil-Marathi, Tamil-English and English-Tamil – are included. Originally these dictionaries are conceived as bilingual and bidirectional dictionaries initially created using the most frequently occurring words ensuring the coverage.

The Tamil Language Manager

This is the most crucial component of Tamil Hyper grammar. It involves the actual functions of the practical aspect of the grammar outlined above. As said earlier, the grammatical description is only a statement about the competence of a native speaker – about his/her language. In order to make it to simulate the grammar, it should involve a working generator, analyzer, parser and lexical accessor, etc. Currently the Tamil language manager includes a word form generator, a morphological analyzer and lexical accessor among others.

a. The Morphological Analyzer

The word analyzer incorporated here is intended to analyze the Tamil words in terms of the lexical root/stem, its category, the paradigm type and the inflectional or derivational affixes attached to it. A morphological analyzer (Morph) engine essentially learns from a morphological lexical database of a particular language. The functional coverage and efficacy of the engine is greatly dependent on the structure and the organization of the database. The database of Tamil Morphological Analyzer comprises of inflectional database and the root dictionary. These data comprise purely linguistic information of the language, which are processed subsequently to enable using it in morphological analysis. It uses the Word and Paradigm Model of analysis.

The Organization of the Linguistic Data for Morph

(i) The paradigmatic-data

The term Paradigm refers to an exhaustive set of morpho-syntactically related word forms of a given lexeme. Based on the inflection, six distinct morphological categories are identified and the paradigms are created. They include the major and minor categories of words.

(*a*) The major word classes which are productive and open class categories (new members are added from time to time) can inflect with distinct but characteristic suffixes which explicit morpho-syntactic functions. The major word categories are listed as below:

1. Nouns
2. Verbs
3. Adjectives

(*b*) The distinct minor categories which are productive but considered as closed class categories (no new members are added) are listed below:

4. Pronouns

5. Numerals
6. Locative Nouns

The other classes of words which are not fallen under the above categories are a list of idiosyncratic word forms. They cannot inflect for any functional categories. They come under functional categories of language with defective morphology. The following words are usually known as indeclinable and have no morphology to process:

1. Postpositions
2. Adverbs
3. Conjunctions
4. Interjections
5. Particles

The above words are listed as 'Avy' (avyayas) in the dictionary.

(ii) Root Dictionary

Root Dictionary is a vast collection of lexemes which contains words, their categorical information and their suitable paradigms. It includes a certain number of minimally distinct words in the semantic system of a language. This is typically called as lexicon without semantics. Input : a valid word formOutput :

1. Root
2. Lexical Category
3. Paradigm Type
4. Morphological Category

(The output may be one or more analysis) Input and Output Specifications in Tamil:

Input

1 koyampuwwUr[1]

2 iraNtAvawu

3 mikappeVriya

4 wamilYYaka

5 mAnakarakam

6 Akum

Output

1. koyampuwwUr unk <fs af='koyampuwwUr,n,n,sg,3,d,0,0'>
2. iraNtAvawu unk <fs af='iraNtu,num,,sg,,o,Avawu,Avawu'>
3. mikappeVriya unk <fs af='mikappeVriya,adj,any,any,any,,0,0'>
4. wamilYYaka unk <fs af='wamilYYakam,n,n,sg,3,o,0,0'>
5. mAnakarakam unk <fs af='mAnakaram,n,n,sg,3,d,0,0'>
6. Akum unk <fs af='Aku,v,n,sg,3,,pp,pp'> |
   <fs af='Aku,v,n,pl,3,,pp,pp'>

b. Word form Generator

A Tamil word-form synthesizer enables a user to generate Tamil word forms. The user is prompted to select some choices leading to the generation of the desired word. This is extremely useful to the learners of Tamil as second language. Such uses can interactively generate the requested word in Tamil. The Morphological Generator of Tamil is based on Word and Paradigm Method. It is built using the feature values, suffix informations with add or delete rules and the root word dictionary with its category and paradigm. It uses the Machine Learning techniques to generate the word form from the given input. The basic resources required for present word synthesizer:

Feature Value

It contains the category, its possible morpho-syntactic

properties. It has five values, each viz., category, gender, number, person and the affix. For instance,

"v m sg 3 nw"

The above is an example for the verb for generating third person singular masculine past tense verb as such vanwAnY 'he came'.

Suffix Information and Synthesis Rule Set

This is generated from the paradigms and its feature values. It contains the rules for words based on their morpho-phonemic processes. It has four columns delimited by comma. For instance, to generate

'marafkalYE'

maram + kalY +E

Eng: tree + plural+ Accusative case

the suffix information table consists,

"Eylakf,m,maram,89"

Whereas the first is an inversed suffix of 'fkalYE' which is to be added, the second is the word which has to be deleted from root and the third is the name of the pardigm as such the word behaves in its morphophonemic process and finally the row number of the feature value file.

Lexicon

Lexicon consists of the root words of Tamil, its category and the name of the paradigm based on its phonological behaviour in its inflection. For instance,

'aNi,v,varE' Eng: put on, verb, draw

Here aNi, the verb act morpho-phonemically as varE.

aNi-nw-AnY as in varE-nw-AnY 'root-PST-3p.sg.m'

aNi-kirY-AlY as in varE-kirY-AlY 'root-PRS-3p.sg.f'

aNi-v-ArkalY as in varE-v-ArkalY 'root-FUT-3p.sg.m'

Input

1. Root
2. Lexical Category
3. Morphological Category

Output

A valid word form Input and Output Specifications in Tamil:

Input

1. kampar NNP <fs af='kampar,n,m,sg,3,0,0,0'>
2. irAmAyaNam NN <fs af='irAmayaNam,n,n,sg,3,o,E,E'>
3. iyarYrYu VM <fs af='iyarYrYu,v,m,sgh,3,,nw,nw'>

Output

1. kampar NNP <fs af='kampar,n,m,sg,3,0,0,0'>
2. irAmAyaNawwE NN <fs af='irAmayaNam,n,n,sg,3,o, E,E'>
3. iyarYrYinYAr VM <fs af='iyarYrYu,v,m,sgh,3,,nw,nw'>

c. Dictionary

The Tamil-Telugu bilingual dictionary is built based on the concepts available in the language. It differs from the conventional dictionary which lists words but not concepts. Here, the lexeme(s) are related to each other on the basis of the concept i.e. the idea of ontological entity. The dictionary which is based on concepts is a better one for obtaining a concise and effective lexicon which can be used in many NLP applications.

d. Machine Translation System

The development of Machine Translation is one of the most challenging tasks of the Natural Language Processing Applications. The development of Machine Translation (MT) System which translates texts from Telugu to Tamil and vice-versa (Bi-directional) are incorporated here. This MT system was developed as part of IL-ILMT consortium project funded by the Government of India at CALTS, University of Hyderabad. This Machine Translation system uses Transfer Based Approach. The System's Architecture is divided into three stages i.e. Source language Analysis module (SLA), Source language to Target language Transfer module (SL-TL) and Target language generation module (TLG).

(*i*) Telugu-Tamil Machine Translation System

The crucial tools used in Telugu-Tamil Machine Translation system includes,

(*a*) Source Language Analysis

Telugu Sandhi Splitter

Telugu Morphological Analyzer

Telugu POS Tagger

Telugu Chunker

Telugu NER (Named Entity Recognizer)

Telugu Parser

(*b*) Source Language-Target Language Analysis

Telugu-Tamil Transfer Grammar Module

Telugu-Tamil Multi Word Expression Module

Telugu-Tamil Lexical Transfer Module

(*c*) Target Language Analysis

Tamil Agreement Module

Tamil Word form Generator

(*ii*) Tamil-Telugu Machine Translation

The crucial tools used in Tamil-Telugu Machine Translation system includes,

(*a*) Source Language Analysis

(1) Tamil Sandhi Splitter

(2) Tamil Morphological Analyzer

(3) Tamil POS Tagger

(4) Tamil Chunker

(5) Tamil NER (Named Entity Recognizer)

(6) Tamil Parser

(*b*) Source Language—Target Language Analysis

(1) Tamil-Telugu Transfer Grammar Module

(2) Tamil-Telugu Multi Word Expression Module

(3) Tamil-Telugu Lexical Transfer Module

(*c*) Target Language Analysis

(4) Telugu Agreement Module

(5) Telugu Word form Generator

Conclusion

The Tamil Hyper Grammar thus described here is the most significant development in the recent applications of Natural language processing of the Tamil language to be used as teaching, learning as well as reference grammar for all kinds of language users.

1 Transliteration Scheme using wx-notation:

Tamil Orthography :

a A i I u U eV e E oV o O H

k f c F t N w n p m y r l v lYY lY rY nY j s h R

Telugu Orthography :

a A i I u U q Q eV e E oV o O M H

k K g G f c C j J F t T d D N w W x X n p P b B m y r rY l lY lYY v S R s h

REFERENCES

1. Arden A.H. 1891. *A Progressive Grammar of the Tamil Language*. Chennai: The Christian Literature Society.

2. ILMT Consortium. 2007. *ILMT SRS and Functional Specifications* (mimeo). Hyderabad.

3. Parameswari K. 2009. *An Improvized Morphological Analyzer for Tamil: A Case of Implementing an Open Source Platform Apertium*. Unpublished M.Phil. Thesis. Hyderabad: University of Hyderabad.
4. Ramaswamy, Vaishnavi. 2003. *A Morphological Analyzer for Tamil*. Unpublished Ph.D. Thesis. Hyderabad: University of Hyderabad.
5. Uma Maheshwar Rao, G. 2002. *A Computational Grammar of Telugu*. (Mimeo) Hyderabad: University of Hyderabad.
6. Uma Maheshwar Rao, G. 2005. *Telugu Hyper Grammar*. (Mimeo and Electronic form) Hyderabad: University of Hyderabad.
7. Uma Maheswar Rao G, Amba P. Kulkarni and Christopher M. 2007. *Functional Specifications of Morphology (mimeo)*. Hyderabad.
8. Uma Maheswar Rao G. and Christopher M. 2010. *Word Synthesizer Engine*. In Morphological Analyzer and Generators. Mona Parakh (ed.) Page 73-81. Mysore; CIIL.
9. Uma Maheswar Rao G. and Parameshwari K. 2010. *On the Description of Morphological Data for Morphological Analysers and Generators: A Case of Telugu*, Tamil and Kannada. In Morphological Analyzer and Generators. Mona Parakh (ed.) pp. 114-123. Mysore; CIIL.

Index